BIOGRAPHY of a
PHANTOM

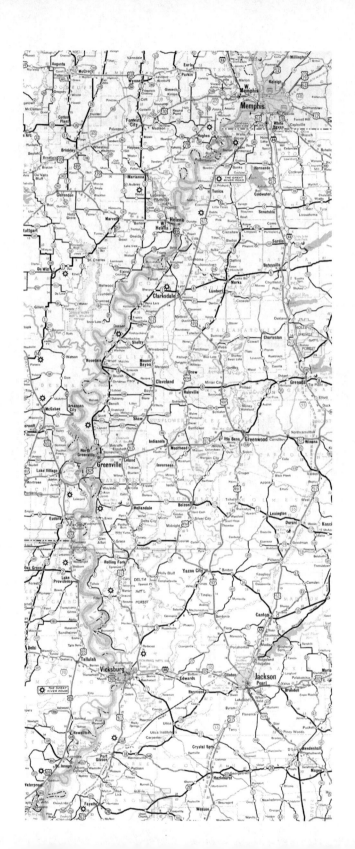

BIOGRAPHY of a
PHANTOM
A ROBERT JOHNSON BLUES ODYSSEY

Robert "Mack" McCormick

Edited by
John W. Troutman

Smithsonian Books
Washington, DC

Published by Smithsonian Books
Director: Carolyn Gleason
Senior Editor: Jaime Schwender
Assistant Editor: Julie Huggins

Copyedited by Duke Johns and Gregory McNamee
Designed by Gary Tooth

This book may be purchased for educational, business, or sales promotional use. For information, please write:
Special Markets Department
Smithsonian Books
P.O. Box 37012, MRC 513
Washington, DC 20013

Library of Congress Cataloging-in-Publication Data

Names: McCormick, Robert "Mack," author. | Troutman, John William, editor.
Title: Biography of a phantom : a Robert Johnson blues odyssey / Robert "Mack" McCormick ; edited by John W. Troutman.
Description: Washington : Smithsonian Books, 2023. | Includes bibliographical references and index.
Identifiers: LCCN 2022047107 (print) | LCCN 2022047108 (ebook) | ISBN 9781588347343 (hardcover) | ISBN 9781588347374 (ebook)
Subjects: LCSH: Johnson, Robert, 1911–1938. | Johnson, Robert, 1911–1938—Death and burial. | Blues musicians—Mississippi—Biography. | African Americans—Mississippi—Delta (Region)—Social life and customs—20th century. | McCormick, Robert.
Classification: LCC ML420.J735 M33 2023 (print) | LCC ML420.J735 (ebook) | DDC 782.421643092 [B]—dc23/eng/20221004
LC record available at https://lccn.loc.gov/2022047107
LC ebook record available at https://lccn.loc.gov/2022047108

Printed in the United States of America
27 26 25 24 23   1 2 3 4 5

Unless otherwise noted at the end of an image caption, all images are courtesy of Susannah Nix from the Robert "Mack" McCormick Collection, Archives Center, National Museum of American History.

For permission to reproduce illustrations appearing in this book, please correspond directly with the owners of the works. Smithsonian Books does not retain reproduction rights for these images individually, or maintain a file of addresses for sources.

Title page: Section from a roadmap of the Mississippi Delta region, cut by McCormick.

CONTENTS

Editor's Preface
John W. Troutman
vii

Introduction
1

Other Johnsons
88

The Town
5

Mississippi 304
102

The Search
14

Leatherman
127

The Map
21

Listening and Remembering
139

Back to the Delta
31

Hindsight
154

Copiah County
48

Greenwood
164

Afterword
John W. Troutman
182

Notes
John W. Troutman
197

Acknowledgments
225

Index
227

EDITOR'S PREFACE
John W. Troutman

His work is a tribute to the untrammeled imagination.
—Peter Guralnick, on Mack McCormick's study of Robert Johnson, 2002

The biggest problem came from Mack McCormick.
—Annye Anderson, sister of Robert Johnson, 2020

The half-century saga of *Biography of a Phantom*, Robert "Mack" McCormick's fabled, long unpublished manuscript chronicling his pursuit of the legendary musician Robert Johnson's story, provides a unique opportunity for a reckoning with the powerful forces, intimate and familial, imaginary and systemic, that have long pulled and prodded at the workings of the blues in American life. The saga comprises much more than just another book on Robert Johnson. It provides an astonishing vantage point for considering the relationships between the material world of the family of a renowned Black composer, singer, and instrumentalist who together experienced the trauma and terrorism of Jim Crow Mississippi; the manner by which a number of Johnson's acquaintances, friends, and family, thirty years after the blues artist's early death, were "discovered" by McCormick, a white, Houston-based, self-taught folklorist and writer; the decision made by Johnson's sisters, Carrie Thompson and Bessie Hines, to share details of Johnson's life and more to McCormick; and then in consequence, and tragically for them all, the toll of their encounter. In more ways than either might suspect, both Guralnick's and Anderson's sentiments about Mack McCormick are true.

In one sense, the book chronicles a short period of McCormick's career, between around 1969 and 1975. During that time, he doggedly researched the life of Johnson by locating and then knocking on the doors of people who knew him, if not loved him. In another sense, however, the book's history asks us to consider the forty years that followed, until McCormick's death in 2015. During that period McCormick wrote, abandoned, and rewrote the book several times, sometimes from the ground up, often entirely revising his claims and in some cases deliberately undermining the findings of his earlier research. Many of his peers throughout these forty years assumed McCormick's biography might be a definitive account of Johnson's life; indeed, throughout the years McCormick would drop tantalizing details about his fieldwork on the subject. They were at a loss, then, to understand McCormick's reluctance to make that work available. It felt like self-sabotage, a betrayal. Some were infuriated by it. Others who knew him well, however, expected nothing less. As scholar Daphne Brooks puts it, McCormick was "the most enigmatic blues mafia figure of them all."

THE MAFIA

The "Blues Mafia" moniker conveys awe as well as disdain. The phrase neatly characterizes a small but culturally impactful, global community of white, male fanatics of southern Black vernacular music who first began to find one another in the 1940s. The members passionately shared, debated, and displayed a powerful esoteric knowledge—knowledge that they could direct to one another to produce admiration or jealousy from within, or wield as a test for those who sought entry to their circle from without. As scholar Marybeth Hamilton put it, they "they were a brotherhood, united by . . . their devotion to authentic blues, a music known only to the cognoscenti, secret, occult, and obscure." They became "made men" through outsized success in scooping up obscure records, or, better, heading into the field to extract previously untold (untold to them, that is) stories of blues artists and their hardships. They communicated through a code of record catalog numbers and song lyric analysis, circulated in mailed distributions of small photocopied newsletters packed with discography or, for the lucky ones, in published liner notes, a form of love letter that they would craft to one another in homage to the Black acoustic blues singers whose ancient-sounding voices popped from the record's grooves when pulled from the sleeve and so gently placed on the platter.

Hamilton identifies the earliest, core members of this ring of white blues enthusiasts as the "mentor," Jim McKune, along with Henry Renard, Ron Lubin, Pete Kaufman, Stephen Calt, Lawrence Cohn, Ben Kaplan, Nick Perls, Bernie Klatzko, and Pete Whelan. While she notes that "none of them had a lot of money to spend," they spent a great deal of time establishing a set of aesthetic judgments about the genre that gained a far-reaching impact that betrayed their humble circumstances. By the mid-1950s, years after first coming together, the group had "dubbed themselves the Blues Mafia." By the early 1960s, McCormick's devotion to the blues and his trading in esoteric knowledge earned him a prominent place in the next set of researchers and writers to absorb and extend the Mafia's growing influence. Many of them were supporters of the 1960s Civil Rights Movement and they saw in their obsession with Black music and celebration of the blues a tangible contribution to the cause. But for most of them, seeking transformative social change was not their driving impulse.

Nor did they seem particularly interested to invite Black researchers and writers into their ranks. Amiri Baraka (writing then as LeRoi Jones), for example, wrote the seminal book *Blues People: Negro Music in White America* in 1963. Baraka built upon the foundation of W.E.B. Du Bois in his 1903 *The Souls of Black Folks*, as well as the works of Zora Neale Hurston, Langston Hughes, Sterling Brown, and other predecessors to further expound on the virtues of understanding Black music—and particularly, for Baraka, the blues—as not only a foundational element for understanding African American culture and identity but also as a critical lens for exploring the literary and social history of the United States.

It does not seem to be the case, however, that Baraka's work was seriously engaged at the time by this small but influential band of white researchers and writers of the blues. Nor did they invite Black musicologist John Work III into their conversations. Work (along with his Fisk University colleague Lewis Jones and graduate student Samuel Adams) had conducted groundbreaking blues field recordings and research in the early 1940s while guiding white musicologist Alan Lomax through the Mississippi Delta and introducing him to Muddy Waters and Son House, among others, who would later become known as renowned blues artists. Of course, Lomax rarely acknowledged Work's involvement in the research project to begin with, which deprived Work of gaining due credit, to say nothing of an invitation to engage his white contemporaries.

Rather than collaborate with living Black intellectuals to study Black music, these white collectors, researchers, and writers preferred to pursue, on their own terms, what they considered the authentic Black experience, the *real*, through their own, self-guided, personal quests of blues discovery. That quest led them to what they considered the most authentic music in the genre, that of the "country blues." For most of them, the "urban blues" of Bessie Smith, Gertrude "Ma" Rainey and other typically female originators and innovators of the genre, in contrast, often were little more than commercial sideshows. Those artists' recordings typically combined piano runs and horn sections that, however swaggering and masterfully executed, seemed to the members of the Blues Mafia to hold no candle to the authority and gritty authenticity of the male-dominated, stripped-down "country blues"—later rebranded as the "Delta blues"—that consisted of vocal performances with little more accompaniment than an acoustic guitar.

Marybeth Hamilton notes that for the Blues Mafia, "the 'realness' of this 'country blues' lay in its rough-hewn sound, its heated, primal emotion, and the primitive character of the song form. As one fan of [the Blues Mafia's independent label, Origins Jazz Library] explained, 'the voice is dark and heavy, often thick and congested, with a peculiar crying quality. . . . and suffused throughout with an emotional intensity that is all but overpowering (the words seem almost torn from the singers' throat).' These were barely songs at all—more a rhythmic wail of anguish, in which 'monosyllabic cries' expressing 'strong, uncontrollable feelings' often 'carr[ied] far greater meaning than do the song's words.'" These recordings, they believed, bore the unfiltered, incalcuable, and otherwise unknowable burdens, pleasures and folk wisdom of the Black artists whose music obsessed, if not haunted them—the music of those blues singers and players who would become their phantoms.

Of course, while there are many phantoms in this book, Robert Johnson is not one of them. He was a brother, father, son, friend, and off-and-on farmer. He was economically impoverished, artistically nourished, and as savvy as any person had to be who grew up Black in the Mississippi Delta's landscape of sharecropper's cabins, lynch mobs, cotton field toil, and planter surveillance. His own stepfather, Charles Dodds Spencer, escaped a lynching in Hazlehurst only after wearing a disguise, fleeing for Memphis, changing his last name, and never returning. No wonder some of Johnson's songs spoke of the devil or of hellhounds on his trail.

Once the Blues Mafia sought to discover his story, decades after his death, the question of who Robert Johnson was and was not emerged as a highly contested and eventually lucrative terrain for white writers, musicians, and critics. All the while, his family, having no idea of this eruption of interest in his work, was left in the dark until Mack McCormick knocked on their doors.

THE MAN AT THE DOOR

McCormick knocked on a *lot* of doors in his lifetime and lived in quite a few places before settling eventually in Houston. His legend among the mafia and its "hangers-on" grew from his vast knowledge of southern vernacular music and his extraordinary success in finding elder blues artists and their families. His intimate knowledge of blues artists was seen by some not simply as his currency but as their gold standard. He achieved such status among his peers despite the challenges he faced in his early years.

His parents, Greg and Effie Mae McCormick, met while training as X-ray technicians in Cincinnati but separated in 1932, two years after his birth. His father traveled the country to demonstrate new X-ray technology to doctors and spent time in Mexico as well, while Mack and his mother moved around parts of Ohio, Missouri, Colorado, Alabama, and West Virginia, with Effie Mae often taking odd jobs as she struggled to find the work that she was trained to perform.

Even though young Robert was frequently moved across the country and sometimes between households, he soon recognized that wherever he lived, the radio was his north star. He became absorbed by late-night big band relayed remotes from swanky nightclubs and hotels on either coast, and he took any jobs he could as a teenager to be a part, somehow, of that world—typically by running errands for radio stations and pushing around equipment for local ballrooms. Meanwhile, his early talent for writing was rewarded by an American Legion of Ohio "best essay" award in tenth grade. That year, 1946, they moved again, this time to Houston.

Bouncing between schools was a hardship—he moved at least twenty times during his first sixteen years—and he remembered his high school years as "really sort of a black period for me." He never received a diploma, and two weeks after moving to Houston, the sixteen-year-old hitchhiked to New Orleans, where he discovered a path for putting his interest in writing and passion for jazz to work. A local record dealer and jazz discographer, Orin Blackstone, charged McCormick with returning to Texas to serve as the Texas editor for Blackstone's later acclaimed *Index to Jazz*.

He hitchhiked back to Houston, but the job did not pan out, and he never heard from Blackstone again. He had found his calling, though. The challenge for Mack at that point, one that remained intact for most of the rest of his life, was how to make a living as a music researcher and writer. To make ends meet, for the next ten years or so he worked the counters, grills, fountains, or sinks of Bantam Buffet, Elliott's Waffle Shop, and a slew of other local Houston eateries.

Jun '43	w/Gregg McCormick
Sep '43	3236 Westminister
	Dallas
Sep '43	Terrill Preparatory School
May '44	5100 Ross
	Dallas
May '44	w/Effie Crowder
	Sparks Clinic Nurses Home
	5006 Ross
	Dallas
	w/Effie Crowder
	St. Francis Hotel
	Denver, Colorado
	W/Effie Crowder
	Boarding House
	Denver, Colorado
Sep '44	w/Effie Crowder
	Red Spot Tourist Camp
	7999 West Colfax
	Denver, Colorado
	w/Effie Crowder
Jun '45	White frame house
	Lakewood, Colorado
Jun '45	w/C.A. Pettibone
	14736 Braemer
	Cleveland, Ohio
Aug '45	w/Effie Crowder
	1514 Prospect
	Sandusky, Ohio
	w/Effie Crowder
	1700 Prospect
	Sandusky, Ohio
	Central Sea Room
	Sandusky, Ohio
	East End Room
	Sandusky, Ohio
	w/Mr & Mrs Smith
Jul '46	909 Vine Street
	Sandusky, Ohio
Jul '46	w/Frank Pettbbone
	Jefferson, Ohio
Jul '46	w/Mr & Mrs Smith
Sep '46	909 Vine Street
	Sandusky, Ohio

Sep '46	w/Andrew Crowder
Dec '46	403 Webster
	Houston, Texas
Dec '46	w/Effie Crowder
May '47	740 Allston
	Houston
	4100 Garrott
	Houston
Jun '47	w/Effie Crowder
	1709 Tuam
	Houston
	w/Effie Crowder
Aug '47	1728 Indiana
	Houston
Sep 47	YMCA
	715 So. Hope
	Los Angeles
	Addington Hotel
Nov '47	735 So. Hope
	Los Angeles
Nov '47	w/Effie Crowder
	1728 Indiana
	Houston
	1427 Hawthorne
	Houston
	w/Larry
Jul '48	710 Avondale
	Houston
	1900 Rosewood
	Houston
Aug '48	2003 Ruth (rear)
	Houston
	w/Ed Badeaux
	Lincoln Hotel
	New York City
	2003 Ruth (rear)
	Houston
Aug '49	Harris County Jail
	Criminal Courts Bldg
	Houston
	2003 Ruth (rear)
Mar '50	Houston

A page from McCormick's carefully documented and lengthy list of former residences reveals that his early years were relentlessly transient.

At the same time, he began to find his people, most far from home. By 1947 he was corresponding with discographers and record collectors across the world, from Australia to Canada and England, hounding them with extensive questions and fielding his own in correspondence that signaled knowledge and built trust. He had a breakthrough in 1949 when he began publishing pieces as the Texas correspondent for *Down Beat* and began work as a press agent for the Buddy Ryland Orchestra out of Nacogdoches, Texas.

Just when he began to establish his bona fides and lay the foundation, however, the cracks became exposed. In August 1949 he was booked in Houston's Harris County Jail for forgery. He had been arrested in Dallas, where a local newspaper reported that officers found in his hotel room "a check-protecting machine, about 50 drivers' license forms, various blank checks, and a memorandum book in which he kept notations of cashed checks," marking perhaps the first instance when McCormick's penchant for holding onto everything he touched would come back to haunt him. He cooperated with police and confessed to keeping additional forgery equipment in Houston, where police found in his room "rubber stamps with names of Houston business firms and street addresses. . . . At least six different names were used by the youth in cashing checks in Houston." Effie Mae was devastated. He wrote her from jail shortly after his arrest:

> I do realize it was a mistake to try to beat the law. But I was fired from
> my fo[u]rth or fifth job because of being late or absent—due to asthma.
> I get desperate and discouraged—I couldn't see how to break out of
> the vicious circle. And I didn't want to ask anymore [*sic*] money from
> you—rather I wanted to start paying you back. All I could see to do was
> to keep some money coming in while I worked out some way of making
> a living in some-my-own-boss sort of thing. And that was just about to
> happen. I had several things that might have worked out.

Despite his predicament, he continued submitting writings to *Down Beat* and other periodicals, while providing jazz research notes to a New Orleans radio personality, Dick Martin, to deliver on the air. McCormick never let on in his correspondence that he was writing from a prison cell, and his friend Ed Badeaux or Effie Mae would mail and retrieve correspondence for him to help disguise that fact. His chosen career path, however, also was a source of friction between Mack and his mother, and she worried that his growing obsession, which she considered an impractical distraction, seemed to be escalating. She had her own struggles, often roving from job to job, sometimes asking him for help along the way, and she hoped he would break out of a vicious cycle that he seemed to inherit. Soon after he was arrested, Effie Mae warned him to limit his correspondence and "forget records etc." Yet, she did as best as a mother could to acknowledge his successes while he was in jail: "I read your write up about Mel and Ryland bands [in] *Down Beat* and it was good your name was printed at the end."

McCormick kept going. At one point he gained access to a typewriter and wrote pianist and bandleader Claude Thornhill, whom he had briefly met while on assignment to cover jazz performances at Houston's new Shamrock Hotel. He described his ilk: "I imagine that at one time or another you've been buttonholed by that weird type of jazz collector known as the discographer . . . one who not only collects the records but also trys [*sic*] to find out the personnel of the recording groups, etc. Therefore this letter won't be too much of a shock to you." He then hit Thornhill up for session information on the trumpeter Harry James, who was the subject of McCormick's latest research. Jail would not slow down his pursuit.

McCormick, however, was slowed down by other forces that likely contributed to his inability to keep any job that required him to show up on time each day to a workplace. Throughout his adult life, he suffered episodes of depression as well as paranoid delusions, both hallmarks of a bipolar disorder. He was released on probation in May 1950 and ordered to pay monthly restitution payments. In November 1951, he could not deliver. He wrote to his probation officer, "During the past month I have had what amounts to a nervous breakdown which coming, as it did, at such a crucial time leaves me with problems at every turn . . . the basis for this col[l]apse was my reaching a saturation point of worry and anxiety following which things lost true perspective and living became an unrealistic venture. That has been my condition these past weeks."

McCormick sold off his record collection and furniture and was able to keep up the payments with the probation officer's personal assistance, but his undiagnosed condition did not improve and could leave him feeling paralyzed for days or weeks at a time. As he wrote in 1960 to a longtime writing collaborator, Paul Oliver, "Have just gotten your letter wondering at the two months silence—which I can only explain as one of those bizarre funks which overcome me from time to time, bringing apathy and leaving me in disorder. So much so that I discovered a letter, or rather two letters, had lain around here unmailed for a month's time even tho I realized you'd be anxious and wondering. . . .

Well, so much for this line of thought, which is simply to say I've been in one of those things."

Throughout the 1950s, he continued to take on jobs when he could, working as a memo machine operator, mail clerk, and shipping clerk, among others. He briefly made a go of living in southern California when an acquaintance found him a job at the Douglas Aircraft Company plant, but this did not last. He would accept and leave jobs in California with the same frequency as he did in Texas, working as a factory assembler, dishwasher (for two days), mail handler (for one day), and freight handler (for two days). In addition to living with his disorder, he also struggled against the expectation that he should pursue a "normal" line of work. The notion that nothing should stand in the way of his calling would determine many of his choices for the rest of his life—choices that, when combined with acute bouts of paranoia, would continue to haunt him. He wrote his mother:

> I've decided to slip into the vagrant-bum-drifter class to which I actually seem to belong. For a very good reason—I feel. Spending eight hours a day at a job then rushing home to go to bed early enough to get up to go work is a life to which I can't adjust. Except for short periods such as the Douglas routing which drove me nearly idiotic. Very simply, I have more important things to do. Which is a very assuming kind of a statement given impetus by a declaring ego. At the moment—as for the past four years—that more important thing to do is writing. Of course that seems exceedingly foolish in that I have yet to produce anything which I haven't been ashamed of for several good reasons. (Otherwise, you'd have seen an example of my efforts). Still I'm convinced I have that ability, that's just a matter of sweating and starving around.

By 1953 he was back in Houston, working as a "balloon dart hanky pank" for a carnival followed by a two-month stretch as an orderly and cook's helper for a construction outfit. In 1954 he joined the Coast Guard, with limited success. By 1957 and for several years that followed, he drove cabs. Once he landed that job, his fortunes began to change, perhaps because of the flexible hours it afforded. He would work when he *could* work. With it he found a semblance of stability. In addition, the job enabled him to drive around town in search of old 78 rpm records, or better, the artists he considered to be phantoms, whose remarkable

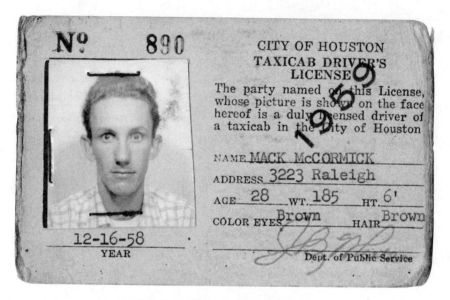

McCormick's 1959 taxicab driver's license.

voices and words ringing out of those records increasingly obsessed and haunted him. In between his fares, he knocked on doors.

Fieldwork formed an important element of what can only be described as an explosively prolific, at times irrefutably manic, period of productivity by McCormick from the late 1950s through the 1960s. McCormick moved on from his pursuit of jazz discography and plunged himself into Texas and Deep South blues, cowboy songs, and conjunto on both sides of the border. He followed his interests and instincts, which led him to take deep dives into wide-ranging topics, such as the history of Hawaiian or bajo sexto guitars, or the ins and outs of hog butchering. He wrote plays, a passion that extended through the end of his life. One of his earliest was staged in London but received poor reviews.

In the late 1950s and early 1960s McCormick booked tours and produced records for local blues artists Sam Hopkins, better known today as Lightnin' Hopkins, and Mance Lipscomb; recruited and recorded numerous musicians for a variety of record label owners; and started his own label, Almanac Records. As the figurative "Texas correspondent" for those in the Blues Mafia, he gained increasing prestige for his knowledge and access to Black Texas musicians, while his liner notes and other published pieces drew widespread praise, or at least as widespread as it could be within such otherwise tight circles of music criticism. Peter Guralnick, one of the most revered music writers of our time, once said of

McCormick's sprawling 1975 liner notes on the life and music of 1920s recording artist and songster Henry Thomas, "Mack went beyond the facts and reimagined the world and music of Thomas—it's one of the most extraordinary pieces of writing on blues I've ever read."

THE FOLK

By the 1950s, Mack had begun to style himself as a folklorist. The field of folklore had increased in stature and provided new sorts of employment opportunities—either to make field recordings for folk labels popping up all over the country or to find "unfound" musicians, who perhaps could be recruited to deliver ancient wisdom, woes of hardship, and murder ballads to an emergent audience of thousands of white progressive college students who could not get enough of such things. Mack became deeply involved in Houston's hootenanny and folklore scenes, producing performances with Ed Badeaux and recruiting local as well as national talent. He sometimes recorded these concerts on tape machines, which coincided with his burgeoning interest in making field recordings of a variety of people who interested him or who seemed to interest other folklorists.

McCormick forayed into the world of prison recordings, for example, following the lead of John and Alan Lomax and other white folklorists who felt that musicians and singers of color incarcerated in Texas prison farms could reveal the real—the unfiltered, unvarnished, vulnerable performances of the unfree, who could not escape the blues hounds who were let inside the penitentiary gate but who perhaps saw opportunity to get an afternoon off, or at least one punctuated by the rewinding of tapes or directions to sing the "old songs," whatever those were. Notions of "field work" versus "fieldwork" held very different meanings for all involved.

In 1965 Alan Lomax encouraged the organizers of the Newport Folk Festival to recruit Mack to find and deliver for the festivalgoers' edification a gang of incarcerated people who would sing work songs while actually chopping wood, demonstrating the unfree, uncompensated labor they provided daily to the state of Texas. The state's attorney general declined Mack's request, so instead he assembled a group of men recently transitioned from prison camps to halfway houses and drove them to the festival. McCormick later claimed to have pulled the plug when Bob Dylan's "gone electric" soundcheck cut into his group's rehearsal time. Folklore bona fides.

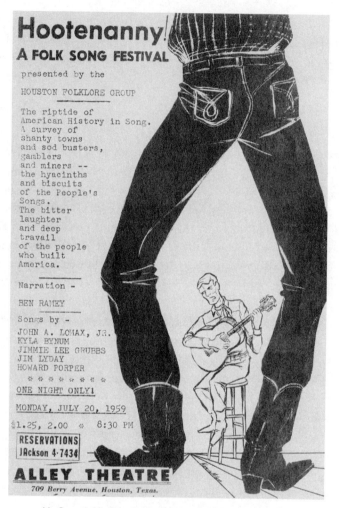

McCormick's flyer for one of several Hootenannies
that he produced at Houston's Alley Theater.

THE BLUES

By then McCormick was several years into what would amount to a decades-long, ultimately doomed book project with Paul Oliver, a British blues enthusiast and writer. Their collaboration on Texas blues was a challenge from the start—living thousands of miles apart from one another, Mack would copy and then send Paul boxes of his fieldwork notes by sea, while Paul would deliver chapter drafts. They would write back and forth, poring over the notes, sharing their esoteric knowledge, finding glee in discovery, and editing the book, which, abandoned due to ongoing frictions and a falling out in the late 1970s, consisted of a monumental volume of original research and writing. Paul had made a handful of trips to the United States during those years, but ultimately the project was reliant upon Mack's ability to locate and establish rapport with often difficult-to-track-down (sometimes because they did not want to be found) blues musicians and their family members and friends.

Indeed, the power dynamic of a white stranger in the 1960s knocking on Black folks' doors, or even striking up a conversation at one of the locals' favorite pool halls or restaurants, certainly led many to turn away or leave the door closed, and for good reason: the threats they endured by white people, often in sheep's clothing, combined with a lack of protection from local law enforcement, left them vulnerable, vigilant, and on edge. Some of the older musicians cited a reluctance to talk due to their church's advice to leave those memories behind, while others provided their own reasons or excuses for getting folks who looked like Mack to leave them alone. Yet, despite those dangers, many ended up willing to speak with him and were often generous in sharing their recollections.

It helped that Mack had learned to present himself as disarming, empathetic, repulsed by the Jim Crow protocols of deference, and genuinely interested in their stories. In consequence of this odd combination of coercion, respect, and generosity (on the part of those who spoke with him), thousands upon thousands of typed, single-spaced pages of fieldwork for this project fill his archive, made up of interview notes and transcriptions with hundreds of blues musicians and their families and acquaintances, as well as vivid, detailed descriptions, from Mack's perspective, of these encounters. The candor expressed through many of the interviews is striking.

McCormick documented his general fieldwork and recording methods in the notes, and his archives are filled with notes to himself about fieldwork preparation. In interviews he often described a "grid system" by which he methodically conducted fieldwork on a county-by-county basis. He estimated working through more than seven hundred counties in the United States. More likely, as expressed in his fieldnotes, he followed leads provided to him by people, one by one, that would often take him on long drives and certainly on many wild goose chases. The work was facilitated, however, by his appointment as a 1960 census taker. The role provided a source of income, but it also facilitated his fieldwork when working in redlined and otherwise segregated Black neighborhoods, since it offered him an excuse: he could knock on doors on "official" government business but then impose upon them a few more questions of his own: "Do you have any records?" "Are there any singers in your family?"

It also helped that McCormick had come to acknowledge and disavow the faulty preconception established by some of his fellow blues researchers that the blues was nonindustrial, an escape from work, and antimodern. In fact, the so-called "country blues" of the Mississippi Delta was, for Black southerners, one of the most radical, modern genres of the early to mid-twentieth century; it was steeped in songs about the excitement of the big city—often Memphis, but sometimes St. Louis, New Orleans, Chicago, and beyond. In the midst of Jim Crow terrorism and white supremacist demands of deference, it was a freedom genre replete with songs about hitting the road or riding the rails and getting lost in adventure, hokum, and romance. For the most practiced and talented, this modern music offered an exchange of one form of labor for another, an intensive form of highly skilled labor that required a consummate command of an instrument and a working knowledge of hundreds of the latest popular hits from Vaudeville to Vicksburg—that enabled escape from the dependency and poverty of sharecropping. McCormick understood the vibrancy of the blues and the context from which it sprang, and could offer a strong working knowledge and deep respect when speaking with or about the masters of their craft.

Despite his productive fieldwork, his sprawling insight on vernacular southern music, his record releases and artists' bookings, and his increasing visibility and promotion of status within the concentric rings of the Blues Mafia world, he continued to live with his disorder. Bouts of depression could leave him unable to work for weeks at a time. Although cab driving, folk festivals, and census work provided income that did not require clocking into a workplace each day, sustainability remained a problem.

One of the most difficult challenges, however, was the paranoia, which started creeping into the work of his calling. As early as 1962, just three years into their book project, McCormick was inserting what he called "hoaxes" into the research notes that he shipped to Oliver. Dozens of them. He would create elaborate stories about individuals and share them as fact. In one case, he contemplated sending Oliver photographs of Black men and women from newspapers, snapshots, and mug shots and making up entire stories about them, changing their identities in the process. In another case, he forged a death certificate of Blind Willie Johnson to reflect that Johnson and his parents originally migrated from the Cayman Islands.

McCormick seems to have laid a hoax about L. V. Thomas, whose story (along with McCormick's story, and his research on Thomas) was broadly commented upon after the publication of a 2014 *New York Times Magazine* article by John Jeremiah Sullivan. The magazine published McCormick's research notes on Thomas, which Sullivan intimated were photographed in McCormick's house and shared by a research assistant without McCormick's permission. Either way, the notes shared with Sullivan did not seem to include the hoax note on Thomas, which McCormick had hidden elsewhere in the archive. For, it seemed, McCormick had begun to convince himself that people around him, even close colleagues and friends, were attempting to publish or trade upon his work without his authorization.

McCormick believed these hidden hoaxes would serve as "traps" in his archive—for when someone published his work without his permission, he later could undermine their effort by revealing the misinformation. Of course, on the one hand, he was right. McCormick's notes in the archive suggest that neither the magazine nor the publisher of Oliver's copy of their abandoned Texas blues manuscript secured his final approval to publish his research, and sure enough, some of his hoaxes appear to have entered the printed word. On the other hand, the hoaxing spoke to delusions, a deep-seated, unsubstantiated, and cyclical paranoia that would fester in McCormick's mind, manifesting as torment of a far greater scale in the years to come. Then again, maybe more than a few of the people Mack cornered for conversation provided him with hoaxes of their own.

THE SEARCH

When McCormick began to pursue the story of Robert Johnson in earnest, he was rolling off an exhausting decade of frenzied and voluminous fieldwork that was richly complex, revelatory, manic, and troubled. Economic stability was a persistent challenge, and he continued to navigate recurrent bouts of depression and paranoia. In 1968, however, he was contracted by the Smithsonian Institution to recruit musicians and artisans from Texas to participate in the Festival of American Folklife, held on the National Mall in Washington, DC. Hired by the Smithsonian again over the next several years, he began recruiting festival talent from multiple states across the country. He regularly traveled by car to Washington and back, and this provided him the support and opportunity to knock on doors all along the way. He recruited musicians from Mississippi to perform at

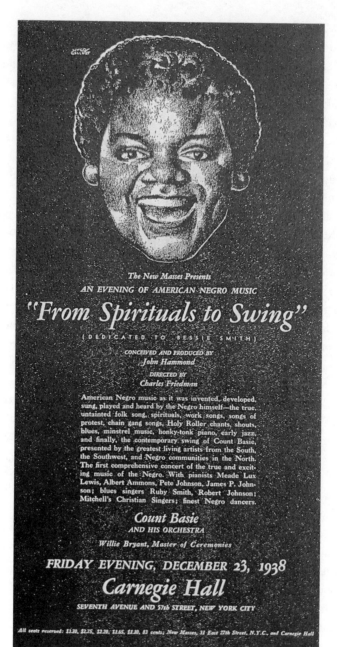

McCormick's photocopy of an advertisement promoting the
"From Spirituals to Swing" concert at Carnegie Hall before
John Hammond discovered that Robert Johnson had died.

the Smithsonian and other folklore festivals, which provided him the opportunity to search for leads on the family and friends of Robert Johnson.

When originally released, Johnson's recordings had gathered some regional sales among Black listeners and jukebox operators but had not made much of a dent in the national market. White music critic and eventual record executive, John Hammond, became a fan of Robert Johnson's upon first hearing Johnson's "Terraplane Blues" record in 1937, and he reviewed it for the left-leaning *New Masses* magazine. Hammond was trying to recruit Johnson to perform at a concert by Black artists to be held at Carnegie Music Hall in 1938 when he learned that only months earlier, Johnson had been killed.

Almost twenty-five years later, Hammond, working as an executive at Columbia Records, oversaw their 1961 release of an LP compilation of Robert Johnson's recordings. In fact, one of the reasons Hammond started the Columbia Archives series was, as he told McCormick, "to put out the Johnson record." For fans of the blues, that 1961 LP, *King of the Delta Blues*, set their world on fire. Among those fans was a burgeoning cadre of teenage white guitarists abroad who first imagined Chuck Berry as their hero but then turned their attention to the astonishing songs on the Columbia release. Listening intently to the album, Johnson's distinctive song-smithing and sometimes brilliant turns of phrase, his dynamic voice, and his guitar playing—which sounded like two people playing at once, with bass line strides underneath fanciful melodies—was unlike anything they had heard before. Echoing the manner by which members of the Blues Mafia had earlier described listening to country blues records, British blues guitarist Eric Clapton recalled listening to the Robert Johnson LP as a teen in the early 1960s: "at first the music almost repelled me, it was so intense." Quickly overcoming that feeling, however, Clapton, along with Keith Richards and other influential 1960s guitar gods, began incorporating Johnson's music into their live repertoires and recordings, giving millions of people their first taste of Johnson's songs.

The question, "Who was Robert Johnson?" then seemed increasingly important (and potentially lucrative) for the Blues Mafia to answer. They had grown obsessed with Johnson over the years as well. Yet they had not found Johnson's family, much to their frustration, and little was known to them about his life, save for what his musician contemporaries such as Son House and Johnny Shines reported in interviews—and even then, much of what House and Shines reported about Johnson was overlooked, ignored, or called into question. But with the attention drawn to Johnson by young rock stars such as Clapton and Richards,

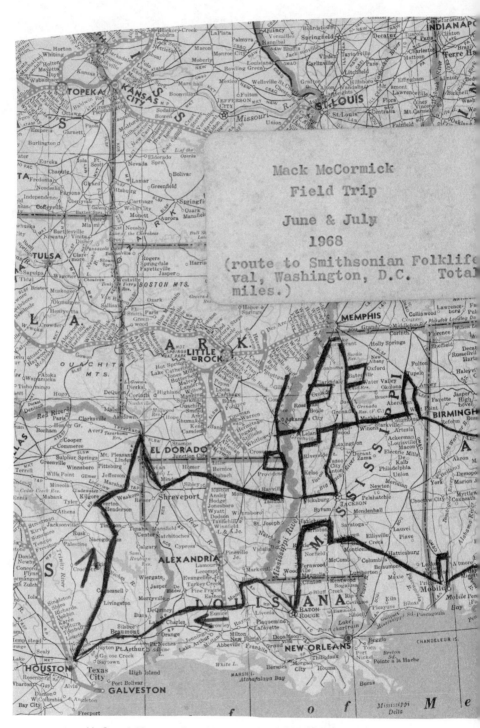

Mack McCormick
Field Trip

June & July
1968

(route to Smithsonian Folklife
val, Washington, D.C.   Total
miles.)

McCormick's route from Houston to the 1968 Smithsonian
Folklife Festival and back, with fieldwork forays in between.

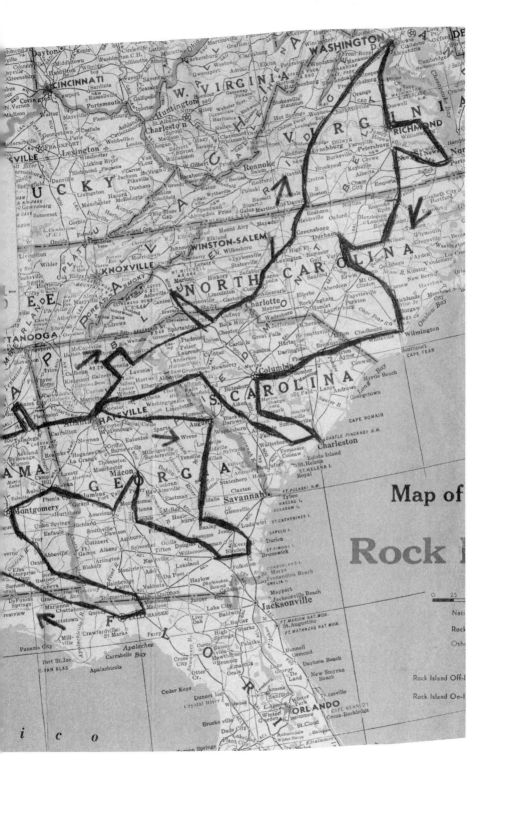

the desire to find his family, or even just a photograph of him, had traveled far beyond the mafia's court. Several researchers began the hunt in earnest in the late 1960s. With work travel for the Smithsonian enabling him to take some Mississippi detours, McCormick began a years-long quest to answer that question.

THE BOOK

The chapters that follow are drawn from early drafts of Mack's book *Biography of a Phantom*. He conducted most of the fieldwork between 1970 and 1973 and completed these drafts by around 1975. His archive, now housed at the Smithsonian's National Museum of American History, includes multiple versions of the drafts incorporated into this version of his book. McCormick was interested not in simply reporting his fieldwork to a small audience of peers, whom he and Oliver would likely engage with their work on Texas blues. Instead, he wrote *Biography of a Phantom* as a crime thriller targeted to a general audience and inspired by Truman Capote's 1966 nonfiction murder novel *In Cold Blood*. He deliberated over the pacing of the book and its character development, including his own. He developed a voice that seemed tempered and wise.

In many instances, McCormick took a great amount of time to sketch his surroundings for the reader. In fact, his portrayals of small-town intersections and bridges, even descriptions of fields and train depots as seen from a particular spot, often hold up remarkably well when looking from those same vantage points more than fifty years later. This legibility of landscape speaks to ongoing economic underdevelopment in many of those locations since McCormick wrote about them. Few of the towns he described in the Delta have grown or been reborn since their years of peak draw for Black families from nearby areas, which took place during Johnson's tragically short lifetime. By the time McCormick arrived on the scene, many families had long fled the Delta for work in Chicago, Detroit, and other northern cities, where they found better pay and less terror and oppression. In consequence of the economic stagnation that followed that Great Migration, we also can confirm the settings, at least, by which many of the stories in the book unfolded fifty years earlier.

The first layer in our telling of *Biography of a Phantom* is McCormick's text—a meticulously crafted tale of his search for people who were close to Robert Johnson, as well as, ultimately, his search for Johnson's killer. McCormick's best tools for doing so at the time included finding Johnson's death certificate in November 1969, identifying research destinations from place names in songs,

By the spring of 1970, when this photograph was taken,
McCormick had begun working on the book.

reading the often guarded interviews with artists who worked with Johnson, poring over dozens of gas station roadmaps, searching through local phone books,
passing a bottle with men on street corners, pursuing their leads, and knocking
on doors. Lots of doors. He introduced and imposed himself on African American families as a white stranger in their towns, absorbed in his own concerns.
This power dynamic casts a pall throughout the book, and it also causes one to
question how we might ever assess the nature of his rapport and the manner by
which it was received and negotiated.

McCormick was also one to record conversations and keep notes. We find
interview notes in small books of the conversations with many of the people
whom McCormick encountered along the way, hundreds of photographs of the
locations and people he met, phone numbers and addresses, correspondence, and
tape recordings of several of the interviews. McCormick did not include many
of the people whom he interviewed when writing this version of his manuscript.
Yet it adheres most closely to his original intention, namely, to cast his pursuit of
information on the life and death of Robert Johnson as an odyssey of personal
discovery. Accordingly, McCormick sometimes takes the reader down paths
that he later realizes were dead ends or pursues theories that he later deems are

erroneous. For part of his journey, for example, he mistakes the spelling of Johnson's mother's last name. He pursues a theory that Robert Johnson and fellow blues musician Tommy Johnson were somehow related. His meandering journey, mistakes included, becomes the story.

His narrative also reveals a fairly nuanced understanding of the power dynamic, as well as the oppressive conditions impacting the families—sometimes the last vestiges of Mississippi sharecroppers—with whom he met. He often acknowledges the generosity expressed by and the racism and hardship experienced by the people he meets; his portrayals of them generally read as empathetic, while he focuses his most biting criticism on local white plantation owners, sheriffs, and others in power. But on a few occasions in the narrative he expresses generalizations or language that is racist or sexist. We have noted when such expressions were editorially excised from this book. In addition, in the early 1973–75 drafts of the manuscript that this book primarily draws from, McCormick used the term "Negro" when describing Black individuals. His archive reveals that he later questioned the use of the term, and his deployment of the term in later manuscripts disappears. For those reasons, along with increasing calls for the word's removal from placenames and other contexts, we have opted to substitute "Black" or "African American" in its place, while recognizing that those two terms can convey different meanings.

It became apparent while reading his drafts and studying the archive, however, that a few more significant interventions were in order. McCormick spins most of his book with the mystery and drama of meeting strangers, chasing down leads, and learning more, bit by bit, from people who knew Johnson. But late in the manuscript, McCormick shares revelations provided in his interviews with Johnson's sisters, Carrie Thompson and Bessie Hines, who were living in Maryland when he met them in 1972. The sisters signed agreements to share the stories with McCormick, but for reasons explained in the afterword, the ethical use of their stories came into question as we further studied the archive. Based upon conversations with the sisters' co-heir and living sibling, Mrs. Annye Anderson, and with McCormick's daughter, Susannah Nix, we decided to remove those passages from the book.

Finally, this edited version of his early drafts excises large swaths of McCormick's now archaic ruminations on 1970s folklore theory, sociology, and the occasional extraneous musings or song analysis that take the reader too far off course and would have caught any good editor's attention. We have chosen instead to focus on and preserve the integrity of his journey, by removing such stones from the passway. Save for the removed sections, then, the pages that follow unfold with minimal editorial intervention.

A second layer of storytelling involves the public research and knowledge that has emerged about Robert Johnson—and Mack McCormick—in the fifty years since he began to craft his manuscript. By no means does our edited version of McCormick's story claim to provide any notion of a substantiated or definitive account of the individual Robert Johnson or his music. Far from it. The cottage industry surrounding Robert Johnson that erupted in the 1970s has not slowed down, and far more details about Johnson's life have emerged by this process in the decades since McCormick wrote these drafts. Even in just the past few years, in fact, when it seemed that nothing else could be said about Johnson, his life, and cultural impact, two major works on Johnson have joined in the conversation, including Bruce Conforth and Gayle Dean Wardlow's *Up Jumped the Devil: The Real Life of Robert Johnson*, a decades-long effort intended to provide a comprehensive history of Robert Johnson. We did not seek to reconcile McCormick's observations and arguments with theirs or others' litany of arguments and assertions about Johnson that have unfolded over the past half-century, with some notable exceptions.

The second of those recently published books *does* require reconciliation in these pages, because *Biography of a Phantom*, and McCormick's archive, is deeply connected to it. Certainly no work on Robert Johnson's life will achieve the clarity of understanding about Johnson as a person, and the legacy of his legend upon his family, that *Brother Robert: Growing Up with Robert Johnson* does. The account of Robert Johnson's life was written by someone who knew him as family—Mrs. Annye Anderson—along with her coauthor, Preston Lauterbach. Mrs. Anderson's engrossing and poignant, at times joyful, at times heartbreaking book is the most important in the bunch to read—and the best way in—to learn about Johnson. She urges us to consider Johnson not as an archetype, not as a dealer with the devil, not as a legend, and certainly not as a phantom—but as a human. She also pushes us to consider the damage done, the decades of lawsuits, rifts, exploitation, threats, and thievery that swirled around his family once the hellhounds appeared on the horizon. She encourages us to contemplate the manner by which Black artists have been memorialized and celebrated as well as neglected or even harmed in service of feeding national mythologies of "the blues."

Mrs. Anderson's book was published after the museum had acquired, processed, and begun making decisions about discoveries in the archive pertaining to her family. Her book, however, has powerfully influenced the questions that organized our undertaking of this volume. Mack McCormick figures ominously in her book. Some of the insight offered by Mrs. Anderson in *Brother Robert* will return in this book's afterword. Here, nearly fifty years after it was first drafted, with all that has changed, is Mack's story.

• • •

INTRODUCTION

Every few years someone shows up in Friars Point, Mississippi, asking questions about a man named Robert Johnson.

Friars Point is sixty-five miles below Memphis on the Mississippi River in the deep Delta, a ferry landing and a river port in the old cotton kingdom. The ferry ran until a few years ago, when they built the new toll bridge ten miles upriver. The port's gone; the roustabouts and the freight handlers are gone. And so are most of the sharecroppers and farm laborers, made unnecessary by new ways of growing cotton on the flat floodplain of the Mississippi. The plantations are still here, diversified into soybeans and rice, and the cotton is tended by walking rows of clattering machines.

You can't see the river from Friars Point, not even if you climb the levee and look on the other side. All you can see is a jungle of black trees growing out of the silt the river left behind the last time it rose and tried to climb out of its walls. You can smell the river, though, somewhere in the distance. It's rank with chemicals and factory wastes.

Friars Point was built to deal in river crossing and river traffic, and now, closed off from its river, it has little reason to exist. It's just an old, half-empty village lying in a crook in the levee. The slope of the levee is grassy, and out of the corner of your eye it looks like an ordinary hill. It's high enough that when you climb it there's a breeze on top, and you can look out over the town and see beyond to the rich checkerboard of fields and the grim shacks that stand at the edge of the fields.

It's not easy to find people here who remember anyone named Robert Johnson. But it's not impossible, either. When someone asks about him, it takes a while for the townspeople to send their thoughts back to the days when the port was busy, the ferry was running, and strangers had a dozen different reasons to come through here. Each fall there was a flood of people, drawn out of the cities for harvest, who came in at high cotton time. Sporting people came too. Hustlers

The levee at Friars Point, Mississippi. Photograph by Robert "Mack" McCormick.

and musicians and gambling people came in to circulate among the riverside taverns and party houses. Robert Johnson was part of that flow, and the people who lived in Friars Point knew him, if at all, as a passerby. They're incredulous when they learn that strangers come here to ask about Johnson because he mentioned the town in a song, because of an old phonograph record: "Best come on back to Friars Point, mama, and barrelhouse all night long."

That particular song lay around for twenty-five years from the time it was recorded, unheard and unreleased, until it was rediscovered in the company files. But the search for Robert Johnson began, tentatively and loosely, long before then. It began soon after his records first appeared. It was in a time when the country was trying to ignore the noises from Europe. The Lincoln Tunnel had just opened, and *The Big Broadcast of 1937* was playing the neighborhood theaters. Newspaper stories were datelined Barcelona and Shanghai and Warm Springs, Georgia. Amelia Earhart was lost somewhere in the Pacific. By the Red Sea archaeologists found King Solomon's old seaport, buried under the sand near Aqaba. It was in this era that a very few people began the search for Robert Johnson.

In the 1930s, among the more curious sidestreams in merchandising were the products sold under the name "race records"—phonograph records marketed to a Black audience. They represented a special world of hot jazz, blues, and gospel singing and fiery sermons, which few white outsiders knew or cared about. Only a handful of record collectors gave them much notice. The curiosity about Johnson began with the small, enthusiastic band that haunted the record shops in Harlem and Chicago's South Side, scouring new releases for blues and jazz to their taste. It was in 1936 that the name Robert Johnson first turned up on the brown and bright gold label of the Vocalion company. Word of his extraordinary performances passed quickly among the collectors. From the first, Johnson's records provoked arguments and generated speculation about the man who had made them. Interest built up, and finally it set in motion an attempt to locate Johnson and bring him to New York City for a performance as part of a concert that was scheduled for Christmas week in 1938. The help of the record company was enlisted. They passed the request on to their southern sales staff, who had originally located and recorded the singer. The Dallas branch office passed the request to a salesman in Memphis.

In time word came back: Robert Johnson was dead. He'd been murdered. The record company people had learned that much and no more. The search for Johnson ended there, but in another sense it only began at that point, becoming a deeper search that continues to the present day.

The stories regarding his death have taken innumerable forms: A kid whose passions got him killed. A youngster murdered by an evil woman. A poet who earned his songs by walking with the devil. Somebody killed him in a fit of jealousy. A musician who was casually murdered. The descriptions are wildly divergent, but they've been oddly consistent on one point: most of them agree that Robert Johnson was poisoned.

Gathering these varied, sometimes exotic accounts of his death has been a major preoccupation of the search, but it has also been directed at the central mysteries of who he was, where he came from, and what shaped his art. The assumption has been that the answers lie with the people who were his immediate audience: the people in Friars Point and the other towns he reeled off in his songs, who could provide the detail, the color, and the life picture to which Johnson belongs.

It's not clear who began the search. Perhaps among the earliest efforts was in 1939, when a record collector living in New Orleans took a vacation trip and stopped at a few places in Mississippi to ask about Robert Johnson. He found only one man who even knew who he was asking about, but with threads like this the searching began. A bit later, someone else went into the Delta and reported talking with Johnson's mother.

From the outset Johnson's life presented a mystery: his songs continually made reference to towns along the Mississippi River, but they'd been recorded in Texas, in two different cities eight months apart. People went to Dallas and San Antonio asking about him, but they learned nothing. For a number of years it was believed that he'd been living in San Antonio and was killed there. But official records gave no support. Others searched for him in Vicksburg, Rosedale, and Memphis—riverside towns, like Friars Point, mentioned in his songs. They tried Hot Springs and West Helena for the same reason. The search even extended to Europe, where others made inquiries among Black American troops and turned up a few of the same stories that were circulating in Chicago, St. Louis, and other cities where Black laboring people had gone after abandoning Mississippi.

Some musicians who remembered him were found and interviewed. A few other recollections began to fit together. Gradually a vague picture of a slender young man with a mark in one eye began to emerge. Still, the essential mysteries remained. Where he'd come from, how he'd died, and the sources of his erotic, tortured, self-damning songs continued to elude searchers.

By 1961, when Columbia Records reissued sixteen of the original records in an album titled *Robert Johnson: King of the Delta Blues Singers*, there was obvious frustration over the mystery. "Robert Johnson is very little more than a name on aging index cards and a few dusty master records in the files of a phonograph company that no longer exists," wrote Frank Driggs in the album's liner notes. "Efforts on the part of the world's foremost blues research specialists to trace Johnson's career and substantiate details of his life have provided only meager information," Driggs complained. "Robert Johnson appeared and disappeared, in much the same fashion as a sheet of newspaper twisting and twirling down a dark and windy midnight street."

1
THE TOWN

My first sight of the town was the water tower, with its black letters spelling out the name "Friars Point." It's on a broken and patchy road that leads along the side of the levee into the town. Brief sections of red gravel alternate with sections of aging blacktop. The road bends and angles with the edges of the flat, wet cottonfields. Most of the traffic is farm machinery and pickup trucks. This is one of the roads that Robert Johnson traveled, but now, years afterward on a rainy day in December, the prospect of picking up his trail seems absurd. Every bend in the road reveals land that's totally changed in the past few decades. The population has scattered and turned over. The town is a shadow of itself.

What seemed like the main street wasn't much. There were only a few businesses scattered along three blocks. The street ran straight toward the levee and then made a sharp right angle. Making the turn, I pulled over to the curb and parked. There were two groups of men gathered on the sidewalks, one on each side of the street. They were lean, worn-looking men.

The post office was in a vacant store with a big glass window. There was a narrow ledge below the glass, and one of the groups of men was perched along that ledge. They looked old enough to have been around when Robert Johnson came through.

I got out of the car slowly, letting everyone look me over. It was the kind of a town where a stranger is noticed and watched. One of the men was paring his thick, yellow fingernails with an old pocketknife. The man sitting next to him was leaning forward, his hands gripping a heavy walking stick. It was very thick, more

A water tower looming over the community of Friars Point, Mississippi.
Photograph by Robert "Mack" McCormick.

in the shape of a slender club than the usual walking stick. There was a design burned into the blond wood showing two entwined serpents, outlined by a series of dots and ovals and some carving at the head of each serpent. The work was crude but markedly similar to some of the African art that I had seen. I walked over to the men, nodding a casual greeting as if I'd lived in the town all my life, and made a few interested comments about the man's curious walking stick.

He was friendly but cautious. He stayed as he was, his weight resting forward on the stick while he said, "It ain't nothing I'd want to sell, you understand?" He shook his head vigorously. "It's a friend to me, this stick is."

He eased his weight back and held the stick out. I took it and turned it slowly, studying the painstaking work that had gone into it.

There were some currents stirring in the crowd. The man with the walking stick was pleased with the interest he'd attracted. The others wanted to get into the conversation, but they were still apprehensive. They watched and listened.

After I handed the stick back, one of the others asked to see it, and they passed it around, looking at the familiar thing with freshened interest. One of the men said something about a story about two snakes he'd heard as a child, something about two snakes wrapped around each other, struggling together, one snake supposed to represent good and the other representing evil. It was a story his grandfather had told, but he couldn't remember the whole of it.

Another man asked, "You know the strongest thing in the world?"

"What's that?"

"That's it right there. Two snakes wrapped together, that's the strongest thing in the world."

The stick was passed back to its owner. He said that years before he'd gone out into the river bottom, cut the wood for the stick, and then burned in the design of tapering eyes and flowing dots that formed the two serpents. The design had come to him one night in a dream. A few nights later he'd had the same dream again, and the next morning he'd gone out in the bottom to cut the stick.

We talked about such things for a time. He said that when he was young, older people used to have walking sticks but not with this same design. This one was his alone. He was proud of it, but a little fearful that I was going to offer him money. He was a poor man, and he didn't want to be forced to make a choice. He'd worked for thirty-seven years as a sharecropper and another ten years as a tractor driver. He was living on Social Security and a little money his children sent him from Flint, Michigan.

Eventually he felt enough at ease to ask me why I'd come to Friars Point. He pointed his stick toward my car, asking, "You come all the way from Texas?"

I told him that I was hoping to find someone who might remember a musician named Robert Johnson. Most of the men ignored the question, but a few shook their heads, withdrawing a bit, not wanting any part of someone who was looking for somebody.

7

The man with the cane said, "I'd help you if I could, but I never did keep up with them guitar players and such." We chatted some more, and then I thanked him for showing me his walking stick and strolled off. As I got out of earshot, I could see that they'd started talking among themselves. All of them were joining in the conversation.

I went around the corner and stopped a man standing by himself. I started off by asking directions and then worked the conversation around to the subject of musicians who used to hang around Friars Point. I tried a crowd of people loafing in front of a store, and a man sitting in a car waiting for his wife to finish shopping. The answers were vague, and the voices sounded worried. Some towns are more suspicious of strangers than others. I found a nearby gasoline station with a soft drink machine and a bench. I sat there counting the empty stores and the vacant lots.

About an hour had passed, and I went back to the men sitting in front of the post office. The man with the knife was still working on his fingernails. I got a friendly greeting from the man with the walking stick, and he asked me if I had found out anything. I told him no, and we talked a bit about how the town had changed over the years and how musicians used to be around all the time when the ferry was running. The man with the yellowed fingernails snapped his knife shut and put it away. He'd been shifting about, snorting as if he were anxious to get into the conversation, and then telegraphing a stony, disapproving look. Finally he twisted about, interrupting us, bursting out, "What you need with Robert Johnson? That man's been killed and put in his grave years ago. So now what is it?"

He stood up and dusted himself off. He didn't want his question answered. He turned his back on me and faced the man with the walking stick. "Ain't it like that?" he said. "Ain't it? It one damn thing after another."

He patted a pocket to reassure himself that he had his tobacco and then shuffled out into the street. The group watched him cross over and join another group across the street, sitting on a similar ledge.

The man with the walking stick shook his head and smiled. He turned to me with a long look, as if trying to make up his mind about something, and then squinted in the direction of an old Ford parked a short way down the block. "I think maybe there's someone there can help you," he said. He called out to the man slumped back of the steering wheel of the Ford, waving him over. The man climbed out of the car and came over. There was a slow-paced exchange of

8

greetings and a little small talk among the group. After a few moments the man gave me a brief, curious glance.

One of the others asked him, "Don't you remember that guitar player used to come through here that went by the name Robert Johnson?"

The new man nodded, "Surely. Surely, I remember him." There were some random comments from the others. They were beginning to talk among themselves, trying to scratch up some memory of the man in question.

The man from the Ford shook his head, "But I don't know nothing about what became of him except what they say that he got killed. Believe I heard he got poisoned. You know how people is. Jealous, you know. Women was crazy over that boy. It was down the country somewhere he got killed. Didn't he have some little gal here?"

"Yeah, Lord, he did," one of the men laughed. "But she's been gone as long as he's been gone, if she's the one I'm thinking about."

"She was a Carter?"

"No. She wasn't none of them." The man shook his head in dismay at the faded memory. "Now what was that gal's name?"

"Oh, she was a little Black gal named . . . now what was it they called her? You know if you'd asked me an hour ago, I might have told you."

"Betty? Wasn't that it?"

"Might have been."

"She used to stay out back of town next to where that house burned one winter. You know that place back over toward Coahoma where it burned? She lived just in there somewheres."

"All them places done tore down now."

"Betty. Yeah, I believe that was what she was called."

"I just wouldn't have no idea, not after all this time."

They were talking for my benefit, but I took no part in it, standing to the side, letting my thoughts pick over the crumbs they tossed out: Robert Johnson was known in Friars Point. He'd had a girl here. Young, dark, small, possibly named Betty. That song that mentioned Friars Point had been a toast to an erotic genius he'd found here; his voice took on a keening brilliance when he sang about her: "She got a mortgage on my body now, and a lien on my soul." There were some explicit, bawdy lines in the song that were probably the reason the record hadn't been released at the time. The girl's name didn't appear in the song, but in another song—an entirely different kind of song, sentimental and uncharacteristic—he did sing about a girl named Betty Mae. That was a curious blues, about a honeymoon and a promise to return with a marriage license in his hand.

As the men talked, I wondered whether both songs—the one maudlin and the other bawdy—might have been inspired by the same girl. Assuming for the moment that such songs can ever be taken in a strictly literal or autobiographical sense, it's possible that two such different songs simply represented different aspects of his feelings toward a single woman. (Later, on checking, it turned out that both songs had been recorded on the same day, one right after the other. Perhaps he intended them to go together?)

The men could add nothing to resolve the question. One of them said, "If she's the gal I got in mind, she was sassy and full of fun." (Robert Johnson had sung, "My Friars Point rider now hops all over me.") Another man added, "Around here, you'd see them together pretty much all the time. Day and night."

The stream of information dried up as quickly as it had begun to flow. The men indicated they'd said as much as they could, and their talk drifted off to something else. One offered some confusing directions to a house where he thought someone might know more. I thanked them and left to search for the house. It was a matter of wandering over several dirt streets looking for a particular combination of green house and white picket fence. I found it, but no one was home.

I drove around for a while on the outskirts of the town. Most of the streets were full of contrasts, from tumbled-down shacks to neat, well-kept homes like the green house. South of town I stopped at a small grocery and then walked along the road to chat with people I came across. Back in town I found another group and stopped to talk with them. Another hour of quizzing people standing on the sidewalk, sitting on porches, or hanging clothes on the line in a backyard didn't produce anything further. There was another suggestion about a man who used to run a local tavern that hired musicians. I found his house, but a neighbor told me he was in the hospital at the county seat.

An hour later, no one was home at the green house with the picket fence, but there were two women on the porch of the house next door. One of them shouted over, "That's my place. You want me?"

She walked over slowly, carrying a heavy shopping bag. It was a time before she felt like talking. She said her feet were bothering her, she had trouble catching her breath during the winter months, and she was still puffing from her trip to the store. She said it was strange that someone should be asking about Robert Johnson, because she'd just heard his name at the grocery store not thirty minutes before. Someone had been asking about a musician by that name, and after he'd left the people had gotten to talking about him, telling each other things they'd been reluctant to tell a stranger. She felt the same: "I don't like to talk about people unless I know what it's all about."

It seemed peculiar to her that outsiders would want to know about Robert Johnson. I explained that I wanted to write a book about him, and she took a while to think that over. Eventually, something I said seemed to satisfy her and she relaxed. She took me into her living room, and we sat facing each other. There were dozens of pictures on the walls of her late husband, her children, and her grandchildren. One wall was a memorial to three assassinated men: the two Kennedys and Martin Luther King Jr.

Her memory was blurred, and she had to go over the little she knew several times before the details sharpened, and to make certain that she wasn't confusing one man with another. Some years ago, while her husband was still alive, she used to take in boarders. There'd been a guitar player who had stayed at her house several times. Probably the man in front of the post office had remembered that, and that's why he'd thought of her. The guitar player was a young man, and the only name she knew him by was Bob. He came through Friars Point five or six different times that she knew of, and he stayed with her several times.

The only thing about him that stood out was a time when he stayed in her house about two weeks, and he seemed to grin to himself all day long. Curious, she asked him about it, but he just shook his head like some bashful child. Then finally one day he told her, "I'm in love with a gal, ma'am."

"I never did get over that," she laughed, "He was a full-grown man and acting like a little boy that's got sweet on a girl for the first time—and him being a musician and among all that goes on at those places where he'd play music."

She went on to describe one particular night when she happened to see him together with his girlfriend. She'd gone to a dance where he was playing, and a girl sat alongside him, sort of leaning against him, as he played. After several hours she started to get impatient for attention, acting playful, pushing the guitar out of the way, and leaning over to whisper at him.

It was customary at dances like this for the performer to take a short pause between every piece. "This night," the woman remembered, "we was dancing, and the music come to an end and we waited, and we waited some more, and finally we all came to realize the guitar player was gone. He and that girl. We thought maybe he'd just stepped outside, but he never did come back that night. They had to get somebody else to come and finish the dance."

11

She said the same thing happened several times around Friars Point. He and the girl would be together, and then somewhere in the middle of the night they'd be gone, and people would be left standing around, waiting for the music to continue. She'd never known the girl's name nor what became of her, nor what became of Robert Johnson. She wasn't even sure it was Johnson—except that half an hour before, when they'd been talking about him at the grocery store, someone had turned to her and asked, "Ain't that the guitar player that used to stay with you?" She thought it was probably the same man. "They say he went down the country somewhere and got killed." She shrugged her shoulders and walked to a room in the back of her house. "He stayed right in this room here and his guitar was always over there in that far corner, if it wasn't in his hands."

She smiled and indicated she needed to get on with her chores. We walked back out to the porch, and she wished me luck: "I told you what little I know." She shook her head. "About where he went from here, you'll have to go and ask someplace else."

I drove out of Friars Point feeling a small moment of satisfaction. The search had come a bit closer to the man. What had been learned was fragmentary, but it was specific and personal. For years almost no personal recollections of Johnson had been found. For a time it was hard to confirm that he even had existed. Now a faint pattern was beginning to emerge, and the visit to Friars Point had helped a fraction.

I followed the road out of town and worked my way south toward Highway 61. The great sprawling buildings of the King and Anderson plantations lined the road for several miles. My sense of satisfaction didn't last long. It was eroding by the time I found a roadside diner along Highway 61. The food was overcooked, and the waitress was careless. My coffee arrived half in the cup and half in the saucer. It tasted bitter. By dusk I was pulling into a motel: a row of little brick boxes with a lot of neon out front. The room was tidy and impersonal. They had cable TV, and most of the twelve channels were full of the same programs from Memphis, Jackson, and Greenville.

That evening I realized that I'd been on the road a long time, and I'd devoted too much energy to something that wasn't getting anywhere. I'd spent too much money. I was tired. It was time to go home. The rest of the search would have to wait.

And looking critically at what I'd learned in Friars Point, it wasn't very much. Friars Point had been the last in a series of stops, and there'd been only one significant piece of new information about Robert Johnson. The rest of it boiled down to some trivia—flickering bits of an unfinished legend. Gathering these threads of an unfinished narrative had been going on for a long time. A lot of people had shared in it. Many of us had been told, "You'll have to go and ask someplace else."

• • •

2
THE SEARCH

I n the beginning it was only a few record collectors, the ones who owned a few of the original 78s or who'd managed to scrounge dubbed copies, who wanted to know more about Robert Johnson. It was only a tiny group with an obscure special interest, but they managed to generate a lot of interest in Johnson, and in time their special enthusiasm spread to many others.

At some point a critical consensus began to take shape, giving Robert Johnson a unique position. The country blues is a rough, crude tradition, but he'd brought it to some kind of ultimate point: his whining, strident guitar and harsh, clenched voice were woven together like the hot colors in annealed glass. There was a totality and a passion that held even the casual listener. It was poetry made meaningful by the performance itself. Phrases such as "blues walking like a man" stung the mind and lingered because of the manner in which Johnson's performance set it there.

His songs were full of abrupt metaphors like "me and the devil walking side by side," delivered in a strained voice that was curiously full of joy. He sang, "I got stones in my passway, and my road seems dark at night" and made it more memorable by almost casually tossing the line away. Moments of poetic imagery came through with the feeling of a confessional. More than once he returned to scenes describing pursuit. He sang, "My enemies have betrayed me."

These somber moods were mixed with an erotic preoccupation that was always there, occasionally bursting through in some pungent double entendre, as when he half-chortled, half-sang, "You can squeeze my lemon till the juice runs down my leg," and then broke into a speaking voice to coax, "Baby, you know what I'm talking about."

In the strongest songs there was a consistency of mood, a sense of possession, an intensity, and a belief that arrested the hearer. The words "blues falling down like hail" created a chill of anticipation for the verse's completion: "There's a hellhound on my trail, hellhound on my trail." But it was neither the words alone nor the voice nor the guitar, but rather the sum total of the performance that made the songs so memorable. Everything about these records made one curious to know more about the man who'd created them.

Meanwhile, something especially direct and vital had been happening in Chicago, where an entire new generation of blues performers had emerged. They were making a loud, pounding blues using grating little amplifiers and crafting a new sound that evoked the lifestyles of the urban ghetto.

There were taverns scattered over the South Side where lean Black men bent over their guitars, using a variety of knife and slide techniques, with odd combinations of drums and harmonica to back them up. I first heard this kind of music in Chicago in 1946, and a little later in Toledo and East St. Louis, but always in the same kind of grim taverns that catered to working people in Black neighborhoods.

By around 1950 this new style had defined its shape and character. The amplifiers had doubled in size, and soon redesigned solid-body guitars with their new fast action gave this kind of blues its own technology. It was a new sound, and yet it owed a large debt to Robert Johnson. The whining, throbbing guitars and the clenched throats of the singers reflected in part his legacy, and some of the pivotal songs were his, too. Many of the blues musicians who thrived in Chicago in the 1950s talked about Johnson's records, or they talked about other performers who'd made the trip from Mississippi north and furthered the transition from the acoustic to the pounding, electric guitar. The pacesetters in Chicago included Elmore James and Muddy Waters, men only a few years younger than Johnson, but whose formative years had been marked by his influence.

There'd been a distinctive kind of traditional blues associated with parts of the Mississippi Delta. With World War II it had moved to Chicago, gotten itself 30-watt amplifiers, and started to evolve. There were arguments that Johnson was a principal source of the new urban blues and counterarguments that held him up as not an originator but rather as a charismatic performer. All these disputes were because real information was scarce and fragmented.

It was obvious that some of the gaps could be filled in if all the original Johnson recordings were reissued. Some of the most avid enthusiasts had only managed to hear six or eight of the songs. The material was owned by Columbia Records, a firm well accustomed to enduring special pleadings from one group or another—the people who collect arias, jazz buffs, country music enthusiasts, or all the others who wanted to burrow into their archives. The major recording companies, because they functioned through marketing machinery set up to sell records by the tens of thousands, were seldom comfortable with reissues directed at a special-interest group.

Columbia Records, however, was eventually prodded and levered into putting together an album of Johnson's recordings. One of the operative levers was the fact that small, independent firms were beginning to reissue the records themselves, taking the position that if the legal owner did not want to put the material on the market, then they would. Copyright in a sound recording was relatively intangible at the time, and US law in this area was murky before 1971. There was a lot of strength to the argument that old recordings, like literature or inventions beyond a certain age, might well belong in the public domain. These broader issues played a part, but within the ranks of Columbia Records itself were several key people—notably Frank Driggs, John Hammond, and George Avakian—who had long been personally intrigued by Robert Johnson, and they were pivotal in urging the company to respond to the growing public interest.

The album, titled *King of the Delta Blues Singers*, was released in late 1961, receiving almost unanimous praise from a wide range of reviewers and critics. It was indeed a superlative production. The sixteen selections had been meticulously chosen, and an unusual amount of care had been taken with almost every facet of the work, not the least of which was a superb job of remastering by an engineer named Stanley Weiss, who cleaned up and reprocessed the original discs so that the sound came through with surprising body and richness. It offered a stunning new look at Robert Johnson.

There was no rush on the retail record stores nor any sudden upthrust that marked the sales charts, but, rather unexpectedly, the album has sold slowly and steadily ever since. It's been a steady trickle that's lasted well over a decade, and to the surprise of some the album has begun gently nudging its way into that same select category where you find Enrico Caruso and Jimmie Rodgers—those few long dead voices that the public continues to want to hear, those that sell not simply to the old fans but to a new group that comes along every few years and wants to hear the man for themselves. A few years after it was issued, guitar

In 1961, Columbia Records released sixteen
previously issued and unissued recordings by
Robert Johnson. Courtesy of Robert B. Campbell
in memory of Dorothy and William Campbell,
National Museum of American History.

teachers began hearing from shaggy youngsters who wanted to be taught the slide technique used in "Cross Road Blues" or the dramatic, whipping accompaniment used in "If I Had Possession over Judgment Day." Later, some of these kids were playing in rock groups that casually accepted $40,000 for a night's work. The influence of Johnson became pervasive and fundamental to the revolutionary popular music of the 1960s. His was a tough, evil sound to emulate: a bag of imagist songs, a dry, clenched throat, and a rushing, knifing guitar style. But that sound now turns up regularly among the groups that climb the sales charts—including Led Zeppelin, Cream, Delaney & Bonnie, and Taj Mahal—and is occasionally heard on prime-time television.

Robert Johnson thus achieved a kind of prominence as an underground figure. His name began turning up in brief, sly references in both *Playboy* and the *Los Angeles Free Press*, in the *Village Voice* as well as in *Newsweek*. Sophisticated Black young people were expected to be acquainted with his name, and *Ebony* would work in a reference to "Robert Johnson, the legendary Mississippi hellhound of the blues."

In 1970, nine years after they'd produced the first anthology, Columbia Records issued a second Johnson album (*King of the Delta Blues Singers, Vol. II*). Since it was basically leftovers, it wasn't as good as the first, and the sound engineering was inferior to the earlier album's. But now every one of Johnson's twenty-nine songs was readily available on modern microgroove discs.

The second album came with a frivolous cover illustration and some faulty arithmetic on the front cover ("Featuring the original 'Love in Vain,' which became a Rolling Stones classic forty years later"). The back had some commentary bragging that another Columbia artist had learned to play guitar from the first Johnson album. Nonetheless, it was an invaluable addition, containing not only significant songs such as the influential "I Believe I'll Dust My Broom" but also incorporating weaker, seemingly uncharacteristic material, which in effect provided a fuller, more honest picture of Johnson's work. The liner notes by Pete Welding offered a detailed assessment, describing Johnson's legacy as "the most expressive and poetic body of work committed to record by any blues singer."

Short pieces about Johnson often share certain characteristics. They verge on superlatives, sometimes to an almost evangelistic excess ("perhaps the most titanic artist who ever traveled the American road," one writer called him), and they typically conclude with or focus on one of the several choice stories of his death. Welding, one of the early enthusiasts who had long sought firsthand information on Johnson, included an unnerving description of his death, drawn from an interview with a musician who said Johnson had been poisoned by a woman. "I heard it was something to do with the black arts," the man said. "Before he died, it was said, Robert was crawling along the ground on all fours, barking and snapping like a mad beast."

Almost no one mentions Johnson without retelling one or more of these stories. It may be because we hear them, or we *feel* we hear them, in the records themselves. Stones blocked his passway, women taunted him, a hellhound trailed him. His favorite themes were loneliness, wandering, all the harsh disappointments and the brief passions of mortality. His own passion may have been destructive in its size and intensity. His mysterious early death became part of an evocative, personal legend that urges us to listen intently and to grow curious about the man. His songs provoke a sense of wonder.

I was not the first to make the trip to absurd places like Friars Point. The searching for Robert Johnson is part of a much larger searching. There has been an emerging concern for better understanding the forces that give substance to American culture. The searchers are attempting to study a complex society: a violent, unhomogenized society caught in the grinding shifts between rural ways and urban ways, a massive collection of people bound up with one another and yet divisible by heritage, circumstance, and the cultural threads that bind individuals to groups, and groups to history. It is history—cultural pressure from what has just passed—that shapes life for the future.

We are many tribes, clustered in cities, who persist in conflicts large and small. The searchers, however, take a closer perspective, in which society is an infinite cellular structure, and strive to understand the rich, varied flow from individual cells. It is as if they were responding to that old challenge made by Walt Whitman:

> Who are you indeed who would talk or sing to America?
> Have you studied out the land, its idioms and men?

They search, perhaps, because secretly they believe our roots may hold more beauty than our future. Their work can become an odyssey: a long, lingering hunt over a haphazard trail. The searching has gone on erratically for over a century; at least three generations of hunters have covered much the same ground. They come like prospectors, roaming the American countryside (in particular the South) and, more recently, the urban core.

The hunters are known by many labels: social documentarian, oral historian, folklorist, anthropologist. They are perpetually confused as to who is the amateur, who is the professional, and who is the teacher, yet for all their disarray they may in time present us with a truly comprehensive appraisal of the American experience.

Some hunters are concerned with what has survived for centuries; others are fascinated with new growth, new manners, new cultural eruptions. Some study regional characteristics, and others explore the mysteries of creative clusters where people inexplicably and abruptly make new things happen. Some go looking for old, near-forgotten skills, and others seek the young revolutionaries.

And for some, such as myself, the obsession is to hunt the blues.

Our search is not simply for the materials—the songs and music that make up the tradition—but more for the most authentic performers, that select group of short-lived creatures, fully as mad as symbolist poets, who roamed through the world, leaving only cryptic clues about their existence. They thrived along the edges of a tough, laboring people's society, fulfilling its need for art, entertainment, and identity, yet responding to their deep-seated conviction that they were in league with the devil. They were born, often the youngest, in strong farming families that suddenly broke apart and scattered, leaving them with a sense of having been profoundly swindled. They experienced love and passion in short bursts and kept on the move, remaking their lives every time they pulled stakes. They existed within the Jim Crow tenant and ghetto worlds designed to segregate Black people, but they accepted few of Mister Charlie's dictates. They mostly followed the promptings of their own egos.

They went by names like Johnson and Thomas and Williams and Smith and Jones, but they earned appellatives such as "Guitar Slim" or "The High Sheriff from Hell." One singer called himself "Peanut the Kidnapper," and another who died under the wheel of a switch engine in Wichita Falls, Texas, was known as "Black Beauty." Casting themselves as mysterious, almost symbolic creatures, they made themselves legends. They thus left behind not simply false trails but a palpable sense of unreality.

Doubts can be banished only in places such as Friars Point, among people who know the legend but also remember the man himself. In the tedious course of following such trails, the hunter grows suspicious and wonders whether the target was real or part of some conspiratorial myth that mocks him. No quest can be quite so tantalizing as one in which the hunter comes, inevitably, to doubt that his quarry exists.

● ● ●

3

THE MAP

As I drove back from Friars Point, the car went stumbling over Mississippi's narrow, crinkled roads. I was distracted and not paying enough attention to driving. Several times I was jolted by a big logging truck roaring up on me.

The country had turned hilly, and it had the smell of damp pine needles. I'd worked my way due south, sometimes on Highway 61 and sometimes on a parallel county road, moving down into the far corner of the state and then crossing into the toe of Louisiana. The roads got narrower and rougher, and one of them took me to the edge of the Mississippi River, where I loaded the car on an old clanking steel ferry that boiled its way across half a mile of water. I drove up the bank on the other side, and after a few more miles I pulled over to the curb in a place called New Roads. I sat for a while in the car, trying to push my lingering discontent back into its own box. Across the street was a massive stucco building with the kind of fine iron balconies you see in New Orleans. It was the local Western Auto store. Next to it was Vee's five-and-dime store. I got out and walked along the sidewalk for a few blocks.

My search for information on Robert Johnson had been haphazard, incredibly drawn out, and unproductive. I'd spent time and money, and they hadn't been spent wisely. There was a disturbing hit-or-miss quality to it. I was depending too much on chance. I'd been merely wandering around, stopping here and there, trying to get lucky. It was at just about this time that the wheels were starting to turn at Columbia Records on issuing the second Robert Johnson album. When it appeared in 1970, the liner notes said, "Little is definitely known

A view of downtown New Roads, Louisiana. Photograph by Robert "Mack" McCormick.

of Johnson's biography." It was the same complaint the first album had made, nine years before. "Reports of his birthplace and date, his early years, musical development and the details of his death remain hopelessly confused, even after considerable research; one gets a different story from virtually every person purporting to have known him."

Clearly, a new approach was in order. I had been making too much of a random, haphazard kind of effort. It wasn't as if the possibilities had been exhausted. On the contrary, there were innumerable leads, but they needed to be prioritized in some order of probable value. My whole project needed a critical reassessment.

On the other hand, I could forget the whole thing. After all, no one had found out much about Elizabethan playwright Christopher Marlowe until he'd been dead—killed in a tavern brawl at the age of twenty-nine—for four centuries. I crossed the street and started back toward the car.

I reminded myself that Johnson must have had relatives, neighbors, and friends, at least some of whom might still be alive. Just one person with close, intimate knowledge might open up the trail to the others. Of all the possible methods that might be used to find such a person, which were the ones that would offer the greatest prospect of success? Where could I turn up close personal information on this man and his people? What if a detective agency were put on the job? What avenues would they pursue? They'd think first of routine sources like credit bureaus, draft registration records, and city directories. Police records in a number of towns and counties had already been checked to no avail. Still, it was that sort of methodical approach that was needed.

I climbed back in my car, swung around the block, and drove out of town. There were important questions that could have been asked at various points along the way, and that might still be asked. There were some leads that might be developed, and I remembered some geographic clues that hadn't been properly sorted.

In a few more miles I started to get into Cajun country. I stopped at Didee's, a rambling little restaurant on South Market Street in Opelousas, Louisiana. It was an unassuming place with a nondescript sign out front. The French-speaking, Black Creole owners had roasted a fat duck slowly for seven hours, basting it in its own juices. They served it with a dressing of rice and giblets, and would only charge you $2. You could run the bill up with a magnificent gumbo or crawfish bisque.

It was midday, and there weren't many people in the restaurant. I found a corner table, placed my order, and then leaned back with a fat red file jacket I'd dug out of the back of the car. It held most of the stuff I'd gathered on Johnson: notes, interviews, and the rest. The oldest thing in it was a letter I'd written in 1948 after I'd passed through San Antonio. Someone had asked me whether I could find out anything about Johnson, and I responded that I'd give it a try. The jacket was three inches thick, with scribblings stretching back for years, an incredible wad of half-truths, rumors, legends, contradictions, and maybe a few pinpoints of fact. It was full of leads that had yet to be followed, and of statements that had not or could not be verified. Its very size was a reflection of what an unsuccessful pursuit it had been.

Only one portion stood apart from the rest of it: I had actually gotten a bit lucky on this trip. The past week had included a sudden breakthrough on the mystery of Johnson's death, and only a few days earlier I'd visited the place where he died. I'd talked to people who were present at the time, and they had led me to his grave and told me exactly how he'd been put there. This was neatly documented with official records and careful interviews with people who had firsthand knowledge and told an essentially consistent story about what had happened.

Yet this episode stood apart, an isolated body of facts that led nowhere else. Johnson was a stranger in the place where he had died, and his death was treated indifferently. I had discovered no relatives, no close friends, no hint as to where he'd come from, no insight into the man himself.

The grim eyewitness story of his death took the zest out of the legends that had sprung up. The story needed to find the man himself, to try to catch some glimpse of the events that had preceded his death, and to illuminate the process that had led him to a lonely, indifferent burial.

My server, a large, brown woman, bustled away with the empty plates and came back with coffee. It came with chicory and lay heavy in the cup. I drank it in little gulps and began skimming again through my red jacket, looking for a new way to put the pieces together. Somewhere there had to be old girl-friends, relatives, neighbors, or perhaps even his own children. Someday someone was going to get the story. It was only a question of going to the right places and asking the right questions.

I left Didee's and went back to my car, tossing the red jacket in the back. In a half-hour I was driving through Lafayette, Louisiana, and in another few miles I picked up Interstate 10 and headed home. It was only four hours to Houston.

My Texas location was how I'd gotten involved in this frustrating search in the first place. By some strange inverse rule, the interest and concern over Robert Johnson seemed stronger as the distance from Mississippi increased. There were interested people in Chicago and California, but the curiosity grew more intense in the New York area and began to peak in Paris and London. A man who lived in Cheshire had published a meticulous transcription of Johnson's song lyrics. A detailed comparative study of the recordings was carried out by a Welsh-man working in collaboration with a man who lived on an estate in Sussex. They checked their work with a wealthy collector who lived in a suburb of Amsterdam. Magazines that carried articles speculating about Johnson were published in Aus-tralia, England, Germany, and Sweden. Some of the records that Columbia did not issue—alternative takes of the various songs—had been issued by a company located near Vienna.

For years I'd been hearing from people, many of them in Europe, asking whether I'd managed to learn anything about Johnson. After all, I lived in Texas, in the very state where his records had been made. Surely something must have turned up. Some of them urged me to investigate some theory they'd evolved from studying the records or from piecing various stories together. I felt com-pelled to try to respond to this interest, coming as it did with such intense curi-osity and from so far away, often from people for whom English was a second or third language, and for whom Johnson's harsh articulation must have been all but impossible to fathom.

Indeed, I did have the opportunity they lacked. I could leave Houston and within ten hours be in West Helena, Memphis, or Friars Point. If I worked it right, I could stop along the way at Didee's for some more roast duck.

I got back from Mississippi in mid-December. Altogether I'd been away from home for three weeks, part of it on a job for the Smithsonian Institution, doing field research in Arkansas, and part of it on my own, digging into Johnson's past. It took a couple of days to unload the car. It was full of tape machines, motel receipts, and wads of notes for the reports that had to be typed up. For a day or two I stayed in bed, sighing over daytime television, but then I started back to work. I waded into the backlog of mail, household chores, and other business that piled up during a few weeks' absence. Even so, within a few days I was beginning to make plans for the next trip into Mississippi and the Delta.

It was around Christmas of 1969 when I started sifting through my accumulated Johnson materials. I sorted everything into one of three piles. One was the three-inch jumble of fieldnotes and interviews I'd gathered myself. I went through them and found a lot of things I'd forgotten and a number of details that might possibly link with one another.

The second pile contained an index and photocopies of various articles that had been published on Johnson. A lot of these were interviews with musicians who said they'd known or met Robert Johnson. Some were plausible, and some were just talk. None were very detailed, but there were points that seemed to link up with others. Occasionally I found myself nodding over some minutiae, remembering something I'd been told that seemed to tie in with something in an interview that Al Wilson or Julius Lester or Paul Oliver had published.

The third pile was the smallest. They were the clues from Robert Johnson himself: the hints and the place names that occurred in his songs.

The easiest way to bring all this together seemed to be a simple geographic approach. I decided to itemize every town and place name, direct or indirect, that had occurred in all three piles and then lay them out on a map and see what it had to say.

From a pile of old road maps I'd found in a used bookstore, I dug out a Standard Oil map published in 1942. This one conveniently put Arkansas,

Louisiana, and Mississippi—plus a corner of Tennessee—on the same sheet. It covered everything from Memphis down to New Orleans, and it showed the roads substantially as they were in Johnson's lifetime. I devised a code for marking the map: a red triangle for a place mentioned in the songs, a black circle for a town that he was said to have frequented, an abbreviated note that would lead me back to the source, and some cryptic symbols indicating my own hunch as to how trustworthy each entry might be.

I started with the primary clues: the places Johnson had sung about. He'd mentioned eleven towns: Chicago, East Monroe, Friars Point, Gulfport, Hot Springs, Memphis, Norfolk, Rosedale, Vicksburg, West Helena, and West Memphis. Three states: Arkansas, California, and Tennessee. Three nations: China, Ethiopia, and the Philippines. And two transportation lines: Greyhound and the "Gulfport Island Road." In addition, there were three words from which some geographic inferences could be drawn: icicles, shrimp, and tamales.

It wasn't a long list, only twenty-two items in all. Taken out of context, they made an odd assortment. Fortunately, the context made it clear where each of the towns was located. Rosedale, for example, was the town on the Mississippi River, but Norfolk referred to the big Virginia city in the Hampton Roads area. The list spanned the globe and reached across the United States from one coast to the other.

Of course, there are any number of reasons why a name might come up in a song. A poet can be attracted by the exotic sound of a name or can use it as a practical matter of rhyme or metrical need. Or simply fumble into it: Gilbert Keyes and Joe Lyons wrote the lyrics for "On the Alamo" while thinking it was a river.

My challenge, then, was to pick out those places that had some personal significance for Johnson. A few could be set aside readily enough. For instance, the three foreign countries named had all appeared in the last verse of "I Believe I'll Dust My Broom," which was recorded in 1936. The news that year had been full of all three countries. Civil war had been raging for two years in China. The Philippines had been granted independence in 1935, and Ethiopia had been invaded the year before. This does say something about Robert Johnson. Several times he'd been described as a young kid who was ignorant of everything outside his immediate world. But that doesn't quite jibe. In this instance he seems like someone who listened to the news and paid attention to what was going on in the world. But it's possible that he simply got the whole verse—or any of these place names—from some other singer. He was working within the blues tradition, dealing in handed-down materials and motifs, but going on from there to achieve his personal compositions and style. It's hard to know which elements belonged partly to the tradition and which were entirely his own.

It took a couple of days for me to go through the list with all the study it needed, considering whether a location had taken on a new meaning or become part of a pattern. A good many of the places fell into a cluster on the map, but others remained hard to evaluate. There's a puzzling line in the song "Sweet Home Chicago," where he sings, "Oh baby, don't you want to go . . . / Back to the land of California, to my sweet home Chicago." After I puzzled over this for a few days, something clicked. There's a California Avenue in Chicago. It's one of those long streets that runs from the Blue Island section up to Evanston, about twenty-two miles. With that in mind, the line could be taken literally. Robert Johnson might have hung around that part of Chicago, probably about where California Avenue crosses West Roosevelt, in the West Side district. A bit later something else clicked, and another interpretation came to mind: there's a Port Chicago in California, a little railhead and dock town on an arm of water that connects with San Francisco Bay. He could have had relatives out there. He might have gone out to visit them.

A great many of the references formed an obvious pattern. Out of the fourteen American place names that occur, eight fall inside the area he'd nicely summed up in one boastful verse:

I got womens in Vicksburg, clean on into Tennessee,
I got womens in Vicksburg, clean on into Tennessee,
But my Friars Point rider, now, hops all over me.

A two-hundred-mile-long corridor with the Mississippi River looping and curling down the middle, Vicksburg to Memphis. This was the ground that's been visited most often, but it's really too large an area—nearly ten thousand square miles—to be searched thoroughly. Visits to specific towns such as West Helena, Rosedale, and West Memphis hadn't yielded much information.

I wanted to explore some new patterns, and so I gave particular attention to towns that lay nearby but outside the corridor itself. Johnson had sung about "East Monroe." It was probably just poetic license; strictly speaking, there is no such place. There's only Monroe and West Monroe, two towns that look at each other across the Ouachita River in upper Louisiana. He'd also sung a line about

A view of Malvern Avenue in downtown Hot Springs, Arkansas.
Photograph by Robert "Mack" McCormick.

all the doctors in Hot Springs, Arkansas. That was a resort that used to attract a snowbird mixture of gamblers and arthritis victims. It was popular with Black tourists and travelers, and one of the Black Baptist church organizations operated a huge bathhouse in Hot Springs.

As I narrowed down the list, one item began to stand out. It occurred in the only song of Robert Johnson's that was predominantly a traditional piece. The blues is often seen, sometimes in a rather oversimplified manner, as a kind of solo performance that evolved from the older work song tradition. Many of the older blues musicians knew songs or pieces of them that were borrowed from the song materials of labor gangs. The relationship between the two is like that between rocks and gravel, but relatively few examples to illustrate a clear transition have worked their way onto commercial recordings. Johnson's "Last Fair Deal Gone Down" is one of this select group, more work song than blues:

> My Captain's so mean on me,
> My Captain's so mean on me,
> My Captain's so mean on me, good Lord,
> On this Gulfport Island road.

28

It retains the structure and the flavor and the cadence of the work song: the short, choppy line that would be punctuated by the fall of an ax or sledgehammer. It was a song meant to help shorten the day, to mix a little sly humor in with the sweat, and to poke some fun or a complaint at the white boss. It's a slavery institution, and it persisted through the era of railroad building and levee building, lingering on to the present day in a few southern prisons. The identical song was sung in 1947 by a convict gang in the Mississippi state penitentiary:

Oh, Captain George, he was a hard driving man,
Oh, Captain George, he was a hard driving man,
Oh, Captain George, he was a hard driving man,
Oh, my road, Lordy, out on the Gulf and Ship Island.

Unlike Johnson, the convict gang named the railroad correctly. It was an obscure, short line that was absorbed by the Illinois Central in 1925, when Johnson was a boy. Somehow he acquired and adapted a song that probably originated—in 1887—with the laborers who cleared the timber and built the railroad. The line took its name from Ship Island, a resort that lies twelve miles offshore. Just opposite on the mainland, the railroad founded the town of Gulfport and then ran up into the piney woods of Mississippi, eventually reaching as far as Jackson. It was built to haul timber and excursion passengers, and it's little remembered except in the immediate area it served—the path from Gulfport through Hattiesburg to Jackson. It's a song most likely to have been remembered or learned in that area.

I spread out the old Standard Oil map and started filling it with symbols and notes: A red triangle for Monroe and another for Hot Springs. A two-hundred-mile corridor from Vicksburg to Memphis, with several red triangles inside it. Some marginal notes about Chicago's West Side and the San Francisco–Oakland area. Another note about Norfolk, Virginia. There was a double red triangle around Gulfport. It was the only town mentioned in two entirely different songs. That was intriguing, just by itself. Off to the side of Gulfport, I wrote the word "Shrimp?" He'd used the term in a metaphor, but the word itself had a coastal implication that was worth noting. Finally, I drew another long corridor, this one 150 miles in length, taking in Gulfport, Hattiesburg, and Jackson.

These were the primary clues, the ones Johnson himself had scattered. The most tantalizing of them that had developed was Gulfport and that second corridor in southern Mississippi. That was new ground.

The next job was a lot bigger. I started wading through the three-inch pile in my red jacket, sifting out towns where people had heard Johnson, said they had seen him, or named their community as his hometown. Some of these were ridiculously faint clues. Dozens of places were mentioned in one way or another: Eudora, Arkansas City, Cairo, Minter City, Carruthersville, Greenwood, Memphis, Helena, Robinsonville, Clarksdale, Greenville, Hughes, Granada.

It took over a week to sort them out and put them on the map. Some of the towns had been mentioned a number of times over the years, and these were duly noted. Next, the final step. I dug into the articles and interviews that had been published in various papers and magazines. This was also a big pile, and it took another week to locate all the items and go through them carefully. Many additional places got circled on the map: Detroit, Commerce, St. Louis, Walls, Banks, New Jersey, Chicago, West Memphis, East St. Louis.

There were lots of others. When I'd finished, the map had 106 places marked on it or noted in the margins. And it showed what I'd hoped it would: there were some particular clusters that stood out emphatically. Along that two-hundred-mile corridor were areas where the circles fell in a tight little grape bunch. And there was a scattering of other markings that hinted at places that I hadn't considered before. A few towns stood out with five or six circles added to them as I'd successively checked through the material.

With the map completed, I felt the task ahead of me was more rational than it had been in the past. I could concentrate on the places where the markings clustered, and I had pulled out many odd bits of information that suggested specific possibilities to check. Above all, the map offered me one of life's rare treats: the prospect of unraveling a genuine mystery. Fiction seldom achieves this; an astute reader can often guess where a plot is going from the inherent structure of the work itself. More often it is everyday life and events that offer the best riddles. The behavior of people is puzzling, enigmatic, baffling, and infinitely absorbing. A strangler plagues a city. A young poet steps off the stern of a ship one dark night. A judge vanishes. A great artist starts doing bad work. A neighbor starts wandering up and down the sidewalks in his pajamas. The search for any answer can become an adventure, and the quest for Robert Johnson's story offered a true mystery whose end was unpredictable. The much-marked map offered a starting point and a guide, but there was nothing on it to give away the ending. I had no way of knowing where each day's questions might carry me.

● ● ●

4

BACK TO THE DELTA

t was April 1970 before I got back to the Delta. The weather was mild, people were out of doors, the days were getting longer. I traveled for five days without turning up anything new. I went into small-town barbershops, and I stopped at crossroads stores. I leaned over fences chatting, and I sat for hours on porches getting acquainted with people, working up to the point when I could ask them to search their minds for recollections of a young musician from years ago whom they might have known only as Bob or Robert.

I spent a Saturday afternoon outside a busy grocery store in Clarksdale, Mississippi, with a group of sidewalk bystanders, talking to nearly everyone who went in and out of the store. It was one of those Saturdays when half of Coahoma County came into town to hang around the courthouse or get their shopping done. Next morning I was a few miles up Highway 61, making gentle inquiries amid a flock of Sunday-dressed people bunched outside the white double doors of a Primitive Baptist church.

Sometimes I was direct about it, but more often I was indirect, spending some time getting acquainted, exchanging small talk, putting people at ease, and letting them know I was no cop, describing my errand in different ways, maybe revealing that I was interested in the best local musicians, letting the talk drift in that direction and then saying I'd appreciate hearing anything they might recall of a certain guitar player. They knew I was there for a reason, and once they understood the reason and judged me to be harmless, they were usually willing to help.

Responses varied from one town to another. In one place people were quick to talk and felt free to answer questions. In the next community they were wary, wanting to ask me a few questions first. With good reason. This was troubled country. Its history is full of night riders, of families suddenly burned out of their homes, and of warnings passed not to make any outside "agitators" welcome. One man looked at me with worried eyes and asked, "I know you, don't I?" He put up his hands as if to ward off trouble. "Ain't you the fellow that comes just before the trouble breaks?" Later I found out there'd been an ugly time over voter registration in that county. From time to time a carload of townspeople would follow me around, wanting to see what I was up to. Usually it was a pickup truck with two or three young white men and a couple of shotguns in a rack against the cab's rear window. Once in Greenville, Mississippi, two pickup trucks began following me. The first had three white men with their shotguns in the rack. Behind that was another truck with two Black men, also with shotguns. So I drove out of town, came back an hour later, and went about my business in peace.

Being the outsider sometimes helps, and sometimes not. On occasion I was gulled by practical jokers. One man promised to take me directly to a relative of Johnson's, but it turned out he just wanted a ride to the next town. Another man solemnly assured me that Johnson was alive and well, had turned to preaching, and had gotten rich out in California. Sometimes people would send me on a wild goose chase just for the hell of it.

But those were the exceptions. On the whole, it's overwhelmingly the custom of rural people to respond to outsiders with courtesy and help. They give strangers the benefit of the doubt. They'll dig around in their memories, call out to other people, talk to their neighbors, or go to the telephone and call up relatives to see if they can stir up anything to help you out.

Even so, my first five days had gone by uneventfully. I'd visited Walls, Eudora, Dundee, Forrest City, Wynne, and Marked Tree. I'd covered some of the places where the circles on my map fell in thick clusters, and I'd come up with only vague memories. Like a gambler trying to change his luck, I switched tactics and drove into Memphis. Looking for someone in a big city is an entirely different thing. People are busy and hard to talk to. The people that have lived there a long time are hard to locate. Still, I looked up some of the local musicians I knew and followed the leads they gave me. I tried some of the men sitting around the barber shops along Beale Street and then, following what seemed like a good tip about a woman who was supposed to be Johnson's sister, I drove out to Bunker Hill, a long-established Black community on the far south side of Memphis, and scoured the place, going from door to door. Nothing resulted.

All I'd heard were jumbled, fading fragments of memories and a few retellings of the death legends. None of the leads had gone anywhere. I drove out of downtown Memphis and spent an evening in the taverns on Eighth Street in West Memphis. The next day I drove south, back into the plantation country.

Finally, I got lucky in Hughes, Arkansas. Hughes was a cotton mill town, just a blip interrupting a flat checkerboard of fields. It had a Pure Oil station, a Chevrolet dealer, and a Planters National Bank. To judge from the phone book, the biggest family in town was named Fong. There was a Fong Department Store, a Fong Grocery, a Dr. F. H. Fong, and half a dozen other listings. There was nothing unusual in this. Small Delta towns often had one or two tightly knit Chinese families, and once in a while a community such as Sledge, Mississippi, would elect a Chinese American mayor. Such idiosyncrasies complicate some of the pat, stereotyped notions that have tended to collect about the Deep South. There was more than enough about Hughes to help reinforce the stereotypes, however. It was dominated by its big farms. As I drove around and asked directions, I heard about Raglan Plantation, Sycamore Bend, the Green River place, Kellogg and Hughey, and the Red Gum Plantation. Black people labored for white people, and the system stretched back five generations or more.

There's a street in Hughes, Love Street, that runs off from the highway at an angle. It featured a row of taverns among some run-down houses and vacant lots. Hughes was and still is a minor sporting center for the area. There used to be droves of musicians working here before the jukebox took their jobs, and there still were some bluesmen who worked there on weekend nights. It could still turn into a lively spot.

When I got there, it was a little early in the morning, but I found the proprietor of one place doing some repair work before the day's business. He was standing on a ten-foot ladder, poking a screwdriver at a neon Falstaff Beer sign that was sputtering and buzzing back at him. He said he knew a number of musicians: "I been running this place or some other place around here since 1932." He took a vicious whack at the neon sign, and it quit sputtering. "There ain't no counting how many musicians I hired to play for me," he continued. "It's got to be a hundred or more. And a lot of them, I wouldn't even know their name."

"What about one named Johnson?" I asked. Musicians named Johnson were of course fairly common. I was curious to see which one he'd recall.

"Lonnie Johnson, you mean?" He shook his head. "No, I don't think he ever came through here."

"Any others?"

"Johnson?" He thought a minute. "You probably mean Bob Johnson. They called him Robert when they put out his records." He climbed down from the ladder and stuck the screwdriver in a drawer. "Yeah, I knew him. I used to hire him to come play music here." He smiled. "What you want to know about him?"

"Anything you can remember."

"I can't tell you much. Except that he's been in here playing for me plenty of nights."

"Know where he might be now?"

"Oh Lord, he's been dead years. Died years ago. Over in Mississippi. Wasn't around here."

"Does he have any people around here. Any kin?"

"No, not now. There was a girl he was sweet with, but she's been gone for years. Went to Chicago or someplace."

He folded the ladder and carried it into a back room. He came back in a minute, dusting his hands, and chuckling to himself under his breath. "I can tell you about a little joke I had with him one time." He eased himself onto a barstool. "There was this one time Bob came around here after I hadn't seen him for a while, so I asks him, 'Where you been?' and he answers back, telling me, 'I been to Texas.'

"He kind of grinned a little, proud like, you know? So I asked him, 'Texas! What you doing over there?,' but he just shook his head and grinned. Wouldn't say nothing, kind of shy. Finally he tells me, 'You wait. You'll find out.'

"Well, naturally enough, I forgot all about it. Then next thing I knew he had put out a record." He stopped, struggling to bring the name of it back. "They called it the 'Terraplane Blues,' that's what it was. You heard of the Terraplane automobile?"

I nodded.

"That was a big, popular car in those days. I expect they're all junked now. So he comes back in here one day, and he says, 'Did you find out yet?,' and I didn't even remember what he was talking about. Then it came back to me, but I was devilish about it. I told him, 'No, I never did.'

"Well, his face got all disappointed, and he says, 'You ain't heard my record?' And I put it on him, I says, 'What record is that, Bob?' So he tells me that's why he went to Texas. I just scoffed at him, and I told him I never heard of nobody going to *Texas* to make records. He was standing there looking hurt, and I was just too devilish to quit. I told him I knew lots of guys that had made records—such as Peetie Wheatstraw and all like that, they'd come here to play for me back in those days—and I never heard of them going to Texas to make records. They had always gone up to Chicago. I told him I figured someone was playing a joke on him.

"So he got to looking at me real straight-on, and finally he sees—he had a little something wrong with one eye—finally he sees I'm having fun with him, and damn if he doesn't break out with the biggest grin, and get shy and hang his head." The man laughed and heaved himself off the barstool. "Just like a little kid."

The Falstaff sign started sputtering again, and the proprietor sighed and went to get the stepladder again. As he set it up, he told me it was going to be hard to find out anything because the area had changed so drastically. Most people had moved away, and farm machinery had moved in to replace their labor. He said a few of the other tavern operators might remember Johnson. "Lots of us used to hire him for a night or two, but I don't know a soul around here that might have really known him, not personally." The man climbed his ladder and whacked the neon sign again a few times. It blinked and settled into a quiet buzz. "I can't think of anyone to send you to," he concluded.

As it turned out, his estimate was correct. Several other people in Hughes remembered Johnson. They recalled him and his records and the fact that he'd died somewhere in Mississippi. I heard several more anecdotes about him, but no one was able to tell me more. There was no lead to anything substantial.

I spent the day wandering around in the area. I drove out toward the river, stopping now and again at one of the big plantations. I talked to several mechanics in one of the maintenance shops, and I pulled up to chat with an older person sitting on the wide porch of a sharecropper's cabin. The road carried me past the Bright Future Farm, Belle Meade, and then the Beck Plantation. I found a YMCA camp, a Civil Aeronautics Administration airway beacon, and an ancient Indian mound. I even found a section of the state of Mississippi, left behind years ago when the river had cut itself a new channel and left a loop of ground on the Arkansas side.

I used up a lot of mileage, heading more or less south along the river, angling around on the back roads, sometimes running down a stretch of road that headed for the river and then dead-ended at the levee. I stopped at country stores and at little settlements, asking the same few questions. Some of these roads were familiar territory. I'd been over some of them a few months before and a couple of years before that, looking then for living, active musicians and people instead of hunting a dead man.

Near the small community of Oneida I'd spent an afternoon with a boot-legger, who'd let me set up a tape machine and had talked freely, giving me a detailed recipe for making mash and setting up a distillery. He was a colorful talker and proud of his skill, despite the fact that it had cost him three prison terms, the last in the Federal penitentiary outside Texarkana. He and many of his customers preferred the hard bite of raw whiskey fresh from the still. He scorned the commercial processes: "Ain't no one ever made good whiskey in no damn factory."

He'd told me that he was thinking of moving into Hughes, but he hadn't done it. Now I found him in the same place, leaning against a junked automobile in front of his house. He seemed genuinely pleased that I'd come back to see him a second time. He said he'd changed his mind about moving, explaining, "This is my groove here." We visited for a while, and just before I drove off he told me he'd been in the hospital and they'd told him his condition was something they couldn't fix. He asked whether I still had the recording he'd made. I said yes, and that seemed to please him. He stood out in the road watching as I drove away.

I began thinking about the subtle changes that had taken place just in the last two years. There were fewer people left in the country. If they hadn't moved to a city, they'd moved to the nearest town. Sometimes it seemed as if there were only two kinds of people left. There were the hopelessly ill-equipped or indifferent ones, who simply stayed where they got put. Then there were the hardheads who loved the land and familiar things and gave that first priority. They were the ones whose talk was so rich and so worth hearing. They knew history—not the dull stuff of politicians and generals, but the immediate personal history that uncovers our mainstreams. They could describe what American life has been and help explain how we got where we were. They could tell us what's been valuable, and what's been worthless.

I drove back up the road, working my way toward Highway 49, with the idea of finding a motel. There were several of them not far away, on the edge of West Helena. As for my search, I felt that something was going to give pretty soon. I was going to pull in a thread that would make things start to come loose. Maybe not today, maybe not tomorrow, but soon. I was due for a break.

But just at the moment I needed a change of pace. My disposition was beginning to sour. I'd been at it continuously for almost ten days. I'd talked to hundreds of people, and they'd loaded me down. They'd tried to answer my questions, but many of them had told me their own stories. It's astonishing how often people will unburden themselves to a stranger. Intimate details, old bitternesses, and their idea of glory all come tumbling out. This usually works opposite to the way you might expect. It's not closeness but distance that makes people want to reach across and achieve some rapport. Go to a town and present yourself as a neighbor and kinsman, and people are usually a bit cautious. But go there as a total stranger—uninformed and unrelated but interested—and the reaction is less guarded. The stranger will learn more, hear more, find more answers, and come away carrying more confessions.

It is not, however, a dispassionate process. The stranger bears a certain emotional load. While meeting people in the Delta, especially people of Robert Johnson's age and generation, I was casually told of epic wandering, of big families always on the move, shifting places year after year, in endless, exhausting searches for a home. I heard of a style of life that mangled too many and was too full of early death or endless, bleak ignorance. Nowhere else in the country was the present day more closely wed to its history.

The people I encountered would speak about their present circumstances calmly, but they would drop in little details that set my teeth on edge. One old woman was living on a diet of beans and laundry starch. Another woman took 30 percent of her husband's paycheck to give to a faith healer. A family rented a house without a north wall and only half a roof. A good mechanic, the father of six, was casually stabbed on a Friday night. And on and on: An accomplished secretary who couldn't find a job. A ten-year-old boy already too far behind to ever hope to catch up with his peers. A little girl needlessly dead of a fever. A young woman without a winter coat. A proud old bootlegger dying of cancer. The past clings to the present. Talking to people in the Delta one hears all these details. And one hears its history, the memory of the steady sequence of changes that occurred, the personal impact of the shifting agricultural method, and the slow, grinding way in which families were uprooted, scattered, and lost to one another. The people left behind are—some of them—the hard-headed ones. The others are merely wretched.

Somewhere near Highway 49 I stopped to ask directions at a confusing, unmarked crossroads. A frail old man came hobbling out on his porch with an obedient air. He didn't know which road led to West Helena. He didn't even know his own address. He just stood there trying to grin, looking helpless, but offering his service. I drove away vaguely angry, oppressed by the sheer number of such sad encounters that had piled up. One fawning old man doesn't represent the whole picture. Only yesterday I'd come across two men, one white, one Black, in a quiet argument about the most economical means of dealing with nitrogen deficiency in the soil. Two agronomists don't represent the whole picture either.

A few days ago, around lunchtime on a construction job at the edge of Como, Mississippi, I'd talked with a man who was chewing on a dry slab of meat crawling with maggots. He knew the maggots were there, and he only shrugged about them. It was an indifference he'd acquired years before, working in a lumber camp where that was the only kind of meat they served and where special deputies prevented anyone from quitting the job. The same man told me that no power on earth and no amount of money, strapped in bales and piled on his front porch, could possibly make him put an oyster in his mouth.

Different people make different choices. After so much of it, the sense of perspective gets distorted. The sheer number of encounters is too much of a burden. It takes a while to sort it out and let the senses restore themselves.

I found a motel and locked myself in a cramped little room with a curious metal door. The television set swung out from the wall on some kind of hinged arm. The picture on the screen was full of fringe-area snow and distortion. I took a short nap, woke up around mid-evening, and resumed considering my situation.

My marked-up Standard Oil map was getting pretty raggedy. A waitress had dribbled water on it, and a few of the symbols and notes were smeared. I stared at it for a while, questioning the logic behind it. Robert Johnson might have come from a small family and gone through life with only a few people close to him. It was not impossible that every one of them was dead or gone from this part of the country. He could have come from a town that had never been mentioned in the source material I was working with. He might have been born in Pine Bluff or Tupelo or any of a thousand other places that weren't marked. I went back over my methodology, noticing all the flaws that could have undermined the whole process of sifting and collating.

Nonetheless, I retained a sense of expectation. A break was due. It was a feeling built out of some irrational notion that hard work will earn a reward. The irrational, however, provides our most comforting thoughts. I stared at the map and felt quietly elated.

Of all its marks and circles, the heaviest were those drawn around Helena and West Helena—two towns separated only by the hump of Crowley's

Ridge, an arc of forested high ground that runs through part of the Delta. In all the interviews, in all the material I had gathered and evaluated, the single place most frequently mentioned in connection with Johnson was Helena, Arkansas. No other town came up so often. And West Helena was one of the towns named in his songs.

Still, I'd been in the vicinity twice before and found hardly a single person who even remembered Johnson. As a matter of fact, it had been difficult to find any substantial or detailed recollections of *any* guitar players. Helena was an old river port, a sawmill town, and the taverns here had traditionally preferred piano players to provide their music. A few people had acted a little insulted when asked about guitarists. One man huffed and said, "We never let them guys with starvation boxes come around here. You have to go out in the country over in Mississippi to hear that stuff, out around some damn cotton patch. What we had here was strictly piano music."

There was a curious grain of truth in this. On this side of the river, blues pianists seem to have been dominant. I heard about Arnold Wiley, Walter Davis, Willie Bloom, Roosevelt Sykes, and Lee Green. Across the river, however, guitar players seem to have been favored. It was only a general pattern, not invariably true, but one that came up often enough to be noticed. Moreover, everywhere in the South, the sawmill towns like Helena seem always to have had a preference for piano music. The reason may simply be that the mill towns were noisy and needed louder instruments to dominate the tavern crowds.

So it was strange and ironic that this stronghold of pianists should be the town most often spoken of in regard to Robert Johnson. All through my interviews and notes, people recalled that he had gone to Helena, or just come from here, had a girl here, or had been seen here. But my earlier visits to Helena hadn't been able to produce any genuine leads. This time, however, I'd come with a different idea, and I had a specific errand to do the next morning.

By the early 1970s, Helena was no longer just a sawmill town. It had attracted some Northern industry—Mohawk Rubber, Chicago Mill & Lumber, and others—and grown into a small city with barges, river traffic, a textile mill, soybean processors, and a fertilizer plant. Moreover, Helena was the home of *King Biscuit Time*. On the air since 1941, *King Biscuit Time* was one of those folksy, down-home radio programs that used local talent to push local merchandise. At a time when radio stations were few and far between, KFFA was the first to come into this part of the Delta, launching a low-power regional station that covered six counties—half in Mississippi, half in Arkansas—where the population was 69 percent Black. Its announcers and farm reporters were white, but much of the entertainment, the music, and a good many of the ads were directed at the 130,000 Black listeners in the KFFA area. If you were selling cosmetics, groceries, or used Fords in this part of the world, your business depended on Black customers.

King Biscuit Time came on the air during the noon hour with a fifteen-minute broadcast selling flour and corn meal mix and featuring two Delta bluesmen. One was a man who featured songs he had learned from Robert Johnson, a man who claimed Johnson was his stepfather and called himself "Robert Junior."

In the morning I drove over the bending, angled road that climbs Crowley's Ridge and drops down into Helena. I parked on Cherry Street and walked over to where I could see the Mississippi River. Driving around in the Delta, you know it's there, but you rarely see it except when you enter a town built high enough to look over the levee. It's a mighty river, but the color's gone bad. Even when you can't smell it you can see the patches of waste and sewage dumped upriver at Alton and Portsmouth and Wheeling.

A little way up Cherry Street I found a trim, neat building that housed the Helena National Bank. Station KFFA was on the fifth floor. The receptionist was on a coffee break, and an announcer in the glass booth was the only person in sight. He rolled back his chair, leaning out the door to talk to me. All he knew about *King Biscuit Time* was that it came on five days a week with a special script and recordings provided by the sponsor. He'd never heard of it being done any other way, but he'd only worked at the station for a few months. In a little while the receptionist came back, and after hearing what I was after, she suggested I go see the program's sponsor. She wrote down the address and told me to ask for Max Moore.

The name she'd given me was the Interstate Grocer Company on Walnut Street. It was in the next block, just one street over: a long, dark warehouse building with an office entrance set in the middle of the block. The office hadn't been modernized. It was dusty and paper-strewn, and the employees looked like they'd been there for decades. Max Moore turned out to be a slight, amiable man sitting at a corner desk in his shirtsleeves. He was pleased to talk about his company and its unusual radio program.

The company had been organized in 1913 as a wholesale grocer supply, bucking the big outfits in Memphis for the business of stocking and supplying the

A view of downtown Helena, Arkansas. Photograph by Robert "Mack" McCormick.

plantation stores in the Helena area. They sold to landlords and storekeepers, but their principal customers were Black sharecroppers. The farmers got their supplies on credit at their landlords' commissary and—tied to a risky system that fostered dependency—paid their bills at the end of the year, when their crops were in.

Interstate Grocer supplied the commissary with its stock, and they courted both storekeepers and their customers, trying to strengthen the tie between what the customer asked for and what they could supply. Interstate soon began packaging products with their own brand names, promoting these brands in the immediate area so as to strengthen their wholesale business. When KFFA started broadcasting in 1941, Interstate was eager to get on the air with a program advertising its own King Biscuit flour.

Moore told me he'd personally recruited the two musicians who had inaugurated the broadcasts. One was a powerful harmonica player known—with some controversy, because there was another popular harmonica player with the same name—as Sonny Boy Williamson. The other was Robert Lockwood, a guitarist from Marvell, Arkansas. In the beginning they were known to listeners simply as "Sonny Boy" and "Robert Junior."

Moore searched a file of old papers and produced an outsized postcard bearing a photograph of the two performers. They were sitting on either side of a

Interstate Grocer Company, the home of *King Biscuit Time*,
Helena, Arkansas. Photograph by Robert "Mack" McCormick.

hundred-pound sack of flour, and behind the sack there was a white announcer
and an old RCA microphone. "That's the first promotion we used," Moore said.
"We sent that card out to people who wrote in asking for a picture of the stars."
The word "stars" seemed a little strange in the circumstances, but it was appropriate. In Moore's mind, *King Biscuit Time* was the same thing as Jell-O and
Jack Benny on Sunday evening, the only difference being the size of the territory covered. The back of the postcard had a brief message that ended with this
paragraph:

> *We hope you'll keep on listening to* KING BISCUIT TIME *on Station KFFA at*
> *12:45, and you'll keep on using* KING BISCUIT FLOUR.
>
> *Sincerely,*
> *Sonny Boy and Robert Junior*

"Why was he called Robert Junior?" I asked. "It's just what he wanted to be
called," Moore said. "What I mean is, who was Robert Senior?"

King Biscuit Time postcard featuring musicians
Sonny Boy Williamson and Robert Lockwood Jr.

"Oh, I see what you mean." Max Moore turned the card over and looked at the picture of the slim young man smiling at the camera. "Back at the time, when Robert Junior came on the program, he used to talk about how he'd gotten a lot of his songs from his stepdaddy," Moore said. "I wouldn't know the names of them, but they went over with the people pretty good."

Robert Lockwood moved to Cleveland in 1960. When I met him later, he sported a goatee and had put on about forty pounds since that old picture had been taken. In interviews he was seldom precise about his relationship with Robert Johnson. When pressed, he would say that his mother and Robert Johnson were never actually married, but that "they were close friends—and Robert would stay at the house whenever he came to town." Lockwood was slightly younger than Johnson, by only a few years, and idolized him as a musician. It was a fragmented, partial relationship, and Lockwood was never able to provide any personal information about Johnson; he appears only to have encountered him on certain occasions spaced over several years' time. Still, he had always taken pride in that alone and continued to identify himself as "Robert Junior."

Moore dug around further in a file drawer and brought out a pile of old crumpled scripts on flimsy paper. They were mostly the copy for advertisements, ending with some tag like "Sonny Boy will play for his first number _____" or "Now let's listen to Robert Junior singing _____." Some of the scripts had titles penciled in the blank spaces. Here and there a familiar name turned up. It was a surprise to see that songs such as "Terraplane Blues," "Dust My Broom," and "Ramblin' on My Mind" had been featured on *King Biscuit Time* in the early 1940s. It suggested a missing link in blues history, which stretched to those later musicians in Chicago and elsewhere who featured Robert Johnson's material or developed a style that was indebted to his performances. Apparently, an early part of this linkage was the local influence of those daily broadcasts, heard and absorbed by a generation of blues singers and guitarists before they went north. Max Moore's dusty old files furnished a new perspective, one that had made this youngster who mimicked Robert Johnson a "star" in 1941, when giants such as Elmore James and Muddy Waters were obscure part-time musicians, only just getting ready to abandon Mississippi and its sharecropping folkways.

Moore talked on about *King Biscuit Time*, describing the improbable relationship between the wholesale grocery business and a flock of scruffy, hard-headed street musicians that had endured for twenty-four years, selling merchandise while perpetuating the Delta blues tradition. From the first, the broadcasts were popular, but after a couple of years jealousy sprung up between Robert Junior and Sonny Boy. They argued about how many songs they'd each do in the program. The tension showed itself on the air, and Lockwood started having a hard time finding the key the harmonica was in, or Williamson would blow the harmonica so loud as to drown out Lockwood's voice. Sonny Boy Williamson was a giant of a man and an extremely powerful showman, and he soon became the dominant, more popular figure on the broadcasts.

As the program's popularity grew, the Interstate Grocer Company leased a telephone line and set up a two-station network—"The Delta Network"—with WROX, a new station in Clarksdale, Mississippi. Between them the broadcasts covered the heart of the big plantation country on both sides of the river. They extended the schedule to include a special Saturday morning broadcast from the stage of the Plaza Theater in downtown Helena. Admission was free, and the theater was invariably packed.

After a few years, Robert Junior left the program. A number of other guitarists came and went on the broadcasts, and in time the group was increased to four or five members. Sonny Boy remained the star, but others—including pianist Willie Love and guitarist Houston Stackhouse—were featured with him. The group was always known as the "King Biscuit Entertainers." Eventually they bought a bus, installed a piano, a sound system, and a drop-down stage, and worked out a method of making fast personal appearance tours in the surrounding area. Every Saturday afternoon, following the theater broadcast, they'd climb aboard the bus and make a quick tour of nearby communities, setting up in front of the local commissary, attracting a big crowd for the merchant, and spending fifteen minutes or so performing, with a drawing for prizes squeezed in, before they rushed to the next stop. A typical schedule for one Saturday afternoon read like this: "Lamber, Miss.: 1:00 p.m. Marks, Miss.: 1:40 p.m. Belen, Miss.: 2:25 p.m. Jonestown, Miss.: 3:20 p.m. Lula, Miss. (L. S. Powell Estate): 4:10 p.m." The stops were only four to eight miles apart, tracking along the plantation communities in the Delta.

They attracted a raggedy and poor audience, people who lived in sagging, unpainted cabins patched with tar paper, but they gathered to hear the music and to buy King Biscuit Flour, Blackburn's Lasses, and Sonny Boy White Corn Meal Mix. (The Interstate Grocer Company started another brand, using their star's name and putting his picture on the corn meal sacks.)

The company thus adapted old medicine show techniques to modern merchandising, but the shows and broadcasts retained that personal immediacy that's possible when the "stars" are neighbors and kinsmen to their audience. A vigorous personal loyalty to the products developed, so that the national brands such as Gold Medal and Pillsbury found themselves all but left out of the market in the Delta.

In the evenings the King Biscuit entertainers frequently played at dance halls or roadside taverns in the area, and these appearances were always mentioned in advance on the program. Occasionally, Interstate Grocer would make a gift of the group, sending them to play for an anniversary, birthday, store celebration, or a dance at a plantation's party house. Moore showed me an itinerary for one short period in 1947:

Sept 17 (Wed. Night):	One Minute Cafe at Sunflower, Miss.
Sept 18 (Thurs. Night):	For Henry Hill, 2½ miles north of Lyon, Miss.
Sept 19 (Fri. Night):	Big Aaron Martin, 1 mile north of Marks, Miss., at Riverside Inn

Sept 20 (Sat. Night):	Mr. Vernon Joiner, at Wabash, Ark.
Sept 24 (Wed. Night):	Mrs. R. W. Purress, at Widener, Ark.
Sept 27 & 28 (Sat. and Sun. Nights)	Lula McCoy, at Widener, Ark.
Sept 29 & 30 (Mon. and Tues. Nights)	Three-Way Inn on Highway 70, at Ellison's place

In an era when the jukebox was driving musicians out of jobs, this was remarkably steady work, with a schedule full of evening bookings, promotional tours, and daily broadcasts. Over the years the Robert Johnson element grew larger or smaller, according to the particular guitarist featured with the group. With the bluff, domineering personality of Sonny Boy Williamson, it was never a large element, but neither was it entirely absent, and touches of "Come On in My Kitchen" or "Dust My Broom" continued to appear. Moore said that after Sonny Boy's death in 1965 it became difficult to hold the program together. The musicians were too erratic, or their personalities not strong enough, or their repertoires not sufficiently varied to stand up to the schedule. Regretfully, Moore said, Interstate Grocer dropped the live broadcasts and turned *King Biscuit Time* into a recordings program, which lasted twenty-four years.

In a corner of the Interstate Grocer office was a huge display labeled "*King Biscuit Time* on Tour," filled with over a hundred snapshots of crowds gathered in front of stores, musicians staring into the camera and playing on porch fronts, people gathered around grocery trucks, and musicians hunched together, playing. The snapshots were old and faded, but the collage had a curiously evocative quality. This jumble of faint, curling, stained snapshots was the best visual representation of Robert Johnson's milieu I'd ever seen. It showed the audience and its bluesmen at a time when the tradition was rich and commonplace. I stared it at for a long while, then broke away, thanked Max Moore, and went back out on Walnut Street.

Later I stopped in a supermarket and found the aisle with the flour and corn meal. The sacks of what the radio program called Sonny Boy Extremely Fancy Cream Corn Meal occupied more shelf space than the big national brands. The face on the sack was an anachronism, years out of its place. It was a drawing—based on the first photograph of Sonny Boy Williamson and Robert

Junior Lockwood—of Sonny Boy sitting on a tree stump. In the distance was a humble log cabin with a Black woman in the doorway and smoke rising from the chimney. Where the photograph had shown him holding a harmonica in each hand, the drawing instead had a kind of rectangular blur that could be piece of corn bread. Sonny Boy had been transformed into a grinning Uncle Tom figure. The altered picture portrayed a way of life that didn't work for those who were part of it, and it managed to show not only the reason but the need for the death of the Delta lifestyle as well as for the music it inspired.

• • •

5

COPIAH COUNTY

At some point early in the search for Robert Johnson's story was the speck of hope that he might still be alive. A lot of the blues artists and other songsters from his generation had been located and heard again. A few of them remained incredibly vital artists. It was almost as if they'd held themselves in readiness during the intervening years, as if they knew that eventually someone would make the effort to come and find them.

If Son House could be found by following a trail to Rochester, New York; if Bukka White could be located by a letter addressed to him in care of general delivery; and if Mance Lipscomb and Mississippi John Hurt could be found patiently waiting in their hometowns, then surely other surprising rediscoveries might follow. It was a tantalizing notion, but in actuality it was little more than a device for sustaining the quest, even when it seemed to reach some discouraging low point.

In view of the persistent accounts of Johnson's death, the notion was ridiculous. And gradually it was put to rest as a small pile of documents began to accumulate, emerging from county clerks' vital records and from other sources that make official note of births, deaths, and marriages. Virtually every office contacted had records on people named Robert Johnson (according to the US Census, Johnson is the nation's second most common surname in the United States, and Robert one of the most popular given names). It was a question of sorting through them, or urging some official to do so, or paying a record search fee, and isolating those details that might pertain to the right man. I had a small bundle of such documents: one from Texas, two from Louisiana, two from Mississippi,

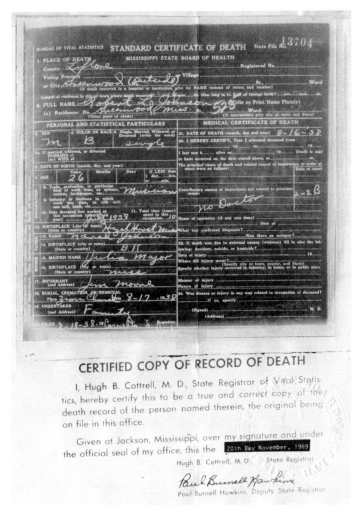

Mack McCormick's copy of Robert Johnson's death certificate.

one from Arkansas, and one from Tennessee—all death certificates for Black males named Robert Johnson, all young men who had died in the 1930s, some of natural causes. There were other records for an Ernest Johnson and for a Willie Lee Johnson that had been singled out because the circumstances of their deaths fit some of the stories about Robert Johnson. A couple of the documents even had "musician" written in on the line for the deceased's occupation. There were also some letters from helpful sheriffs and police whose "dead files" had turned up something on a Robert Johnson who seemed to fit in one way or another.

These documents had been amassed over several years, and the most likely looking ones had provoked a trip, phone call, or some kind of effort to follow through. Most of the time it had been established that the dead man wasn't the one in question. Eventually I narrowed down these leads to one particular photostat that had come from the state of Mississippi. It was a death certificate for a Robert Johnson, a Black male who had died in 1938. Although it was otherwise a sparse, uninformative piece of paper, it did include his parents' names, and it listed his place of birth as Hazlehurst, Mississippi.

Hazlehurst is in the hill country of southern Mississippi, much closer to New Orleans than to Memphis. It was miles from the area where my searches had usually concentrated. But an interesting thing happened when I circled Hazlehurst on my annotated Standard Oil map. Just a little to the east was that long corridor marking the Gulf and Ship Island Railroad. The word "shrimp" and the double red triangle marking Gulfport weren't far away. There were circles around two other towns in the general vicinity. It was too flimsy to say it represented a pattern, but when I spread out the map, that heavy concentration of marks and notes in the area below Memphis immediately hit my eye. There were other marks scattered around, but the only other place where anything approaching a cluster stood out was this area in southern Mississippi.

It was the only really strong new lead I had, and I had been tempted to start there on this trip. But I'd gone instead to the Delta, back to the same ground that had been searched by different people so many times. I was saving Hazlehurst as a kind of ace in the hole.

The two days I'd spent in Helena, Arkansas, hadn't come to anything. After I had talked with Max Moore, I'd drifted around the town trying to find out why Helena was mentioned so often in connection with Johnson. I spent the evening in the Kitty Cat Cafe on Missouri Street. There was a sign on the window that read "Colored & Mexicans," and I bought beers for a few of the patrons. It was an edgy, uptight crowd, and they started ragging me about my fool's errand, trying to find out if I knew the rules.

One guy said, "That sign on the window—we just keep it there for old times' sake." Another one whispered, "We keep it there so one day we gonna get a Mexican in here and we gonna stomp his ass."

This went on for a while, and finally I challenged the whole crowd. I told them that if one of them would go buy the milk, I'd buy the scotch. They agreed. I went next door to a liquor store and one of the crowd went around the corner for the milk. We were probably breaking a couple of local laws, but the man

The Kitty Cat Cafe, Helena, Arkansas. Photograph by Robert "Mack" McCormick.

behind the bar didn't seem to care. Someone got paper cups and started mixing the drinks.

One of the guys who'd been picking at me, trying to find a nerve, said, "Scotch and milk—now that's what I call a nasty drink."

"But think of how healthy it is," I replied.

"Yes, it's better than stomping Mexicans."

A Mexican at the next table looked up and gave a solemn nod.

Someone had gotten drunk enough to stumble against a table where some men were playing dominoes. A small fight started up, and the crowd drifted over that way to see how it would develop. While I was left alone, a man of about fifty came over and said he'd once seen Johnson at a place down the street, a drugstore that, like a lot of shoeshine parlors, barbershops, and grocery stores, kept a piano in one corner. Anyone was free to play, and sometimes they'd even hire a pianist to help bring a crowd into the store. The man told me he'd seen Robert Johnson playing piano there.

"I don't think that was the right Robert Johnson," I said.

"No, I expect not," he admitted. "Besides, it's been closed down for years."

It was a vague evening, not worth much until I went next door and had a meal at Eddie's Cafe. They specialized in chicken dinners and homemade sweet potato pie.

The next day I wandered around the same area until I drew a kind of final blank in a pool hall where I'd been directed to a man who was said to know every musician who'd ever played around Helena. He listened to me without blinking, then calmly finished his shot before he looked up. "Didn't you," he asked, "come here a couple of years back and ask me that same damn question?"

"Yes," I told him. "I might have."

"So why come back again? I don't know any more now than what I knew then, and that's nothing at all." He rapped the pool cue on the floor. "I heard of Robert Johnson, but I never even saw him."

That was the turning point. I was due for a change of luck, and overdue for a change of locale. I walked straight to my car and drove out of Helena across the new bridge into Mississippi. I was tired of the Delta and its flatness and its persistent stink of insecticides. I drove east to the edge of the Delta and then swung south on Interstate 55. It was a two hundred–mile trip to Hazlehurst, and I drove it without stopping.

Interstate highways give you a false impression of the land. Half the time you can't tell whether you're driving through Vermont or Alabama. The broad, manicured rights-of-way look much the same everywhere, the only significant difference being whether the landscape beyond is green or brown.

Southern Mississippi is green. The land is hilly, occasionally flattening into a field or a bottomland washed by a small river. A hardwood forest gave way to pine trees, and then a bit later a big sign came looming up to announce the exit for Hazlehurst. I swung off and then drove a short uphill mile into town.

Back when I'd been marking up my Standard Oil map, I'd done some homework on Hazlehurst. If you write letters to small-town librarians and historians, some of them will send you curious things. One of the things I'd ended up with was the program for the Mississippi Tomato Festival of June 8–9, 1939. It was full of pictures of area businessmen and farmers and ads from the local funeral home. There were some background articles that explained that some of the ridges in Copiah County have patches of fine yellow loess deposits, in which tomatoes thrive. The area had a flourishing truck crop industry.

The booklet noted that Copiah County called itself "Mississippi's most diversified county." A map showed how business was split up among seven major enterprises, each in a different segment of the county, with Hazlehurst, the county seat, right in the middle. The booklet observed that local forests supplied the wood which the town's box factory turned into crates and lugs farmers used to ship their vegetables north on the Illinois Central's fast freight trains. The climate was such that a shrewd farmer could get in a crop of early vegetables—cabbage, Irish potatoes, or tomatoes—and then produce a second crop of cotton or corn. It sounded like a busy, industrious place, somehow, not the kind of town where a Robert Johnson might have come from. But maybe it was just that kind of pre-conception that had made my search so drawn out and unproductive.

I got out of the car and started looking around. Evidently, the town's slogan hadn't changed in thirty-one years. In the middle of the main street was a huge neon sign reiterating that this was "Mississippi's Most Diversified County." Nearby was a historical marker explaining that the town was named after the chief engineer who'd built the first railroad between Jackson and New Orleans. The last spike had been driven on March 31, 1858. The marker also noted that the town had been raided by Union commander Benjamin H. Grierson's cavalry in 1863.

Hazlehurst turned out to be a fairly prosperous-looking place, with many strange little bridges arching over the Illinois Central tracks that cut the town in half. Everything was relatively clean and trim, and there was a feeling of vigor about it. It made a tremendous contrast to the declining towns of the Delta.

The Black neighborhood centered around West Gallatin Street. One rather hopeful prospect caught my eye almost immediately: a sign for a restaurant named after a Johnson. It actually was two adjoining businesses, one a cafe and the other a pool hall. Several people were moving around in the vicinity.

I angled the car into a parking slot and switched off the engine, slumping back a moment in thought. What was I going to find here? Or, rather, what was I looking for? Family? Neighbors? Friends? Possible, but not likely. Things aren't that stable. Everything gets torn loose and moved around. You can't just pop into a man's birthplace sixty years after the fact and expect to turn up his life story. Not unless he was the kind of upright citizen they keep files on at the local newspaper or library.

More to the point, what exactly could I hope to turn up here? Some trace of relations, perhaps. Some family lineage.

I had two names to work with: Major and Johnson. According to a death certificate I had obtained, Major was his mother's maiden name. It only took a few minutes to establish that Major was a rare name in the vicinity. None of the people on the sidewalk could recall any family past or present with that name. I guessed that there might be twenty to twenty-five African American families with the name Johnson; getting in touch with each one wouldn't be an impossible job, and the task would be even smaller if I surveyed only those in the Hazlehurst area instead of the whole county. Johnson's Restaurant looked like a good place to start.

There was no one on the restaurant side of the establishment except Mrs. Johnson, who suggested I talk to her husband, Early Johnson. He was next door, playing pool with a slightly built young man. Mr. Johnson was an open, easygoing man, and he took an immediate interest in the problem I described. As the local pool hall operator, he was well acquainted with most of the people in the area. He said he knew of four different families named Johnson. He thought about each of them, ticking off names, and came up with two Roberts, but both of them were young men. He mentioned several more families and even remembered several musicians with the surname Johnson, but there was no apparent connection. I asked whether he knew any family by name of Major.

"No, but I'll tell you a funny thing, I know a guy that's got both those names you're asking about." I must have looked puzzled, because he laughed as he explained, "This guy is named Major Johnson."

That was curious. Maybe he'd somehow been named after Robert Johnson's mother's family? On the other hand, at one time Major had been a familiar given name within Black families. It turns up on old census reports and city directories, there'd been a bicycle sprint racing champion nicknamed "Major" Taylor, and many boys had been named after him.

"On top of that, he's a guitar player," Early Johnson added.

"Does he play now?" I asked.

"I think he do. You could go and see him."

While we were talking, the young man who was playing pool with Mr. Johnson seemed to want to ask a question. While Mr. Johnson was studying a shot, he finally asked, "What do you want with this man you're looking for?" He seemed skeptical. I explained my interest, but it didn't seem to register. A little bit later he asked again, "Did that man do something?" He was having trouble accepting the idea that I was interested in Robert Johnson because he was a musician.

Meanwhile, Mr. Johnson had laid aside his cue and gone over to the window between the two halves of the establishment. He asked his wife to pass over the slim telephone book that covered most of Copiah County. It was only an eighth of an inch thick, and the various towns produced only a total of forty-five listings under the name Johnson, two of which were businesses (one an insurance agent and the other Mr. Johnson's own place). Mr. Johnson seemed to know or be able to place nearly all of them after a bit of concentration. He estimated that about half were white families.

As Mr. Johnson studied the phone book, his pool partner circled the table, setting up a few tricky practice shots. He tried a three-ball shot but muffed it. He still seemed curious. "This guy was some kind of musician, huh?"

Before I could answer, Mr. Johnson gave a shout: "Here he is, right in the phone book!" He and his wife had their heads together in the window, straining over the book. They'd found a listing for a Robert J. Johnson on Thomas Road.

Mr. Johnson immediately launched into an elaborate set of directions to the man's house. I should drive north on Highway 51 until I came to a new school building, and then make first a right and then a left turn. He went on through several additional steps, but suddenly his words trailed off, and he shook his head ruefully. "No. That ain't him," he said. "I know this boy's daddy. He ain't near old enough to be the one you want."

He came back over with the book and pointed to the listing. "Fact of the business is, that's the guy I was telling you about a while ago: Major Johnson. That's his telephone. His son is named Robert, and they got the phone in his name."

I'd hoped to pick up some dim memory that might lead to Robert Johnson's family, but as Early Johnson reviewed the various listings one by one, reading out the names and addresses and identifying the people, it didn't seem to lead anywhere.

Toward the end of this process, the young man at the pool table, obviously a little bored, looked up and unexpectedly asked, "You mean Robert Lee Johnson? That who you looking for?"

I was struck by the middle name he'd used. The death certificate had given the name as "Robert L. Johnson," and that was the first hint I'd ever had of a middle name. I looked at the young man with more interest. He was too young to have known Robert Johnson, but clearly he had something in mind.

"That could be the one," I told him. "Was he any kind of musician?"

"Yeah, he played guitar. He was my stepdaddy."

Mr. Johnson had stopped to listen to this. "How come I don't know him?" he asked.

The young man just shrugged and set up another pool shot.

"This guy was with your mother?" Mr. Johnson asked. "When was that, Cain?"

"I don't know. Way back sometime."

"Wait a minute, just a minute now." Mr. Johnson closed his eyes, trying to bring up some detail. "I do remember the guy you're talking about. I saw him around here, I believe, but I never did know anything about him. I never would have thought of him if you'd mentioned him."

Until then we'd had the pool hall to ourselves, but soon both the pool hall and the restaurant started filling up. It got busy, and the mood changed. The young man clearly didn't want to say anything in front of other people. He went out and stood on the sidewalk down the street.

I told Mr. Johnson I'd come back later when he wasn't so busy, and then strolled down to where the young man was standing with several others. I used the name I'd heard Mr. Johnson mention and asked him, "Can you tell me anything more about him, Cain?" It was a mistake. With his friends and peers around, he didn't want to say anything more. He said his mother would know more, but then he wouldn't tell me how to find her. Finally, he said, "She's dead," and walked back into the pool hall, apparently hoping to get rid of me. I remembered that Mr. Johnson hadn't spoken of her in the past tense.

I walked around town for a while, trying to decide what to do next, and stopping to talk with people. Nothing more turned up, but a lot was said about peripheral matters. There was a Johnson Road and a Johnson Bayou in different parts of the county, and people assumed they'd probably been named after some big landowner who had lived there.

African American families in the area named Johnson often got their last name from an ancestor who had been enslaved by a white family named Johnson. It was therefore entirely possible that Robert Johnson's grandfather or great-grandfather had worked on a plantation along what was called Johnson Road. It headed west toward a village called Dentville, which was in the cotton-producing part of the county, where the region's early Black population had been concentrated.

Speculation like this could go on endlessly. But what I really needed was to revisit the young man who had decided he didn't want to talk to me. About an hour had passed by the time I got back to the Johnson Restaurant. The pool hall wasn't too busy, and Mr. Johnson had time to talk. He said he'd thought about it and decided the young man had been right. "I do remember that Virgie stayed with a musician some long years back. In fact, I think he was the daddy of her boy. Not the boy that was in here, but another boy."

"Is she dead now?"

"No, she ain't dead. I can take you straight to her."

He went to the little window and explained to his wife that he'd be back in a few minutes. He suggested that I follow him in my own car. He climbed into a pickup truck, waited for me to make a U-turn, and then with a wave drove over to the street that carries Highway 51 through town, turned north, and drove out of town. In about five miles we arrived at an intersection, and a mile further there was a church sitting on a hill on the right side of the road. Mr. Johnson flashed his brake lights a few times, then turned and pulled up in front of a house down the hill from the church. He walked over to my car and said, "I'll just introduce you, and then I got to get back."

We climbed up onto the porch, and he called out a name. After a while there was a bustle from inside, and the door opened. There were five or six people gathered in front of a television set in an otherwise darkened front room. Mr. Johnson ushered me inside, and there was a blur of greetings but no names were exchanged. Chairs were hastily dragged in from an adjoining room, and there was a lot of small talk about how everybody had been. It wasn't clear which of the people we'd come to see. There were two women old enough to have known Robert Johnson.

After a few minutes, Mr. Johnson announced that he had to leave, saying, "I brought this man out here because I believe you can help him." He left, and I sat there trying to decide how to start. The size of the group was awkward. Most of them seemed content to continue staring at the television set. I realized that over in the corner was Cain, the young man from the pool room.

Finally, trying to see in the bluish glow from the television set, I tried asking a few general questions. Had anyone known a musician named Robert Johnson? The younger people glanced at me, then went back to watching their program. The older people answered the question with a shake of the head, except for one of the two ladies, a short, heavy woman with graying hair and a round, benevolent face. She just nodded faintly.

It was an aggravating and difficult situation. Here I was in the midst of a family gathering, asking embarrassing questions about old, possibly carnal relationships. No one seemed to take offense, however. The person I took to be the man of the house was smiling and cordial, waiting patiently to see what I wanted. Finally, I looked at the woman who had nodded and asked whether I might have a drink of water. She went off to the kitchen and I got up and followed her.

She poured the water from an ice box bottle. As she handed me the glass, she said, "He was daddy to my oldest boy." We talked for a few minutes, standing in the light from the open refrigerator door. She told me in a slow, quiet voice that she had a son named Claud Johnson who'd been born in 1931. His father had been a blues musician named Robert Lee Johnson. She said she'd met him at a house party where he'd been singing and playing. She remembered that one of his most popular songs was called "Terraplane Blues," and she could even quote some of the words. Her husband came in the kitchen and stood by smiling and looking unconcerned as she repeated some of the old double-entendre lines: "I'm gonna heist your hood, and I'm gonna check your oil." She giggled a little. "That was in there."

It had been a long day. I was tired and a little taken aback by the sudden, unexpected developments. Clearly, it would be easier to come back the next day and try to get the whole story. I made arrangements to return in the morning and thanked them, saying I didn't want to interrupt their evening.

On the way out of Hazlehurst I'd noticed a place called the Edwards Motel. I drove back there and checked in. I'd managed to miss dinner, and now I didn't feel like going out to hunt for a restaurant. I got a small case out of the car where I kept instant coffee and snacks. Supper was smoked oysters and two antique jelly doughnuts I'd acquired a few days earlier.

I was skeptical and confused by the events. The coincidence of being in that pool hall at just that moment was remarkable. No one else I could have talked to in Hazlehurst would have led me to that woman: just that one young man, and he wouldn't have said a word except that I had happened to arrive at a time when the place was empty.

I'd come to Hazlehurst because this was supposed to be Robert Johnson's birthplace, and I'd been looking for his mother's or his father's family. Instead I'd found a stepson, and a woman who remembered him singing "Terraplane Blues" in 1930. That actually was discouraging; the Terraplane automobile hadn't been manufactured until 1932. Still, that didn't mean she was lying. Johnson could have made the song about any automobile, and he might have been singing it in 1930; then later he could have particularized it when the Terraplane came along. Since it became his best-selling record, she might well have learned to think of it by that title. Or maybe she was just wrong about whether she'd heard it from him or from a record. Memories are tricky and unreliable about such things.

I hoped that she was telling the truth about knowing Robert Johnson, and there was surely no reason I could see why she'd invent such a story. But I'd been gulled a few thousand times by wanting to believe what I was told, by people trying to tell me what they imagined I wanted to hear.

As it turned out, I needn't have worried. Her story checked out in every essential detail, right down to a birth certificate for Claud L. Johnson, son of Virgie Mae Cain and R. L. Johnson, born December 18, 1931.

Virgie Mae Cain had been just seventeen years old when she left home to stay with her aunt in Martinsville, Mississippi—a flag stop on the Illinois Central, exactly five miles south of Hazlehurst.

Martinsville is not a town but a rural community that spreads out along half a dozen roads running through an area of small farms. The land is hilly and covered with pine, but some of the level stretches have been cleared and cultivated. Anise McClain, Virgie's aunt, lived in the section known locally as the "It" community. Highway 51 was just a gravel track in those days, and it ran past a small country store known as the It Grocery. A dirt road forked off behind the store, curving through some hills dotted with poor cabins and shacks around the Chapel Hill church. This part simply took its name from the store where the road turned off.

Most mornings Virgie's aunt would catch a ride into Hazlehurst and walk into one of the quiet residential sections on the town's west side. She worked as a day maid doing cleaning, ironing, and washing. When Virgie came to stay with her, she took the girl along to help and to teach her how to take care of other people's clothes. There was a stark contrast between the aunt's crude cabin, with so many of its boards falling away, and the neat houses where she worked, with sunny rooms and flowered wallpaper. There were baskets full of clothes to be washed and ironed, and most of them looked like Sunday clothes. After going with her aunt to several different houses, Virgie asked her, "These rich white folks, huh?"

Aunt Anise laughed and shook her head. "No, they ain't rich." Later, on the way home, she pointed out one of the largest homes in Hazlehurst. "That's the rich people there," she said. "I used to work there, but they got another woman to come instead." The girl asked why. "They complained about how I done the

59

work. Said I don't iron things good enough to suit them." Virgie thought about it a minute, then giggled. "Damn, if they don't like the way *you* iron, what would they think of the way *I* do it?"

The aunt got to giggling with her. "That's the fact, girl, you ain't much on that ironing." Actually, Virgie wasn't terribly interested in learning housekeeping, not at the age of seventeen. They stood on a corner of Extension Street, waiting for their ride home, hoping there wouldn't be any mix-up. Sometimes they missed connections, and then they had to walk the five miles home.

Virgie remembered that particular conversation because it was just a day or so later that a girl about her own age invited her to go along to a party to meet some people. It was just a casual house party in a house near the Martinsville depot. Virgie never knew the people who gave the party. It cost a dime to get in, and there were snacks and drinks for sale in a back room. It was the kind of gathering that could be found in nearly every southern rural Black community many afternoons and most nights of the week, except Sundays. The young people always had something going. It was at this party where Virgie met Robert Johnson in the fall of 1930.

After they had talked a little while, they realized they'd seen each other before. Virgie told him that her parents' home was in Wesson, a small town ten miles farther south, and he said he'd performed there a few times. She thought that she might have seen him around Hazlehurst on Saturdays, when everyone came into the county seat. He was about a year older. She remembers teasing him, asking him, "What you gonna do when you grow up?"

He told her, "Same as I do now." He teased her back and was rather blunt about it, telling her, "I needs me a girlfriend."

They stayed together about nine months, both of them living with Aunt Anise. He had a few jobs during the time. He worked briefly as a porter at a store in Hazlehurst and then as a freight handler for a farm supply warehouse. For a few days he worked for a family near the It community, but he didn't like farm work.

During this time he was playing gigs at least several times a week, and he'd sit around the house playing guitar, listening to records, or making up new songs. From time to time he'd leave for a week or more. Virgie wasn't sure where he went or why. Sometimes he'd hitchhike, going out to Highway 51 to flag a ride, and at least once around ten in the morning he caught the northbound train, going somewhere up the line (it was due in Memphis at midafternoon). Virgie felt lonely and left out when he made these trips, but in a few days he'd be back, grinning, looking pleased.

Robert was a professional musician in the sense that it represented his primary way of supporting himself and Virgie. He was still too young to bring it off entirely, and the income was erratic, but increasingly he turned away from any other way of earning money. He played most of the familiar blues pieces popularized by records, and when asked he could entertain a crowd with "How Long Blues" or "It's Tight Like That," but he put the emphasis on his own original songs.

Virgie remembered him sitting on a corner of the bed in their cramped room, leaning over his guitar and singing or talking the words in a low voice. Sometimes he'd get up in the middle of the night and work on a song. She asked him about it, and he told her, "I get some of my songs that way. They come to me in a dream."

He'd practice the same song over and over, changing the words and then repeating them as if he was afraid he was going to forget them. He never wrote down the words. Virgie once suggested that he try that, but he got mad. It may have been because he couldn't read and write, or because he didn't think that was the right thing to do. Virgie wasn't sure. All he said was, "After I got it like I want it, then I don't forget it."

She remembered that he was possessive about his music, and he seemed to prefer that she not pay any attention to him when he was playing around the house. Out in public he was a little more outgoing, but still much more reserved than most of the other musicians. Sometimes when people wanted to dance or cut up at a party, he'd start singing something in a voice so low others couldn't hear, as if he were playing for himself, ignoring the people he was supposed to be entertaining. "He was just a private person," Virgie said.

After nine months or so they broke up and he went off, letting her know he wouldn't be coming back this time. She didn't know where he went, except that it was "up the country somewhere." She was about three months pregnant at the time.

She decided to go back home, outside of Wesson. Her son Claud was born there in December 1931, and her mother acted as midwife. Two days later the birth certificate was filed, but Virgie's mother couldn't answer some of the questions about the father. In the space for the father's occupation the word "labor" is written, and the spaces for the father's age and place of birth are filled in with "Don't know." Other spaces about the father were left blank.

Virgie thought Johnson's family lived in Memphis, but she wasn't sure where. She wasn't clear whether it was in Memphis or simply near the city. The birth certificate asks for the father's full address, but that space simply shows "Memphis, Tenn."

Virgie thought Johnson had lived in the Hazlehurst area most of his life. He was well acquainted with the area, knew every tavern and store nearby, and spoke one time of playing around the railroad tracks when he was younger. He also mentioned going to school for a short time. Virgie had gotten the idea that he had once had relatives in the area, but that most of them had left before she knew him, with his parents moving up close to Memphis. She remembered one particular house near Martinsville where Robert had told her "some of my people live there," but the house wasn't there any longer, and she couldn't remember exactly where it had been.

He'd never brought her in touch with any of his family, and the only person she knew about was a "stout, bright lady," who might have been an older sister or an aunt who lived for some years in the Cato Quarters part of Hazlehurst. As a young girl, away from home for the first time and caught up with a guitar player, Virgie had felt that her life was full enough. She hadn't bothered to collect much information about him. She couldn't even recall how she knew the stout, bright lady was a relative of his. She used to pass her regularly on the streets in Hazlehurst up until as recently as eight or ten years ago. Virgie didn't know the woman's name, but she promised to try to find out something about her.

Robert Johnson came back to the area in 1933 to see his son, when the boy was eighteen months old. He played with the child several hours one afternoon and then went away again. He returned at least once and maybe twice again to see the boy. One time he brought two records with him as presents for Virgie and the boy. She remembered that he complained that the record company hadn't sent him any copies of his own records. He'd gone to a store to buy the two he brought them.

Virgie never owned a photograph of Robert Johnson, but she said she had something that might do instead. She went to a bureau and lifted off a small, gold-framed photograph of a young man. It was sepia-toned and cracked across the middle.

"That's my boy, Claud," she said. "He was just about eighteen when that picture was taken, and he looked just like his daddy did." There was warmth and tenderness in her voice for the first time. The photograph seemed to stir a memory but it was nothing she could articulate.

She carried the photo over to a window to study it in the light. She enumerated the likenesses between father and son: "They both have round faces, and their hair's kinda back on their forehead, with round brown eyes." She tilted the photograph a little. "Their color is light brown, both of them." She came back and handed the photograph to me. "They both tote their shoulders kind of round. And they walk just alike." She said the picture looked so much like Robert that she sometimes had to study it to see that it was the son and not the father.

It was a photo of a young man sitting slumped and relaxed, staring pleasantly into the camera in what appeared to be a studio or perhaps a carnival photographer's booth. There was a distracting background of badly painted trees and flowers. He looked young and inexperienced, uncomplicated and placid. Quite ordinary. It seemed impossible to associate that face, or anyone whose face resembled that one, with the vivid musician who'd made such extraordinary recordings.

Later the photograph was shown to some of the musicians who'd known Robert Johnson. Usually it was mixed in with other photographs, and several times, without coaching or any leading questions being asked, it was picked out and identified as a photograph of Johnson. "That's the thing about it," one musician said. "Robert looked just like anybody. His music would take you by surprise."

Virgie took the photo and studied it some more. "Robert Lee was maybe a little lighter and a little taller than Claud," she said. "More like Claud's own boy, Gregory." She told me that Claud Johnson had a steady job as a finish painter for a factory that made the kind of big transformers you see hanging from utility poles. She said that he lived on a street where most of the houses were unpainted tumbledown places, but that his home was a neat white frame house with a brick front. She gave me the address and told me it was about five miles away, in the next town north. After I wrote down the address, she asked, "But you ain't going there, is you?"

I said I'd like to meet him. She went over to the window and drew aside the curtain. "That's him there," she said. There was a group of three men who'd just arrived and were getting ready to do some work on the church building next door. "He comes by every Saturday morning to help with the church repairs," she said. "I called him last night and told him about you being here."

As I walked toward the men, Claud Johnson said something to one of the others and came forward to meet me. He was the one, as it turned out, who had most of the questions to ask. He knew little about his father, and his curiosity had largely gone unsatisfied. He knew only that his father had been a musician known in parts of Mississippi and that he'd once made some records. He had no idea that the records had been repackaged and were currently on sale in stores as close as New Orleans and as far away as Australia. He was curious and excited that someone had traveled a distance to inquire about his father.

His interest was momentarily frustrated while an Illinois Central passenger train flashed by, its red and gold cars making a rainbow-like blur against the pastures. The roar was too loud for conversation, so we briefly stood, looking at each other. He'd put on about thirty pounds since Virgie's photo of him as an eighteen-year-old had been taken. It felt odd to be looking at Robert Johnson's son, standing in front of the Gallman Chapel AME Zion Church, with Highway 51 on one side of us and the northbound train hurrying past on the other. It was about ten in the morning. Unless they'd changed the schedule, that was probably the same passenger train Robert Johnson had caught the time that Virgie had described.

When the train had passed, Claud Johnson started asking questions. He wanted to know whether what he'd heard about his father being murdered was true. He'd heard it several ways—mostly that a woman had poisoned him. He wanted to know if his father had any other children, if there was any money still coming from the recordings, and if anyone had a photograph of his father. I told him I was trying to find answers to all the same questions myself.

Claud did have a distinct memory of his father's visiting one time, taking him out on the porch of the house and playing guitar for him, even trying to get him to sing some church songs together. Claud must have been six or seven at the time. His memory of the incident seemed crisp and clear, perhaps made so by the fact that it was one of the two or three occasions on which he'd seen his father, and the only such visit when he'd been old enough to realize who his father was.

After that visit, which lasted only through a single afternoon, Claud decided to be become a musician. He marched around for a time, banging on tin cans, playing drums with all kinds of tubs and boxes, and singing scraps of songs. Later, when he was grown, he started wondering whether he'd inherited any of his father's talent, so he bought a guitar and attempted to teach himself. "But," he said with a smile, "I never got too interested with it."

To me there was a striking parallel between the fascination of the blues collectors and the way in which Claud Johnson thought of his father. For both Robert Johnson remained a mystery—a man remembered by a child, but largely unknown, often spoken of but never in full focus. Questions about him went unanswered, for there was a limit to what Virgie knew or was willing to tell him. Virgie said that while Claud was growing up, he'd been given to periods when he'd repeatedly ask questions about his father. One of the most poignant was, "How come a guitar player can't stay in one place?"

That afternoon I drove out Highway 51 to Martinsville. Now that it was established that Robert Johnson had spent time here—not simply been born, then moved away—there was a good chance of learning more. I even had an idea of where the search would lead.

When the name of Hazlehurst first came up, an obvious thought presented itself, since the town lies a mere ten miles from the home of another blues artist of great stature and influence, a gifted musician who had produced some of the finest performances in the genre. The fact that two such artists, even a generation apart, should have come from the same corner of the state seemed a little unlikely. The fact that both were named Johnson suggested that more than coincidence was involved.

The two men concerned:

Robert Johnson, from Hazlehurst, Mississippi, a gifted but tortured blues singer who died of women and youth.

Tommy Johnson, from Crystal Springs, Mississippi, the eloquent stylist of "Cool Drink of Water Blues" and "Big Road Blues," who succeeded in drinking himself to death in 1956.

Both were remarkably talented men, among the most influential of all bluesmen. It seemed probable, after discovering that both Johnsons came from one and the same county, that they would turn out to be relatives. Tommy Johnson was old enough to have been Robert Johnson's uncle. I was expecting that some sort of connection would offer itself as I followed up on the leads and covered the territory that Virgie had described.

Just south of Hazlehurst, the road dips, then climbs a small hill and swings past a box factory, then drops into a long valley, and after a couple of miles rises through a cut to the top of another hill. As I climbed the hill and the road leveled out, I saw the It grocery on the right. To the left, a rough-surfaced road branched off and ran a half-mile over to the Illinois Central tracks.

The center of Martinsville was where the road crossed the railroad tracks: two houses and a store. The depot was gone, but there was an old, weathered sign on which the name was still legible, even though long slivers of wood had rotted

The grocery store marking the center of Martinsville, Mississippi.
Photograph by Robert "Mack" McCormick.

and fallen away. The store was new; the original store had been on the other side of the road.

Every ten or fifteen minutes a car or pickup truck would skid to a stop in the patch of gravel in front of the store. A good many of the people who showed up seemed old enough to have known Robert Johnson or his family.

One of them, a man named Lloyd Roman, took enough interest in my questions to stay for over an hour, passing a few words with neighbors and people who showed up at the store, asking whether they could recall the Johnson family. None of them could help, but everyone agreed it didn't necessarily mean anything. Martinsville had been a bustling crossing, a place where wagons lined up as far as you could see every June bringing loads of tomatoes to the depot. This wasn't sharecroppers' territory, but rather a place where Black farmers rented or owned their land, hustling twenty acres or so each year and bringing in good crops of corn, tomatoes, and cotton. There was also sawmill work and day pay for log cutting and hauling. All this had supported many families scattered over these ridges. There'd been too many for anyone to remember them all with certainty.

When the talk turned to musicians in general, a number of different names came up. There'd been a sizable group of casual musicians here, many about the same age, all guitar players. The best of the group, a man named Willie Hudson, was said to be still living about twelve miles west of Hazlehurst near a place called Dentville. They said he was probably around eighty, which would mean he'd been born around 1890. They assured me that any youngster who'd grown up around Martinsville with a bent toward music would have heard and taken a keen interest in Willie Hudson—or in some of the others, such as Wade Coleman, Willie Lomax, or Thomas Taylor. They had all been playing for "frolics" back in the 1920s and earlier. Other musicians were named and described. There was a youngster named Lonnie Johnson, but he wasn't the famous one who had made records. There were the two Williams brothers, Joe and Henry, and an Ira Williams, who wasn't related but who played with the other two. There were Tommy Johnson, Clarence Johnson, and their brothers. There were Alpha Eps and his son, who they called Little Alpha Eps.

The most frequently mentioned combination was Willie Hudson and Wade Coleman. They appeared together a great deal, and sometimes Ira Williams joined them. Most of the musicians mentioned seemed to be from the era of the earliest blues. They sang songs with lines like "I'm going away to wear you off my mind" and "If you knock me down, I'm going to fight back up again."

All these musicians had played around Martinsville, and a few had lived near here, but they were more often associated with the area around Dentville. The land was flatter there, and there had been some big plantations with as many as twenty or thirty families working at a single place. Places like that always had more need for musicians.

The more people I talked to, the longer the list of local musicians grew. Virgie herself had mentioned two brothers named L. C. Hill and Archie Hill, who'd been part of the second generation of bluesmen, Robert Johnson's generation. But she didn't think he'd ever played with them and had no idea what had become of them. Later someone mentioned a one-legged musician named George Smith who turned out to be Virgie's uncle. She just hadn't thought to mention him herself.

Some of the names—particularly Willie Hudson—came up repeatedly. Musicians named Johnson were mentioned several times, but they seemed to be different, unrelated people. Often people would mention a local Lonnie Johnson, explaining that he wasn't the "real" Lonnie Johnson, but someone who called himself by that name. The better-known Lonnie Johnson was a refined, polished blues singer whose recording career began in 1925 and spanned forty-five years. By his own testimony, he was from New Orleans, but his name was often and confusingly brought up by residents of Copiah County. One man said that there was a local guy by that name but that "he only mocked Lonnie Johnson's records." Someone else thought this fellow was still living nearby, but someone else contended that they were thinking of a different person, not the one we'd been talking about. It all got quite confusing.

Later in the afternoon I drove out toward Dentville, trying to find Willie Hudson, but I drew a blank. There'd been sharper changes in this part of the county. No one there seemed to know a Willie Hudson, and it was hard even to find people who had lived in Dentville for any length of time. Some of the housing was new, almost suburban in style, and there were villages of mobile homes. It was hard to develop any picture of the community as it had been in years past.

I returned to Hazlehurst, trying to decide what my next step should be. I was beginning to get a feeling for the place. There was only a little of the Old South antebellum flavor there, even though Copiah County had been well-settled at the time of the Civil War. The Confederacy's great cotton-producing regions centered on Natchez and Vicksburg, and Copiah County was just on the fringe of that area. Nine million pounds of cotton were picked in the county in 1859, transported to the river by wagon or shipped on the brand-new railroad to New Orleans.

In some ways Copiah County hadn't changed much. I parked on South Extension, the main street, and walked over to the courthouse. Just inside the door was a rack of leaflets for the Southern National Party, which advocated the South's right to manage its own affairs. There was a racist tone to some of it: "The Southern Anglo-Saxon race—when the South was free, and in control of her own destiny—produced the brains and the ethical standards that ran America."

This was George Wallace country. He had won 59 percent of the vote in 1968. The strange thing is that even though the segregationist thinking hadn't changed, the local economy had made a tremendous adjustment. Copiah County had accomplished much of what the rural South was still trying to manage. Over the years the county had made a transition from a near total dependency on labor-intensive crops into diversified truck farming and then manufacturing. County development officials had brought in a shirt factory, a company that made school laboratory equipment, and Kuhlman Electric—the plant where Claud Johnson worked.

The boll weevil got here in 1909, and that had quickened the changeover. Farmers shrugged off their dependency on cotton, moving into different kinds of cash crops and turning some of the local timber into crates and boxes. As a result, there wasn't that deadly, falling-down kind of poverty that marked so much of the rural South.

It was, of course, the Black population that made the biggest adjustments, most of them by simply moving away. Between 1910 and 1920, the decade in which Robert Johnson was born, about five thousand African Americans left Copiah County. The families that moved away went mostly to the Delta, particularly the parts of the Delta that were settled relatively late, such as the areas around Clarksdale and Tunica. New planters moved into the Delta, clearing and draining new sections of land, and then sending labor agents to the hill country to lure more families to work the new fields.

There was a kind of hard logic to it all: Let the people go where they're needed. Cotton had required hordes of laborers, but Copiah County was going into other things, and new plantations in the Delta to the northwest were starting up, making big promises to those families willing to relocate. Everything boomed when World War I pushed up the cotton prices. The by-product of these trends was that Black families were scattered. For most of them, the Delta became a temporary stopping place, for a year or maybe for a generation, between wherever they'd started and some city.

It was those disrupted, dislocated generations that produced the blues singers. The Delta blues came about not by some gradual development, but abruptly, almost explosively. There was no long pregnancy; just the labor pains, then the birth.

The next morning I decided to try a different approach. Virgie had told me that Robert Johnson's sister (or relative of some kind) lived in Hazlehurst. She hadn't seen her in some time, and it seemed likely she'd moved away, but Virgie had told me about a Mabel Washington, who had been a friend of the woman in question and might know where she'd gone. She could only furnish me with a vague address in a neighborhood known as Cato Quarters, but she suggested that I could find her by asking around.

Cato Quarters turned out to be a poor section with several deep gullies used as roads. A big truck with engine trouble had gotten jammed in one gully, and the other gully was full of parked cars. I left my car at the edge and walked into Cato Quarters. Almost immediately a gang of teenagers encircled me and started teasing, acting tough. They wore oversized sunglasses and bell-bottomed slacks in Day-Glo colors. One of them wore a dashiki. The apparent leader was sitting on a motorcycle. He kept inching it forward while the others flung insults. Some of the talk was about paying a "road tax." They tossed it back and forth among themselves.

"You know he can't come in here without paying the road tax."

"No, he can't!"

"Well, how come he gotta pay when there ain't no road."

"That's what the tax is for."

"You mean first you pay the tax, then you got the money to build the road?"

"Now, it ain't that way at all."

"First you collect the tax, but you don't *never* build in the road. Not down here in Cato Quarters."

A few times before I'd faced gangs of real toughs, the sort capable of mindless violence just because the urge takes them. But these didn't seem like the type. They made a pretty good show of it, but it didn't ring true. Besides, it was Sunday, and these were probably college guys home for the weekend, with an idle day on their hands and some curiosity about me. One of them asked about the Texas plates on my car.

Situations like this, even when they're a lot closer to violence than this one was, seldom need to develop into anything. The trick is to respond in an unexpected way. I walked over to the leader and started talking. I told him in explicit detail what I was doing and why. I told him a lot more than he wanted to know. I told him about the hardships of traveling, about the evil food in truck stops, the misleading directions to places you couldn't possibly miss, and the number of swindlers who run gas stations. I told him I was looking for a woman named Mabel Washington and explained why I wanted to find her. I talked for at least a full ten minutes.

It was soon plain I was beginning to bore them. The joy had gone out of their game. By the time I'd talked another five minutes, half of them had drifted away. Finally the guy on the motorcycle gave up and surged up the gully with a blast of sound.

The next hour passed quickly. I walked up and down the streets of Cato Quarters asking for Mabel Washington. Finally someone pointed out a big corner house with a sagging porch sitting on the crest of a hill. A scared-looking young girl came in answer to my knock on the torn old screen door. She took me inside to a senile old woman who tried but never did manage to remember her name.

The girl who was taking care of her said indifferently that she didn't know the old woman's name. "I'll just be here until they come back," she told me.

"Who's they?" I asked. She looked at me as if I were stupid. "Them that asked me to come stay with her," she answered.

I tried talking to her for a while, but I couldn't find out the family's name or who the old woman was. The girl just didn't know. She was fourteen, and she'd lived across the street for only three years. This didn't seem to be getting anywhere. It was too far out at the end of a string of maybes.

As I walked back up the gully, one of the young men fell in step with me.

"Walk with you?" he asked.

"Sure."

"You really doing what you said?" he wanted to know. "You hunting some old funky blues singer?"

"That's straight."

"But why, man? Dead is dead."

"Well, you know what they say about the blues."

"No, what *they* say?"

"The blues are 'the fullest expression of the Negro's individuality.'"

"You believe that?" he asked, a little appalled.

"No, it's bullshit. I don't like the finality of it. Full, fuller, fullest."

"Who said it?"

"They said it."

"Who's *they?*"

"A guy who wrote the blurb on a book jacket. It was a book by LeRoi Jones."

The young man said he was a student at Jackson State College. I asked him whether he'd been there when the police had opened fire on a crowd of students.

"No, that was a year before I started. That was 1967."

"You into Black studies?" I asked him.

"Yeah."

"How's it going?"

"It's bullshit." He shook his head. "Black guys who made it as generals or judges or civil rights leaders. That ain't history."

"No. But that's the way they write it."

He laughed and thumped my arm. "Who's *they?*"

We climbed out of Cato Quarters and got to my car. He asked if I'd drop him a couple of blocks further down the street. He climbed in the other side.

"Maybe one day they'll be teaching about this blues singer you say was born here."

"Not too likely," I told him. "At least not yet. You know the thing about a prophet in his own land."

"Right." He smiled at a thought. "Wouldn't it be weird if he turned out to be the most famous guy that ever came from Hazlehurst?"

"He's that already, I suspect."

I pulled the car over and he got out, "Who says?" He stuck his head back in the window. "Is that something more *they* say?"

"No, that's something I say. But it's only a guess. Depends on who else came from around here."

He pulled his head out of the window and gave me a gesture with a flexed forearm. "Luck, man. I hope you find out about him."

I drove on down the street, turned on Extension, and drove back out to the motel. I went into the motel office and sat down with the telephone. I'd removed a phone book from a booth, and Mr. Johnson, the genial pool hall operator, had marked the Johnsons who he thought were Black families. I started down the list, calling every one of them. It was midday Sunday, a good time to catch people at home.

It took about an hour. Several of the people I talked to had uncles or cousins or brothers named Robert, but a bit of conversation eliminated them. Several people mentioned Lonnie Johnson, not because he was related, but because he was a famous musician with the same family name. Tommy Johnson came up only twice, once from a man who'd known him but wasn't related, the other time from a man who turned out to be Tommy Johnson's nephew. But the one I was looking for never came up. I talked to many Johnsons who were related to one another and who, together, told me enough to sketch out a good bit of a genealogy chart. But none of the Robert Johnsons who were mentioned were the one I was interested in.

I pushed the telephone away with disappointment. It was time to try a more indirect approach. The day before I'd heard the name of man who'd lived in the Martinsville area all his life, and he was somewhere in his eighties. I was told that he ought to know all the history about the local Johnsons. I had an instinctive good feeling about this man. I even liked the ring of his name: Alpheus Brown.

It took only a few minutes to drive back to Martinsville past the store and along a red dirt road that shot off to the south. I drove up into the hills and, after stopping to ask a few times, found Mr. Brown's house on a wandering back road.

He came forward to meet me as soon as the car stopped. He conducted me to his front porch and offered me a chair. He wore overalls, a heavy, tattered sweater, and a knit skull cap. His skin was leathery and deep brown, with blackish highlights. He had a broad, blunt nose, but most of his features were more finely etched. His eyes were deep set. Something about him reminded me of the actor Leigh Whipper. It could have been the erect way he carried himself, or the easy grace of his hospitality.

Alpheus Brown knew little and cared little about the outside world, but he was thoroughly acquainted with his corner of Copiah County. He sat on his wide, breeze-swept porch and talked, rambling on about anything and everything. I hadn't yet asked him any questions about musicians or about the Johnson or Major families. I just leaned back and let him continue.

He told me he'd been born in 1888 near Dentville. He'd moved into these hills, bought his own land, and did as he pleased. He had supported his wife and raised his children by hunting, cutting timber, and working his steep hillside fields.

"See," he said, "I was smart. I never got nothing that anybody else wanted too bad. So they left me alone."

In October he would set up his sorghum mill with the long copper pan and boil the juice into syrup. Some of the area farmers still planted sorghum cane, and they would bring him their crops in the fall; he would give them back gallons of the rich, dark molasses.

It used to be a special occasion. Young people would come and sit up all night as the syrup was being boiled and skimmed down the length of the long copper pan. Neighbors would sit around chewing stalks of cane, sipping the juice from the mill, playing counting-out games, challenging one another with riddles, or just gossiping. Usually someone would boil a washtub full of freshly dug peanuts, and then they'd pass around the hot goobers. Sometimes the occasion might turn into a real frolic, if someone had brought a guitar or a fiddle and if none of the stricter parents made objections. They'd get a broom, sweep part of the ground where it was packed hard, and dance barefoot on the earth itself.

Alpheus Brown pointed up to the hill where his old mill stood, and told me that some nights there'd be fifty or sixty people up there, the mules walking their circular track at the end of a long pole, someone feeding in the cane, others toting buckets and helping skim the syrup, and a whole crowd of people off to the side, dancing and hugging each other while the music charged the night air. He said that city people usually had a mistaken notion about country people going to bed early. In fact it was often the other way around: city dwellers might stay up until 2:00 a.m. and think that was late, but country people at a frolic could stay up the whole night long, dancing and partying until the roosters crowed for daylight. They couldn't go home, not with a horse that might fall and break a leg in the darkness. So frolics that lasted all night were the usual thing. "That didn't change until these good roads and automobiles came along," he said. "That was what allowed people to go home at night. But even then, the custom was if you went to a frolic, you'd figure to stay the night."

The bigger frolics, he remembered, were held near the railroad tracks, where the depot platform was sometimes used. On other occasions partyers would clear the inside of a cotton gin and then sprinkle the floor with bran for dancing. And a few people held frolics in their houses, two or three nights a week. Some fried chicken and barbecue, some whiskey to sell, a couple of musicians to play, often taking turns, and a platform, porch, or big room were enough to attract a crowd on Friday or Saturday nights.

Brown seemed to sense what I was interested in, or perhaps he noticed the way I hitched my chair forward as he talked about the frolics. He mentioned some of the better musicians he knew, several of them fiddlers who'd learned from an uncle or a father, and he recalled the names of a few guitar players. One of them was named Robert Amico, and Brown's description made it sound like he could have been Robert Johnson. But then the old man said that Amico was still alive, living on the north side of Jackson, Mississippi.

We walked up the hill to the rusty old sorghum mill, and Brown described how he'd clean the brick oven and set up the copper pan next fall. It wasn't hard to imagine his hilltop full of people on an October night. There was a crackling sound as I walked over the old dried cane stalks scattered around the base of the iron mill. I wondered how many more years he would go on making sorghum molasses.

Brown looked at me and smiled. "I know most everything about this part of the country, but what I don't know, there's a lady that knows the rest. She was the schoolteacher here for the colored for as long as I can remember."

As he gave me directions to her place, I realized he was describing the It community, the area across the railroad and on the other side of the highway, behind the grocery store. Her name was Minerva Cain, and he cautioned me to be careful because she was old: "You best do her like you did me. Don't ask no questions. Just let her talk a while."

I drove back down and across Highway 51 onto another winding road, stopping only once to ask directions to her house. Minerva Cain was home, watching television, but pleased to have a reason to turn it off. She was easy to talk to, and she didn't seem too surprised that someone would come by to ask questions about the children she'd taught. She said there'd been hundreds of them, and she often wondered what had become of them all. She said too many of them had quit school to go to work, going out into the world in their early teens with little knowledge beyond being barely able to write their names.

Gently, I asked if there had been any particular child who seemed more interested in music than anything else. Almost immediately she mentioned a Robert Johnson, a youngster she'd had in school for only a few months. She'd tried to teach him to read and write. He was about twelve or thirteen at the time, and wherever he'd gone to school before, he hadn't learned much more than the alphabet and some simple math.

She remembered his father and his mother. She wouldn't say a word about his father, except that his name was Noah Johnson (she pronounced it as "Norah"). His mother was named Julia, and she had been one of the Majors girls from a big family that lived on Miller's Hill around the Antioch Church. There had been a Madison Majors who'd lived on Miller's Hill, and he'd had four children, all girls. Julia was one of those girls, or else she was first cousin to them. After she married Noah Johnson, she'd had a raft of children. "That boy Robert was about the only one who came to my school," Minerva said. "He was about the youngest."

Another of the Majors girls, Mary, had worked for a Mr. Rempke, who ran a sawmill at Martinsville. At some point he'd closed down the mill and gone back to Ohio, maybe Cincinnati. He asked Mary Majors to go with him because she was such a good cook, and the Rempke family was so fond of her. Later she wrote and told her family about life in Ohio, and another one of the girls decided to join her. That might have been Julia, but Mrs. Cain wasn't sure. It might have been one of the other girls.

The more she reflected, the more likely it seemed that these events had occurred long before Robert Johnson was born. The old lady's memory was sharp and clear on the way things had been when she was a girl. The rest, however, was fragmentary, like odd frames snipped at random from an eighty-year-long motion picture.

She didn't remember where Robert had been living when he went to her school, but she thought that Julia had moved away a good while before that. He'd probably come back to Hazlehurst to stay with relatives, she thought. For a moment she seemed to glimpse some frames that she wouldn't tell me about. She

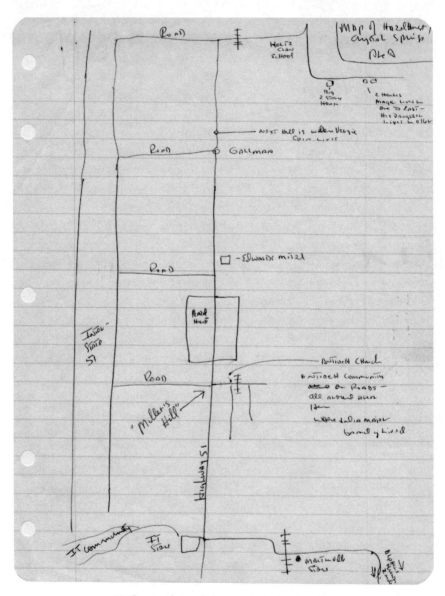

McCormick's hand-drawn map indicating the
Majors home on Miller's Hill, just south of Hazlehurst.

simply said, "That family had more trouble than they was due." She shook her head, as if the memory angered her.

She searched around for some other fragments. Whatever had become of Madison Majors was missing, and she couldn't recall what had become of Julia. She'd seen Julia on the street in Hazlehurst one day, but she had no idea of when it had been or where it fit into the sequence of events. She wouldn't say a thing about Noah Johnson; on that she was adamant.

There wasn't a single relative of Robert Johnson's whom she could think of to send me to. She asked me what had become of him. Apparently she hadn't heard the stories, and I simply told her that many people now thought of him as an important musician. That didn't particularly seem to surprise her.

She talked on, dropping back into the days of her own youth, mentioning the frolics and the dances that sparkled in her memory. She said it was just about then, around 1900 or 1905, that people got tired of fiddle music, and musicians started playing guitar a lot more. She named a few of the musicians who'd lived nearby, but she'd never paid them too much attention. Some were people from around the county, and some were just people passing through. A few of the names she mentioned and some of the occasions she talked about dovetailed with what the people around the Martinsville store had previously described.

When I got up to leave, she asked me a question: "Robert is dead, ain't he?" I nodded.

"I expect he died young?" I nodded again.

That seemed to confirm what she had imagined. She gave me directions to Miller's Hill and the Antioch Church, then went back inside to switch on her television set.

Miller's Hill turned out to be the first rise just outside of Hazlehurst, but it was one of the areas that had totally changed. No one remembered a Majors family nor anything else that went back more than few years. There wasn't any point in spending time there.

Driving along the street in Hazlehurst, I saw the young student who'd walked out of Cato Quarters with me, and I stopped to give him a lift. I told him a story that Alpheus Brown had shared with me. He'd called it "The History of the World" and said it was something he'd heard when he was a young man:

The Lord made the three races—the white man, the Black man, and the Indian—and he lined them up to pass the work out. There was three bundles laying on the table there, and He say to the Black man, "You gets first pick." So the Black man picks the biggest bundle, which is a mule and a plow. So he got himself out to the cotton patch. Next, the Indian had his time to choose, and he took the next pick, which was the bow and arrow. So he went off into the woods. Well, that left nothing for the white man except a little bitty bundle, which was a writing pen. So the white man took up the pen, and he sat down and went to figuring against the Black man and the Indian.

The young student didn't say anything. He just turned and gave me a big, benevolent grin. After I dropped him off, he walked on down the street, nodding to himself, the Day-Glo colors of his clothes flashing in the sunshine.

The cast of characters in my quest had enlarged considerably: the Majors family including Madison Majors, Mary Majors, and Julia Majors. Rempke, the sawmill operator. Noah Johnson. The "stout, bright lady." Julia's other children—a raft of them, but bearing some other last name I hadn't been able to learn from the old schoolteacher.

I spent most of the next day trying to get a line on any one of the group. I tried at the county courthouse, the post office, and the George W. Covington Memorial Library. I was sent to some of the older white residents, who would ponder the various names, saying something about, "Now, that sounds kinda familiar," but then start muttering about how long ago all that had been. I found people who thought they remembered someone named Major or Rempke but not well enough to tell me what had become of them.

When I read over the notes I'd made and listened to the interview I'd taped with Virgie Mae Cain, I was impressed by the number of musicians that had been mentioned at one time or another. It came to a total of thirty-two different musicians, give or take one or two, owing to confusion over nicknames and possible duplication. The name of Lonnie Johnson continued to plague me. It had come up a number of times, describing someone much younger than the blues fiddler and guitar player who'd been so famous at one time. But several old-timers had insisted that they distinctly remembered "the real Lonnie Johnson coming through here." That was possible; it was only a short train ride from New Orleans to Hazlehurst. In any case, his name appeared on the list twice.

With only a few exceptions, it was a list of resident musicians, players who'd lived and worked in the area over a period of years. The ones who passed through hadn't usually stayed long enough to make an impression and weren't known by name. At least three generations of musicians had been described. First were those who'd been actively playing when Minerva Cain had been a girl. Next were those who took over from them: the players who'd been on the scene from the time of World War I through the 1920s. The following third generation was the one that produced Robert Johnson. He'd come into a rich musical community.

Yet it was by no means a complete list. Oddly enough, one notable musician who was still active in the area had never been mentioned. I decided that my next goal was to check in with that unmentioned musician: Houston Stackhouse, a bluesman from Robert Johnson's generation, who still lived and played in Copiah County. He'd been a member of the *King Biscuit Time* program for several years, one of the guitarists who came in after Robert Lockwood Jr. departed, and he sang in a nasal, clenched voice that at moments was strongly reminiscent of Robert Johnson. Around Helena, he was best remembered for the rumpus created when he went on the air singing a song that opened, "I got a sweet Black angel . . . and I love it when she spreads her wings."

He was born in 1910 at Wesson, Mississippi—the same small town in the southern part of the county that had been Virgie's home, the town where Claud Johnson had been born. Houston Stackhouse started playing guitar when he was about seventeen and joined a group of local musicians who went around with each other, borrowing songs, lending guitar strings, and chasing jobs together.

Later, following a familiar pattern, he spent increasing amounts of time in the Delta, where there was more demand for musicians and looser money among the cotton pickers and sharecroppers. He continued to maintain this geographic duality for years. When I asked him once how I could stay in touch, he'd reminded me of the man in *The Captain's Paradise* by providing two addresses: 932 Phillips Street, Helena, Arkansas, or 215 West Piazza, Crystal Springs, Mississippi. "You'll catch me one place or the other," he'd said.

When he was in the Delta, he played in the taverns around West Memphis, Hughes, and Helena, and when he was in Crystal Springs, he worked a few jobs and hung out with friends at a corner gathering spot, a drive-in grocery called the H & T. I'd stopped by there several days in a row, but I hadn't found him. All of a sudden, there he was, standing outside the store, talking with several friends. After a moment he recognized me and flashed his incredible smile.

Houston was getting used to being interviewed and having people poke at him with questions. Given that he remained the most persistently active Delta

Houston Stackhouse performing with the Joe Willie
Wilkins Blues Band at the Smithsonian Festival of
American Folklife, Washington, DC, July 1, 1970.
Photograph by Robert "Mack" McCormick.

bluesman of the 1970s, it was natural that a number of different people sought him
out. He was a strong performer but not an innovator. He absorbed material but
didn't often originate it, and for this very reason represented a kind of unintended
amalgam of the Delta and Mississippi blues.

One night a couple of years earlier he'd appeared at a West Memphis tavern in a powerhouse group playing pure, throbbing blues with a relaxed good
feeling that stayed in the room even after the music came to an end. He'd been
working with another guitarist, a drummer, and a tough, angry harmonica player
whose body twitched as he played shattering phrases, clutching both the microphone and harp to his mouth. Over the course of the evening, they had evoked

the spirit and style of half a dozen major blues artists. At one point Stackhouse's voice rose above everything with the eerie, unmistakable falsetto of Tommy Johnson's "Cool Drink of Water Blues." It's one of the most copied of all performances, and Houston Stackhouse did it immaculately, as if in tribute to the man who had created the song. Each syllable and each note were honed and studied, every nuance shaped and set in place just so, to become part of a gentle, floating structure.

In recent years Tommy Johnson had generated much the same kind of intense interest that Robert Johnson had received. Some of the same ground I was covering in Copiah County had been tramped over by ethnomusicologist David Evans, who'd come here four years earlier doing research on Tommy Johnson that developed first into a master's thesis and then a book published in England. And only two years before, a writer-photographer-anthropologist named George Mitchell had recorded and interviewed Houston Stackhouse. A number of other enthusiasts and researchers had talked to him, so I didn't expect to learn anything new.

But Houston surprised me. He was a bullet-headed man—his bald skull had almost the exact configuration of .32 caliber ammunition—with a dark, brooding face that would break into a bountiful, overwhelming smile when anyone gave him a kind word. He promptly told me that he had known Robert Johnson, played with him at times, and heard him in several different towns. I was skeptical, thinking that perhaps he was being kind, telling me what he thought I wanted to hear. Sometimes when a person has been interviewed by successive writers and researchers you'll get a kind of feedback, and he'll start talking about people that he learned of from those earlier interviewers. It may all be perfectly mean well intended; after all, a name like Robert Johnson sounds familiar to most people. It's easy to agree with the question, and say yes, I knew him. But Stackhouse had always struck me as a straightforward, honest person. He didn't seem like the kind of man who would exaggerate and embroider the facts. Maybe no one had ever asked him about Robert Johnson before? But that was incredible, particularly when you consider that Houston Stackhouse continued to alternate between the Helena area and Copiah County in the same fashion—as it was beginning to appear—that Robert Johnson seems to have done. Could it be that no one had poked the most obvious of all questions at him? That didn't seem probable, yet when I thought back, I realized I'd talked to him on three or four occasions and never asked him about Robert Johnson.

In any case, my doubts were rapidly dispelled by the firm, full detail that Stackhouse included in what he knew of Robert Johnson. He said he wasn't sure when he'd first come across Johnson, but they'd gotten better acquainted sometime during the 1930s when they were both playing in places near Helena, such as at a crossroads store or at party houses. For a while they crossed paths quite often, and then a short time later Johnson had shown up in Copiah County. He'd stayed around a little over a week.

"He played around here two weekends," Stackhouse recalled. "It was during the cabbage shipping season, I remember, so that'd make it toward the last of May. It was somewhere in the '30s, just at a guess I'd say 1936 or 1937." He remembered the occasion because Robert Johnson's records had just begun to appear, and that was making him something of a regional celebrity. Stackhouse was able to recall the titles of several records that were current at the time, pieces that were being played on phonographs and that Johnson was playing around the county. He named "Terraplane Blues," "Sweet Home Chicago," "Kind Hearted Woman Blues," and "Cross Road Blues."

This information checked out neatly. Robert Johnson's first record had been issued in January 1937. From January through August a new one appeared each month, but after that the releases became more erratic. If Johnson had been in Crystal Springs in May 1937, a total of five records—ten songs—would have been available at the time. All but one of the songs Stackhouse named would have been included, and that one was issued the next month.

Stackhouse said that he'd played at the Burney Farm one Saturday night, and that Johnson had played there the previous Saturday night. During the evening, someone came in and told him that Johnson was playing that night over at the Frank Ford Farm. So Stackhouse wrapped up his job as early as he could and drove over to "help" Johnson. They spent an hour or two backing each other up, occasionally launching a hokum song, swapping verses, and kidding around.

Stackhouse explained that the two farms were regular venues for musicians in the area. They were on opposite sides of Crystal Springs: the Burney Farm about three and half miles west on Burney Road, and the Ford place about three miles due east of town. During the week or so that Robert Johnson was in town, Stackhouse saw him on the street a few times. He got the impression that Johnson came to Copiah County during the cabbage season every year to play music and visit relatives. "His people was all from here," Stackhouse said. "I moved off so many times myself, I never did know him when he was growing up,

The corner of Marion Avenue and Jackson Street, Crystal Springs, Mississippi.
Photograph by Robert "Mack" McCormick.

but I believe he told me this was his home. But you understand, I never did just keep track of him."

It seems almost certain that the occasion Stackhouse described was the same time when Robert Johnson brought records to his son, Claud. And it was the following month when he returned to Texas, this time to Dallas, to record again. Probably some of the songs he was playing in Mississippi at the time were ones he was working on, preparing to record. But Stackhouse didn't recall these nearly so well as the ones already out on records.

I questioned Houston some more, but he'd said all he could. I went over all the other family names with him, but none meant anything to him. I asked whether he had any idea of where Robert Johnson's people had moved to. "Up close to Memphis," he said. "Seems like it be around Tunica."

"Tunica County? Or the town itself?"

He shook his head. "I just wouldn't know. It just seems like he said Tunica."

As we talked, we'd walked the several blocks along the street toward his house. Most of the houses we passed were simple frame buildings, a good many of them in pretty bad shape. One house stood out from all the rest: It was neat and well trimmed. There was a brick front to it, a lot of fresh paint, touches of aluminum grill work, and attractive shrubbery. Something about it rang a bell, and I asked Houston if he knew who lived there. He told me it was a man named Claud Johnson. "He works over at the Kuhlman factory." I asked him whether he thought he could be related to Robert Johnson, and Stackhouse shrugged. "He might be. I never thought about it."

The irony was not lost on me. Here I was, tramping all over the state of Mississippi and a good bit of Arkansas, and I end up getting a good many answers from a man who could have told me on a number of previous occasions that Robert Johnson's home had been Copiah County. It was a matter of my not asking the question. Then, when I finally do get around to asking it, it turns out not only that he was a one-time cohort of Johnson, but that he and Robert Johnson's son were living nearly side by side. When he was in Crystal Springs, Houston Stackhouse was at 215 West Piazza, and Claud Johnson was at 211 West Piazza. They were neighbors.

There were other coincidences that had piled up.

I didn't like the fact that I'd just happened to walk into the pool hall when the only customer was practically the only person in the county who could have told me about Virgie. It was too much of a chance. Yet the only alternate explanation seemed to be to postulate some conspiracy at work, staying ahead of me, setting things up. There was another major coincidence in the astonishing, almost incredible fact that both Robert Johnson and Tommy Johnson had come from the same county. That one didn't take me by surprise, but it had narrowed down a great deal. I knew that Tommy Johnson's younger brother lived in Crystal Springs, and I'd passed his house a few days before.

What was so hard to accept was that I had wandered over thousands of square miles of territory looking for Robert Johnson, while someone else was looking for Tommy Johnson, and both stories had ended up being concentrated in the same tiny piece of ground.

Claud Johnson and Houston Stackhouse lived on the same street. It was just about 1.1 miles from there to where Tommy Johnson's younger brother lived. A crow could fly it without blinking. And from his house to where Virgie lived was another 1.7 miles.

The real puzzle was why nothing had yet turned up to tie these two stories together. Two extraordinary bluesmen named Johnson, with relatives living in the same neighborhood, and yet nothing linked them up. The small coincidences

I might accept, grudgingly. But this major incongruity was too improbable. By this time I'd become a fixture at Johnson's restaurant. The very name of the place was the first of the coincidences that had struck me. The menu there featured something called buffalo fish, and I decided to experiment with that. While I was waiting for my order, Early Johnson poked his head into the window between the two halves of the business, and said, "I thought of who you ought to go see. Don't know why I didn't think of him before."

I creaked forward a bit on my stool.

"There's a fellow up at Crystal Springs, name of Stackhouse . . ." His voice drifted off as I shook my head. "Damn, I was waiting on you to tell you about Stackhouse. You already been to see him, huh?"

I nodded. "He couldn't help?"

"He helped, but he couldn't tell me anything about his family. That's the place I can't get past."

"Yeah, I know." He told me he'd been asking people about anyone named Noah Johnson or a family by the name of Major. He said he'd asked thirty or more people, old-timers. He shook his head again. "I believe we must have just about covered it."

Mrs. Johnson brought some silverware, and then Mr. Johnson's head popped back through the window. "There was one guy that said some people named Major lived down in Brookhaven."

"How far away is that?" I asked.

"About thirty miles. Next county south."

I went to the telephone and asked for information in Brookhaven. There was an Alberta Major listed. I dropped forty cents into the slot and called the woman. She was a little cagey about talking to strangers on the telephone. She said she'd never had any relatives in Copiah County, and no relatives anywhere named Julia, Mary, or Madison. That didn't sound quite right to me; everyone has a relative somewhere named Mary. I deduced that Major was probably her husband's name, but that she didn't know much about his family history. At any rate, she wasn't interested in discussing the matter. I could go on with this game. I could call people in Jackson. There were three Majors listed in that phone book, and it was only about thirty miles in the other direction.

Before I'd left Houston, I'd done some statistical research, just to see what kind of odds were involved. The 1910 census listed 19,981 Black people in Copiah County. Over the next decade, almost 25 percent of the county's Black population left, according to the 1920 census. Out of an estimated black population of

85

nearly twenty thousand, about two hundred would have carried the surname Johnson, if the census's statistics on the nation's most common names are accurate. Thus, in 1914, this group of two hundred must have included both Tommy Johnson (then around eighteen) and Robert Johnson (age two).

I wonder what kind of odds Nick the Greek would give on something like that. What are the probabilities that out of a given group of two hundred, two of them will become outstanding in the same field? What are the odds on two of them being the object of far-flung searches and researches fifty years later? What are the odds on even two of them being noteworthy in any way?

In short, how do you rationally explain Copiah County's ability to produce two extraordinary blues musicians named Johnson? The most probable explanation is that there was a family link, a connection, or a relationship between the two. Even if a common last name were not involved, two musicians of their rank coming from the same place would automatically suggest a connection. One would expect to find that one of them taught, inspired, or at least set an example for the other.

Many musicians of any stripe, and almost all blues artists, tell about a relative who started them off. It's sometimes a father, mother, cousin, or sibling, but most often it's an uncle. Given that Tommy and Robert Johnson seem to have shared the same community roots, it wouldn't have been a shock to find that they were uncle and nephew. On the contrary, it would have been close to the typical pattern. Yet so far I hadn't been able to establish more than pure coincidence and proximity. The best I had was the prospect that young Robert may have hung around when Tommy and his brothers played on the streets of Crystal Springs.

Robert Johnson's parents had lived in Copiah County, at least for a while. His mother's family had lived here, but they'd all drifted away. He'd been born and perhaps raised here, but it didn't look like he'd lived here for a great part of his life, although he had sporadically reappeared in the area over a wide span of years: once when he'd attended Minerva Cain's school; later, when he met and lived with Virgie Mae Cain; a short time in the mid-1930s; and again in May 1937. Those times had been pinpointed, and it was even possible, as Houston Stackhouse had thought, that he had returned every year to visit relatives.

But nothing I'd tried had put me in direct touch with those relatives, and nothing had pointed in the direction of Tommy Johnson's family. Meanwhile, I felt I was beginning to wear out my welcome. A few of the people that came into Johnson's restaurant glanced at me sharply. They were beginning to doubt my story about looking for a dead musician's family. They suspected there had to be something more to it. I knew there was a rumor going around that a big inheritance was involved. People often assume that great wads of money are involved whenever someone's made successful recordings. That could be a cruel rumor if it managed to reach Robert Johnson's family.

Suddenly Early Johnson's head reappeared in his little window. "Did you try that fellow I told you about?" he asked.

"Which one is that?"

"You know, the first man I told you about—the guitar player that lives up at Crystal Springs, around back of the school. Major Johnson."

For some reason I'd forgotten all about that suggestion. His name had come up, but then it had been obscured in the process of locating Virgie and her son. Now it came to me who he had to be: the Major Johnson Early was talking about must be Tommy Johnson's brother, whom I'd avoided going to see except as a last resort. The thing that had thrown me off was the fact that his name had appeared in several interviews as "Mager" Johnson, and I'd never heard it pronounced as "Major" until I got to Hazlehurst. I got up and thanked Early Johnson. I told him I was going straight up to Crystal Springs to see the man he'd just reminded me of. It was time for last resorts.

• • •

6

OTHER JOHNSONS

When I drove up to Mager Johnson's house in April 1970, a group of women was out in the yard, gathered around a huge iron pot. They'd just butchered a hog, and they were rendering the lard, cutting the rind to make cracklings and turning the small intestine into chitlins.

Mager Johnson wasn't at home, so I stood around a few minutes watching the work. They'd set up a long table in the space between the two houses (Mager and his family lived in one, his son and his family in the other), and they were hacking up the meat, sorting it into different pots. The big iron pot sat over an open fire.

I made arrangements to come back later and then drove off to see whether Claud Johnson was home from work. He was, and we talked a while. He hadn't managed to learn anything yet about the "stout, bright lady," but he appeared more relaxed than he had before. This time he told me about his great-uncle, a one-legged musician named George Smith, whom the people around Martinsville had also mentioned.

It was George Smith, more than his mother Virgie, who used to talk to Claud about his father and answer his questions. When Claud was young, Smith used to repeat, "Your father was a guitar player, and you probably got his talent." He'd often urged that Claud take up guitar.

Smith had told Claud that when his father was young, he himself had taught him a few things and that soon he was playing better than Smith himself. Like most teachers who find themselves outdistanced by their students, Smith

The hog rendering at Mager Johnson's home,
Crystal Springs, Mississippi. Photograph by
Robert "Mack" McCormick.

had been awed by his pupil. It also seemed clear that Smith had known Robert Johnson some time before Virgie had met him. Claud recalled that on one particular occasion when he was a teenager, he and his great-uncle were sitting in the kitchen, and Smith had reminisced about Johnson coming to his house: "He said when my daddy was just about the same age as I was, he'd come around to him asking how to make this sound or do this thing on the guitar. I was about thirteen or fourteen when he told me about that." Assuming that Robert Johnson had been in his early teens, this might have been about the same time that he'd gone to school in Martinsville, as Minerva Cain had remembered.

There were a number of other times that Smith had sat around the kitchen, playing guitar, and talking about music and musicians, trying to provoke his grandnephew's interest. "He used to tell me a few things about my daddy," Claud said.

"What sorts of things?" I asked.

"That he was a famous musician and all like that. He tried in the worst way to get me to get interested in music," Claud said, looking away with a shy grin. "He said about my daddy that he had made his reputation up in the Delta."

"Was any particular place mentioned?"

"No. He just said 'up in the Delta,'" Claud answered. "He did tell me my daddy had a brother up in the Delta by the name of Tom Johnson who was a famous musician too."

I felt myself wishing he hadn't said that. I knew it wasn't going to turn out to be that simple. My neck creaked a little as I leaned forward, but I managed to keep my voice casual.

"Did he ever mention anything more about the brother?"

"No"

"Or say anything about musicians around here that might be related?"

"No."

"Did he say where this brother lived?"

"Just up in the Delta. That's all I know." I asked where George Smith had lived. "Sometimes he lived here, and sometimes he went off to the Delta," Claud said.

I asked whether he knew where George Smith had first known his father. "That was around here. But I guess he knew him up in the Delta too. Both places."

There was no sure way of distilling the facts from these childhood memories of what an admiring great-uncle had said. I drove back to Mager Johnson's house, hoping he could set the matter straight. If Tommy Johnson and Robert Johnson had been brothers, it should have come out before this. All I could do was deal with the possibilities as they came along. Sometimes I felt like a trained seal that tooted horns and balanced a ball on the end of his nose. If I banged my flippers and barked, someone might toss me another Johnson.

It was dark when I got back to the two white frame houses on Thomas Road. The fire was still going under the cauldron. Mager Johnson opened the door and motioned for me to come inside. We tiptoed through a room where some children were asleep, and he took me into the kitchen, where the women were still working. The odor was overwhelming. Hog butchering in the open air is one thing, but inside a house it creates a staggering stench. Johnson sat down at the table and motioned for me to sit across from him. The hog's head rested on a big plate at the end of the table.

After we had talked a while, we made another tiptoeing trip out to my car to bring in the battered guitar I carried with me. Mager Johnson wanted to sing some of the blues he'd learned from his older brother. Neither of us was exactly at ease. The women kept frowning disapprovingly at him, probably over the fact that he was having a good time while they worked, and the slaughterhouse odor was nauseating me. Mager sang a few songs, and I heard again that unmistakable phrasing, that sudden falsetto, and the tumbling fall of the words. Tommy Johnson had a vocal style as distinctive as W. C. Fields's, and he was imitated in the same closely mimicked way.

Desperate to escape the kitchen, I mentioned that we might take a ride down the road. Mager readily agreed to what he recognized as a euphemistic suggestion of a bottle out in the car. He got in the back seat with the guitar, and I sat in front. We passed the bottle back and forth a few times, and he sang another song. There wasn't any point in driving anywhere, so we just sat there.

Bit by bit I got him talking about his family. He named most of his brothers and sisters and even some of their children. But it was a big family, thirteen children altogether, and he was next to the youngest, so he couldn't cover them all. Some had died or moved away before he was old enough to remember.

Nonetheless, he largely destroyed the notion that Robert Johnson and Tommy Johnson had been closely related. The brothers in his family who played guitar were LeDell, George, Clarence, Tommy, and Mager himself. There was no Robert Johnson—at least none who was a guitar player—in the family.

Cautiously, trying not to put words in his mouth, I asked whether there had been anyone—a cousin, nephew, or anyone else in the family—who played guitar and was five to seven years younger than Mager himself. He shook his head and couldn't think of anyone who fit that description.

He talked about his mother's family—the Wilson boys—and the big string band they'd had, which had "given all of us the idea of music." He recalled how he and his brothers had played around Utica, Dentville, Georgetown, and Hazlehurst.

"Martinsville?" I asked.

"Yeah, we went there too. And down to Wesson. And sometimes Vicksburg. All over." He frowned trying to get the guitar into tune. "And we went up into the Delta."

Slowly his story came together. Mager and his brothers had been born on a plantation a few miles north, and by 1919 all of them had married and were living on the Lem Barren Farm. A man named Troy Slay was in charge of the property, and he also doubled working as the Crystal Springs constable. Mager lived there from 1919 to 1929, when another man bought the property. For a time Tommy and his wife and Mager and his wife lived in two houses side by side on the Barren Farm. Tommy traveled more frequently than the others, but when he was at home, the brothers would play at various venues in the area—on the streets in Crystal Springs, for Friday and Saturday dances, and on other occasions.

"We played for white folks as much as we could, 'cause we got more money from them, 'cause quite naturally they had more money," Mager said, nodding over the truth of that. "So when we'd get into a rainy spell and couldn't do no work, everybody would want to party. We might go to work ten different places—four or five white places, house parties and such, and the same number of colored, but we'd earn twice as much money from the white. So we did as much of that as we could. Tommy was a great favorite with the white people all around here and up in the Delta too."

Tommy Johnson and his brothers were known as a family string band that played the usual numbers like "Hesitating Blues" and "Sitting on Top of the World." As Tommy developed his individual style, they increasingly featured him as the lead performer, while the others backed him up. They stayed together for many years and frequently spent Saturday afternoons playing on the corner outside the Crystal Springs City Drug Store. By the late 1940s LeDell had moved to Jackson and George long before that to Birmingham, but Clarence and Tommy were usually in the vicinity, and Mager himself stuck particularly close to home.

When I asked him where the Barren Farm had been located, he leaned forward and pointed due south. "Just across the fields straight through there, about a half a mile. That's where we all stayed for so long." He waved at the two white houses on each side of the car. "Now I own this place here, so I didn't get too far away."

Tommy Johnson had died in 1956, he told me. "He was at my niece's house, hitting on his guitar, and he just keeled over. She called to him, but he was gone."

"And Clarence got killed," he added. "He was the one who played jazz horn." I wasn't sure what he meant, but I assumed it was something like a kazoo or one of the toylike instruments that were often featured in such groups.

"It was about twenty-five years ago it happened. He walked up to the porch of this store, and he sensed that someone was there, and he called out, 'Who is that?' And a voice come back, 'Me—Goddamn it!'" Mager pantomimed the action of someone putting a shotgun to his shoulder. "*Boom*! Killed over a

Mager Johnson plays the guitar, Crystal Springs, Mississippi.
Photograph by Robert "Mack" McCormick.

girl. The guy that done it was the father of the boy who was screwing the same girl as Clarence was. They had some words about it, and the boy's father come and killed Clarence. He went to Parchman [State Penitentiary] for it."

Mager eased himself back in the car seat and sang another of his brother's songs, his voice now more forceful and under better control. The whiskey had loosened him up. He tried for a lot of Tommy's effects: the falsetto and the carefully wrought mood. Occasionally he couldn't manage it, but by and large he recaptured that distinctive sound, and the words came in that tumbling cadence.

Lord I ain't goin'
down that
big road
by myself—
Now don'cha hear me talkin', pretty mama?

The following day I drove the thirty miles into Jackson, worked around the state capitol building, and found my way to LeDell Johnson's house on the west side of town. He was the oldest brother still living, and Mager had suggested I go see him if I wanted more family background.

The previous evening, Mager had told me that Tommy Johnson had a son, whom he called an "outside child." He didn't know the boy's name or anything about him other that the fact that he had been born somewhere up in the Delta. I mentally toyed with the possibility that Tommy's child might be Robert Johnson himself. They were about sixteen years apart in age, so it was possible, but it didn't fit the other pieces of information that were coming together. Moreover, Mager was pretty certain that the son had been born in the 1920s during one of Tommy's longer stays in the Delta, so he could have been younger than Robert.

All during the evening I'd been studying Mager Johnson, trying to spot specific points of family resemblance. The only known photograph of Tommy Johnson was one taken when he was a young man, showing a smiling, undistinguished face, and it was hard to see any but the most general traits that he may have shared with the sixty-five-year-old Mager.

With this in mind I'd gotten out an envelope full of old photographs that I carried with me. It was an odd accumulation of pictures of old blues singers, along with a few preachers and an insurance agent. I used it in much the same way that police use their lineups, to see whether people can identify the persons they say they've known or seen.

In this case, however, I just wanted to see what Mager would say as he flipped through the pictures. He glanced briefly at most of them until he got to an old Victor Records publicity picture of Tommy Johnson, which he nodded over before picking it out and saying, "That's him." A minute later he pulled out another photo and said, "That's him too."

The second picture he had handed me was of Lonnie Johnson, taken about 1937. I studied it, comparing it with Mager and the picture of Tommy. After a while I saw, or imagined I saw, a family resemblance. There seemed to be something in shape of the face and the set of the eyes. I could see why he'd mistaken it for his brother.

I'd come to this part of Mississippi trying to learn more about Robert Johnson and wondering whether he had a family tie to Tommy Johnson. Instead, people kept tossing Lonnie Johnson at me. At first I'd dismissed it, but it kept coming up so often that it was hard to ignore.

What Mager had to say was quite specific. "We're related to Lonnie Johnson somehow or other," he told me. "In fact, first time that Tommy went off

LeDell Johnson in his home, Jackson, Mississippi.
Photograph by Robert "Mack" McCormick.

to make records, Lonnie Johnson came and helped him make the contact and helped him out on the records too." A bit later he mentioned the other Lonnie Johnson, a local boy who played guitar and went by that name. "But I ain't seen him or heard of him for years now."

I sought out LeDell Johnson in the hope that he might help clarify the confusion. He didn't. On the other hand, he didn't increase it either. He simply confirmed and elaborated on what his brother Mager had said. They were related to Lonnie Johnson on their father's side, but there was no one in the family named Noah nor any guitar player named Robert, nor could he remember anything of a Major family in the Hazlehurst area.

Being much older than Mager, he could speak with authority about the family's background, and he spent a good part of the morning sorting his memories for me. His father, Idell, had had a twin brother named Mance. There was an Uncle Jim and an Uncle Robert. He knew some but not all of their children.

After considering the ages and birth dates of those concerned, it seemed possible that one of Tommy Johnson's first cousins was Lonnie Johnson. There is nothing to support this except the general family understanding that they were somehow related, and LeDell couldn't recall any member of his family having moved to New Orleans and raising a family there. By the same token, it was possible that one of Tommy Johnson's cousins had fathered Robert Johnson, but there was nothing but geographic proximity to suggest it.

Throughout the time I'd spent in Copiah County, it was repeatedly made clear that Robert Johnson had been born in a rich, musically active community. I'd heard vivid accounts of the frolics and the kind of excitement that prevailed. Every conversation seemed to bring forth the names of more musicians, some new to me, some already familiar. In all, I'd now heard about thirty-four musicians resident in different parts of Copiah County among the three generations concerned. Nonetheless, I had not found a clear link between any one of these men and Robert Johnson.

I could only assume that he had heard some of them, had been influenced by some of them, but specific roles—either in terms of family kinship or musical contact—couldn't be assigned.

When I drove back from Jackson, Mississippi, after seeing LeDell Johnson, I began a final sweep around Copiah County, revisiting places where I'd missed people before or had some loose end I hoped to follow up. Of all the musicians who had been described, the one most frequently mentioned, particularly in the Hazlehurst area, was one Willie Hudson. He wasn't necessarily the best of the group, only the best-remembered. He might have been an extravagant personality or simply a more active performer than the others. But when I finally found Willie Hudson, he was a complete disappointment. He was long retired from both work and music, unwilling to discuss either, and inarticulate on most subjects. Whatever he had been, he was no longer. A dead end.

Yet another of the old musicians I located also refused to help me. He said he was preparing his soul for its Maker and begging forgiveness for all the evil he had done by playing guitar and making sinful music. His deep, heavy voice trembled as he dismissed blues as the devil's music, played by people who were doing the devil's work. "I know that youngster you're asking about," he said. "But it ain't my Christian duty to talk about such as him. I thank Jesus I saved myself." I gritted my teeth and went away.

I drove back to Early Johnson's pool hall and talked to him about an idea I'd been considering. He agreed, so I brought in my tape machine and a reel containing copies of old blues recordings that might help stir up memories. There was a fairly wide assortment of the early "race records," but sequenced especially for this trip so that every third or fourth selection was by Robert Johnson. The others were by his contemporaries and predecessors.

I played this ninety-minute tape for the customers of the pool hall one evening, Some of the recordings were familiar, and some were not. The younger people listened briefly and then went away. The older customers gathered around, listening nostalgically and sometimes with surprise to music that had been blurred by memory. In the course of it nothing was said about Robert Johnson. I said nothing to call particular attention to Robert Johnson's records.

People drifted around the room, half-listening, half-watching the pool games. Generally they'd listen to the beginning of a new number to hear whether it was anything they particularly remembered. A lot of things were said as the tape played. People said they used to own a particular record or had once run across the musician who'd made it. Extravagant and ridiculous things were said, mixed in with other comments that seemed straightforward and factual. When a Charley Patton song was played, one man said he'd run across him once in Sunflower County during a cotton pick, and when a Bessie Smith recording came up, another man remarked about how she'd died on Highway 61 up above Clarksdale.

There were not a great many comments on the Robert Johnson records, but four people identified them as by a musician who'd lived around Hazlehurst for a while. The fourth identification was the most interesting. It came from a man who'd left Copiah County in 1930 for Flint, Michigan. He was only back for a family funeral. He'd never heard the records, but he said he'd heard two of the songs being played by a guy he used to know in Hazlehurst. He described him as a young man with one eye that drooped a little bit. He had played guitar with the neck of a beer bottle stuck over one finger, producing the slide effect that was popular at the time. He said that the fellow he had in mind tended to hunch over the guitar, slipping his bottleneck back and forth, and getting his mouth close to the sound box so that his voice and the instrument would "sound" together.

"He didn't hold the guitar like most guys," the man said. "He'd heist it up across his chest, laying it so it was cocked out at an angle, and stoop his neck over it. That way, his singing and whatever the guitar was saying, would come at you from the same place."

He said one of the songs he heard sounded "pretty near the same" as what he'd heard years ago, before he'd moved north. It was a small but significant point. It suggested that Robert Johnson's style had begun to take shape when he was young, living here in Copiah County.

I asked him if he'd known the singer. He shook his head. "I don't know anyone that made any records," he said. "The guy I knew lived right here. He was named Bob Johnson."

"How well did you know him?" I asked. "Pretty good. He had a gal I wanted," he laughed. "Funny thing. I remember his name, but I don't remember her name."

I glanced at Early Johnson, but he acted as if he wasn't paying any attention. I ran the tape back and found "Terraplane Blues" again. When I'd played it for Virgie, she'd said, "He sounded just like that. That's sure him."

Now the man from Flint was saying essentially the same thing. It's illuminating to listen to this particular recording—accepting for the moment at face value the statements that it reflects the way Robert Johnson played as a youth. The characteristics of his style are there: the keening voice, the intensity, the melding of voice and guitar with all the interplay and the accents moving back and forth. Still, it sounds a bit rudimentary and less refined than his other performances.

The implication is that Robert Johnson worked by developing a song and its particular performance to a certain point, and then afterward played it in much the same way. Thus, "Terraplane Blues" may represent him at an early point, somewhere past merely copying and assimilating other artists, when his own style was beginning to emerge but still was short of the flowering achieved in many of his later songs.

This interpretation is conjectural. The essential facts for me in that moment were that those in the pool hall who recognized the songs associated them with a local musician who had lived in the Hazlehurst area around 1930, perhaps coming back for visits in later years. The recordings of "Terraplane Blues" and "Come On in My Kitchen" seemed to closely resemble what the man from Flint had heard Robert Johnson sing in 1930. But he'd never heard "Hellhound on My Trail." Even so, no real conclusion could be drawn from this. Johnson might well have avoided playing his most personal, expressive songs in party situations. He was not simply a demon poet; he was also a working entertainer.

A bit later the tape played one of Tommy Johnson's recordings, and I studied it anew, trying to hear some trait or similarity that might musically link the two Johnsons. They were far, far apart: one harsh and intense, the other cool and beautiful. They established entirely different moods. They seemed as far apart as two musicians could possibly get within the same immediate tradition.

Robert Johnson was innovative, seemingly the creator of much of what he sang. Tommy Johnson drew mostly from familiar, standard verses and gave them freshly magnificent performances. Yet they did share one characteristic: each song was carefully hewed, with a specific guitar part worked out for it, and it was developed as a separate, discrete work. In this aspect they both stood far apart from most of the era's bluesmen, whose performances contained a less conscious artistry, resting more on impulse and improvisation.

The next time a Robert Johnson record came up on the tape I asked a few more questions of the man from Flint. I suspected that he was going to try to send me back to the Delta when I asked where Robert Johnson might have gone from Copiah County. The answer was, "I left before he did, so I don't know where he went from here, but I know he said he had people up in Tunica County, up close to Memphis." I knew what that meant, and I rankled at the thought of leaving the pine hills again and journeying into the Delta.

The man told me several stories of his times with young Robert Johnson. It was mostly about what he'd done, not so much what Johnson had done, but I listened carefully to hear what he might dredge up from forty years ago. He said they'd been the same age, very close, and that he himself had been born in 1911: "Bob wasn't more'n a few months different." He didn't know anything of his background or where he'd come from. " 'Bout all we did was some drinking together," he said.

Rather diffidently, he asked me to play the "song about the Chevrolet" again. I looked puzzled. "You know, that one all about 'I'm going to get deep down in this connection, keep on tangling with your wires.'" I ran the tape back again. "I thought it said something in there about a Terraplane?"

"It might have," he said. "You know how a guy'll change stuff like that around. The way I remember, it was about a Chevrolet." Unlike most of mysteries that Copiah County had generated and left unsolved, this minor one seemed settled. Apparently "Terraplane Blues" got its start as "Chevrolet Blues." That would explain how Johnson could be singing it several years before the Terraplane went into production.

After I'd exhausted everyone's patience, I piled my equipment back in the truck and thanked Early Johnson again for all his courtesy and help. He shook his head ruefully, sorry that no one had turned up who seemed to be related to Robert Johnson's family. "But you know," he said, "I got relatives I don't know anything about. I expect everybody's got some. There's no telling where he could fit in. Maybe even somewhere back in my family, and I don't know it."

The next morning before leaving, I took care of one more detail in Copiah County. I thought I might have given too little attention to the Antioch area. I'd visited there toward the end of a long day, and I'd been impatient to get to a meal and shower. The rural neighborhood around the Antioch Church is where Julia Majors's family is said to have lived, and it needed a second look.

Hazlehurst had grown out, so that the Antioch neighborhood was just on the southeast fringe of town. The Illinois Central Railroad is doubled-tracked, and on each side of the right of way was a dirt road. Here and there a road crossed the tracks, making an H pattern, and the church was near one of these crossings. The houses seemed occupied primarily by people who'd lived there only a few years and had no knowledge of people who had lived in the area earlier.

The Antioch Cemetery was a mile away, but a walk through it proved futile. Many stones had fallen over or been broken up. The only grave markers still legible were those the federal government had furnished for veterans of World War I.

Finally, after an hour or more of my poking around, a man living near the church said he vaguely remembered a family by the name of Majors. He said there'd been a bunch of girls, and they'd all married and had many children. Then they started moving away. Some went north, probably to the big cities, and some went up into the Delta. Compared to the Hazlehurst area, there was money to be made in the Delta on the big plantations back in those days. "I expect those people all went off up the country. Up to the Delta, most likely," he said, with his arm pointing up the railway tracks. "They went up the country. That's about all I can tell you."

I thanked him and walked back to my car. I drove over to the highway and obstinately turned south, heading for Gulfport and its broad, shallow-surf beaches. The country was lovely. The rolling hills were covered with green, and the forests smelled of pine needles. I was looking forward to the drive. About ten miles down the road, however, I started having second thoughts. The drive would be nice, and there were abundant restaurants and motels along Gulfport's thirty-mile strip of beaches. But the answers I wanted seemed to lie in the other direction. I knew that I needed to go back to the Delta and try again. I pulled off to the side of the road and grumbled for a while. Then I swung around and started driving the other way.

• • •

7

MISSISSIPPI 304

Robinsonville, Mississippi, had always been an unprofitable place to stop. It had the look and feel of a ghost town: empty and largely deserted, with no one remaining who seemed to remember or care. The railroad depot was abandoned, and across from it sat a line of unpainted shacks with broken screen doors flapping in the breeze.

The first time I'd stopped here, I'd held high hopes. Robinsonville had been consistently mentioned as the place where Robert Johnson's family had lived. So years before, I'd driven straight here, calmly expecting to learn something. Instead I'd been met with a mostly empty cluster of buildings. The handful of people I'd encountered were cranky and uncommunicative and looked blank when questions were put to them.

The last time I'd been here was only a couple of weeks before. At that time I'd driven around enough to find about twenty people to talk to. Half of them were too young to have been able to help, and the others didn't seem to know what I was talking about.

Other researchers had been here too, a number of times. In fact, it was here that a group of three record collectors from New York City found the clue that eventually led them to find Eddie "Son" House, one of the great Delta blues artists, whom they found alive and well in Rochester, New York. Son House had offered a number of succinct recollections of the young Robert Johnson, and he consistently associated him with the depot-and-crossing town of Robinsonville.

Moreover, before Son House had been located and interviewed, Robinsonville had been mentioned as Robert Johnson's "home." Most of these comments apparently stemmed from the fact that this was where the agent from the Brunswick Record Company had his contacts with Robert Johnson. He'd recorded an address where he could get in touch with him through his family, apparently somewhere in the Robinsonville area.

In spite of all these promising factors, my visits to the little village had never offered much. On the contrary, it was in Robinsonville that the entire search seemed at its most pointless, and I felt a dull resentment at the appalling bleakness of the surrounding landscape.

Still, the most recent testimony in Hazlehurst had continued to point in the same direction. Near Tunica. In Tunica County. Close to Memphis. That basically spelled out Robinsonville. So I'd come back. The first thing that happened was that someone sent me on a wild goose chase to Hernando, Mississippi. I spent an hour in Robinsonville trying to find people to talk to, and then an elderly man peered at me for a moment and said "Him? That guy that played guitar?" I nodded. "You'll find out about him over at Hernando." He wouldn't explain how or why he knew but simply insisted that I'd have to go to Hernando to find out.

Hernando is about twenty miles due east of Robinsonville, a slow drive over a narrow road through places like Banks and Eudora—both of them mentioned at different times in connection with Johnson, but offering little when I stopped to ask around. The road then abruptly climbs out of the flat, wet Delta land into the Mississippi hill country. A town of 2,500 people, Hernando was the county seat of DeSoto County. It lies along both US Highway 51 and the Illinois Central line between New Orleans and Memphis, the same highway and railroad that skirt the edge of the Delta and then pass through Hazlehurst.

I parked in a lot that stood along the railroad, facing the town's businesses, and walked over to a group of men standing on a corner. I greeted them casually, said a few words about the weather, and explained that I was trying to learn something about a blues musician named Johnson who used to live here. I had no idea of whether he had lived here or not, but putting it that way gave the question more emphasis. They said they didn't know the man, but they agreed that many musicians used to pass through the town, especially because of the railroad.

There was another group of men on the next corner. This time I put it a little differently: I didn't say he'd lived in Hernando but that he'd been around a lot. Then I asked several men who were waiting in the barbershop. They were probably loafing because the two barbers were sitting in their own chairs talking with other customers. The replies were uniformly negative.

The answers seemed genuine, but it's never easy to know whether people think it's worthwhile to give you a frank answer. They simply may not want to bother. The safe thing to do is say no. The handicap can't be overcome, but it can be tilted back a little by a few details of technique. It's good to emphasize the person sought is or was a musician and to underscore that the real object of concern is the music itself. It helps to let people see you get out of a car with an out-of-state license plate. It's a help to dress and talk differently than they do locally. People are more liable to help a stranger who's traveled a long distance for whatever curious reason.

It helps tremendously if you have an English accent, or better yet, only a modest command of English heavily accented with French or German. That's why visiting Europeans have had such success when they've come into the South looking for the ones that made certain records. People will go to great lengths to help someone from London who's done such an incredible thing as come to Friars Point or Hernando to ask questions about musicians.

Still, an outsider asking about local people is always suspect. Too often, trouble comes in that form. People are skittish where trouble has been such a familiar thing. Again, it helps to avoid looking like trouble. You can study, for example, the manner in which a deputy sheriff goes about hunting for a man. He'll take a single Black man aside, question him closely, joshing with him and then pressuring him with little trick questioning and an implicit threat in the way he stares him down. A lawman looking for someone would never walk up to a bunch of men on a street corner to ask his questions. Therefore, that's just the thing to do. And when you first approach people, be casual and let them look down on you at least a fraction. If they're sitting, hunker down alongside. If they're standing, put a foot on a fire hydrant and hunch over a bit. Don't stand over people if you want to come away with well-answered questions. An outsider who avoids looking like a cop or acting like any of the familiar kinds of harassment stands a pretty good chance if he strolls up to groups of people and blandly asks about music and musicians. With luck and a few questions that manage to arouse their interest, it can happen that they'll start talking back and forth, recalling this musician or that one, a man wondering aloud whatever became a certain one, and someone else chiming in with the answer. When this sort of thing has developed, it's easy enough to throw in, "Was there one named Johnson?"

Still, for all the technique and exercise, I'd talked to three separate groups of people here in Hernando and come up with nothing at all. I knew it was a wild goose chase. If I was going to waste my time like this, I could have done it in Gulfport just as well as here. I decided to make the next effort a passive one. About two dozen men in Hernando had heard the name and the question I was asking. If any of them did know anything of Robert Johnson, they'd be discussing it among themselves, or at least thinking it over.

I strolled back to my car. It was sitting in a municipal parking lot almost a block away, but within sight of the barber shop and the two street corner groups I'd just encountered. I pulled the door open and sat down sideways, letting the door hang open and with my legs sprawled out along the side of the car. I was resting, looking discouraged, wondering what to do next. They were talking about me in each of those three groups, speculating about what I was doing here, trying to decide whether I'd given them the real reason I was asking questions. None of them were looking directly at me, but they knew I was there. Now that I was out of earshot, they were probably telling each other what they knew about Robert Johnson.

These street corner clusters of men are fluid. Some of the men are all-day bystanders and town-watchers, but mostly it's men who came into town on an errand or someone who drove his wife down to do shopping and he's just waiting. From time to time someone breaks off to go help his wife with a sack of groceries or drifts over to another group. They climb back into pickup trucks and drive off down dusty roads, and other men come out of stores to join the others on the corner. There was a good chance that so long as I was sitting in plain sight that they'd continue to wonder about me and mention the question I'd asked to newcomers. In a surprisingly short time, the question would have passed around town pretty thoroughly.

After twenty more minutes of my resting and looking discouraged, a dull red, rattling pickup truck started up at the far corner of the parking lot and swung around toward me, sliding into the slot alongside my car. The driver leaned out the window and said, "Hope you find that guy."

"It doesn't look like I will," I replied.

"What are they after him for? What'd he do?"

"Nothing like that. The law isn't after him. People are interested because of the music he played."

The man looked at me and then nodded. "Made some records, didn't he? That the Robert Johnson you asking about? The one that made 'Terraplane Blues'?"

"That's the one."

"I guess I knew him." He sat there with his engine running, his foot on the clutch, ready to disappear if the matter proved to be trouble after all. "He used to come through here pretty often. He came here to catch the train. That's about all I know, except he was a good musician."

"Do you happen to know where he lived?" I asked.

The man shook his head. "I heard him play over at the joint there, and I used to give him money, but I don't think I ever really talked with him." He dropped a foot on the accelerator, shifted a noisy gear, and eased the clutch in. The truck moved away slowly. It was only about fifteen feet away when it braked and then backed up. I hadn't moved. This time the driver left the engine running but climbed out of the cab and stood alongside of me. "There's just the one thing I can tell you. There was this one time I saw him come into town." He raised an arm and pointed. "He got out of a car right there. It was a Ford Model T. He was catching a train 'cause of the time of evening it was, and there was people around the stationhouse waiting."

I asked which train.

"The southbound, out of Memphis, going on down. I figure he caught that train. He could have been in New Orleans that night."

Or Hazlehurst. Or a couple dozen other towns. That wasn't the issue. What I needed to know was not where he was going, but rather, assuming his family lived somewhere around here, where'd he come from? I asked the man whether he knew which way the car had come from.

"Came from back over that way," he said, pointing west toward Eudora, Banks, and Robinsonville. The road I'd just come over. "Back at that time, there wasn't hardly a paved road anywhere in Mississippi. Highway 51 here was gravel-top, and that road going back over that way"—he pointed west again—"was just a dirt track. I remember that Model T was all covered in mud. Let him out right at the corner there."

He stared at the corner as if trying to remember something more, then shrugged and climbed back into his truck. I thanked him; he nodded and drove off. When he was out of sight, I realized I should have asked him whether he'd known the person driving the car. Maybe that was why he knew which direction it had come from.

So I finally had another scrap to work with: Robert Johnson had come to Hernando to catch a southbound IC train. He'd come from somewhere to the west, along the road from Robinsonville. People kept sending me back there.

The train depot at Robinsonville, Mississippi.
Photograph by Robert "Mack" McCormick.

The twenty miles of road going back seemed a lot longer. I stopped at various clusters of houses along the road and at a small general store. My questions got the same negative answers, from different people. I drove into the forlorn little town for the second time that day. I pulled up alongside the same abandoned depot, a two-story shedlike building. Some of its windows were broken, and the big, wide loading platform was empty. In its day it had held tons of cotton, but now it looked like an empty stage. I climbed up and walked around on the platform with its thick, polished boards. I felt like an actor trying to get the feel of a deserted theater.

A thought suddenly struck me, and I jumped down and ran off to find the post office. It had hit me that Johnson's mail had probably come through Robinsonville. Maybe an old postal employee might remember the name and what rural route it had gone to. I tried the post office but drew another blank. They told me that there was no possibility of remembering all the people who used to live here.

I went back to the depot and climbed back up on the platform, looking across the fields that stretched in every direction. Unbroken miles of them lay before me, with the faint rim of the levee off to the west. The land was wet with recent rain, waiting for the spring seeding. The earth still produced the same cotton, but the work was now done by machinery, and the people who operated the machines were the only ones still around. And most of them lived in larger towns such as Tunica or even Memphis.

Given distance and detachment, a scholar might innocently ask questions about the roots of the blues tradition and the circumstance of its birth. But here on the old broken loading platform at Robinsonville, such questions didn't arise. It seemed obvious that people set down in this desolate place would react. Gases rush in to fill a vacuum; people will rush to decorate social and environmental drabness.

Bright, defiant music comes out of revolutions: "Yankee Doodle," "La Marseillaise," and "La Cucaracha." Times of prolonged stress may produce a revolution and sometimes a new music: the bracing shouts of the Holiness churches and the hard, abrupt sounds of a brass band turning to jazz.

Here, in this purposeful, weary land dedicated to cotton, something like the blues seems to have been inevitable. Take a few thousand families, break them up, scatter them around the country, toss in lynchings and assorted pressures, then set the remnants to sharecropping in the Jim Crow South. Come back in twenty years, and it's likely that the people will have reacted—and perhaps not with armed rebellion as might seem appropriate, but rather by some social behavior. They might evolve a new religious movement, build a monument, develop new music, or create a sculpture in the levees. The value, richness, and nature of the reactions would depend largely on families' various cultural heritage and traditions.

Even in 1970, as I stood grumbling on the empty depot platform, the state of Mississippi still tended to rank at the extreme end of American statistics. It had the lowest per capita income and the highest incidence of poverty. The largest percentage of an African American population. The most frightened whites—people who become literally pop-eyed with fear, knowing that the Black majority is going to start running things around here.

The thing that was hardest for an outsider like me to believe was when a Black Mississippian who'd been through the whole wringer would tell me, "I like it here. This is my home." I'd even heard it from young people. An African American activist once told me, "I don't want to run Newark or Cleveland or some other sewer that whites have used up and dirtied and then left. No, baby, I'd rather run Mississippi." He told me his state was "pretty," and I wondered

Jack Hudson's Rolling Store. Photograph by Robert "Mack" McCormick.

whether he'd meant to include the Delta. It didn't make any difference. It was his home, and many people tend to fall in love with the place where they grow up.

I knew I needed the kind of informant I'd never been able to find in Robinsonville, someone for whom this was home. Suddenly I glimpsed a flash of yellow in the distance and eventually realized that it was a school bus. On impulse I decided to go talk to the driver and see if he or she could help. I hopped off the depot platform and ran over to my car, quickly swinging it around and barreling down a dirt road.

I caught up with it about two miles away. It looked like a school bus, and it chugged like a school bus, but it was something else. There were black letters painted on a sign reading "Jack Hudson's Rolling Store." I followed it for a few miles, watching as it pulled up in front of a group of houses, where people would come out to buy various groceries and cosmetics. Wherever it stopped, there was a small line of people waiting to get on and a trickle of people coming out with canned goods, loaves of bread, and school supplies. It was revealing to see how many people really lived in this empty-looking region. Every quarter or half mile, the bus would stop at some broken-down houses at the edge of a field, and some people would emerge. I began to realize what an opportunity I had been missing.

At the bus's next stop I parked the car and went up to talk with Jack Hudson. He turned out to be a vigorous young man, with his sleeves rolled up above his elbows. It took a few minutes for me to explain what I had in mind, but we soon struck a bargain: he'd take me along with him and help me talk with his customers if I'd promise to mention his business in whatever I wrote about Robert Johnson. I cautioned him that the publicity probably wouldn't do anything to help his business. He nodded, but said, "Still, it can't hurt, can it?" He grinned and cleared a place for me to sit.

Jack talked about needing a bigger bus, one where people could come in the front door and go out by a rear door, like on big-city buses. He'd bought this bus at a county auction, overhauled it, and turned it into a store himself, ripping out most of the seats and installing four rows of shelves on each side of the center aisle. Toward the back was a small cash register and a vegetable scale hanging from the ceiling. Waving at the surrounding fields, he told me that there used to be several small stores around, but that they'd closed down as more people had moved away. But there were still people living miles from town who needed occasional groceries, so he'd built the rolling store to serve them.

Between stops he drove the bus gingerly, turning corners slowly so that the mayonnaise and ketchup jars wouldn't hop over the lip he'd built on the front edge of the shelves. As he drove, he talked about this part of Tunica County. "All this land," he said, "is still owned by the same people that used to have it, it's just that most of the working folks have gone off. But the land and the gins and cotton compresses and all like that, it's still the same as it was. Every mile or so, you go from one plantation to the next." He waved a hand out the window, "Like that's the Irwin Company Farm over there on the left, and on the right, that's the Kirby Plantation."

"Joe Kirby?" I wondered.

"Yeah, right." Jack gave me a puzzled look. "How'd you know that?"

There'd been a record, a long time ago, called "Joe Kirby Blues," I told him.

"A record by this fellow you looking for?"

"No," I answered. "That particular record was by another musician, a man named Charley Patton."

Jack shrugged. "I guess there must have been musicians all over here, back in those days," he said. After a couple of more stops, he pointed ahead, saying, "Now I'm going to get over onto the Darrow and Cox place. That place runs from here all the way over to the river."

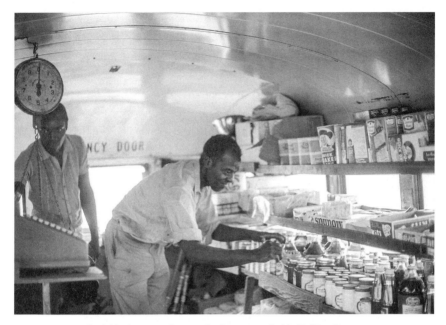

Jack Hudson tending to the inventory in his Rolling Store.
Photograph by Robert "Mack" McCormick.

My questioning went smoothly with Jack Hudson's help. He introduced me to his many regular customers, saying things like, "Maybe you can help this man. He's looking for some kind of word about a guitar player used to come from around here." At each stop, three to ten people would board the bus and do a little shopping. The tempo was efficient but not particularly hurried. There was always a little small talk and time to ask a few questions.

When I'd begun to ride along with Jack, the levee and its trees had been a hazy blur in the distance, but after an hour or so it came into sharp focus. We were within a half-mile of the levee when a man huffed his way up the steps, listened to the introduction, looked at me expectantly, and waited for me to tell him the name of the musician I was interested in. I asked whether he knew anything about a man named Robert Johnson.

He glanced at me quickly and said, "You mean Robert Spencer." It wasn't a question but a declaration, and I got a little tingle out of the way he said it. He had the air of a man who was sure of what he said.

But that was all he would say. He just shook his head at my other questions, insisting, "You should go talk to people that knew him better than I did."

When I asked where I could find them, he shook his head again. It was a little maddening. But as he turned to leave, he said something to Jack. They had a brief, quiet conversation, and then the man left. Jack Hudson turned and smiled. "He says," pointing to the man, who was climbing the sagging porch of a dingy old house, "that there's lots of people just down the road that know that fellow. We'll be there in three more stops."

"That's the Polk Plantation next, and then we'll be coming up on the place you want," Jack said. He seemed to have complete confidence in the man's knowledge.

For some reason, I shared that confidence. I wasn't at all surprised when, three stops further along, an old woman got on the rolling store, listened to me ask about Johnson, and then calmly replied, "Oh, you mean Robert Spencer, I expect."

All of a sudden I was surrounded by people—customers who'd emerged from a row of battered old houses—who all knew Robert Johnson, and they all told me that his name was really Robert Spencer. These were the neighbors I'd been seeking all over Mississippi. And here they were, right where they were supposed to be: within a few miles of places I'd investigated on three other trips into this northwestern section of Tunica County.

Everyone who came out to the rolling store said the same things. When asked about Robert Johnson, they talked about Robert Spencer, who'd played guitar and had an older brother named Leroy Spencer, who played both guitar and piano. The boys had been raised on the Polk Plantation, people said, and their mother was named Julia. Robert had died same years back, and Leroy had died about eight or nine years ago. After talking to some of the people in detail, I learned that most of them hadn't personally known Robert Johnson or Spencer, but knew of him by reputation and through his family. They had known his mother or his brother.

There was an element of raw comedy about the scene. After all this time, all my traveling and small talk and all the suspicious looks, here I was with a crowd of excited people all trying to talk at once, naming different people I ought to see. They tossed out names quicker than I could write them down. Several people started giving me long, complicated directions to various houses. Sometimes it was hard for me to tell whether the directions were to a place nearby or fifty miles away.

Gradually some of the hubbub died down, and I got a chance to sort out what Jack's customers were saying. Apparently there were four or five people who

Building on the Abbay & Leatherman Plantation, Commerce, Mississippi.
Photograph by Robert "Mack" McCormick.

could tell me about Robert Spencer in some detail. They all lived in the immediate vicinity, and three of them lived in the same row of houses, within a quarter of a mile from where the bus had stopped. Some of the people were off at work, so I'd have to see them later in the day, but everyone agreed that I could probably find Cleveland and Lula Smith at home. They pointed out their house.

I thanked Jack Hudson and climbed down from his rolling store. I negotiated with one of the customers for some impromptu taxi service, and he drove me back to where I'd left my car.

This place, where everyone seemed to know or know of Robert Spencer, was exactly two miles due west of Robinsonville, straight down State Road 304. About a mile and a half farther down the same road is the community of Commerce. The cotton gin, store, and post office of the largest property in the area, the Abbay & Leatherman Plantation, were located there. The property was snugged into a corner where the Mississippi River and its levee makes a sharp bend. The people I'd been talking with all lived at the eastern end of the "Leatherman place," where a wing of the property stretched along the road, facing the southern edge of the Polk Plantation. Because of the bend it makes, the river lies both to the north and to the west. It's almost two miles to the water itself, but the breeze carries the odor of the mud flats and the industrial sludge from the far side of the levee.

I found my car and drove back to the place within fifteen minutes, parking in front of the house that had been pointed out to me. It was a larger house than a lot of those scattered along this part of the road. Still, it was a classic example of the region's vernacular architecture. The siding was brown and yellow asphalt, imprinted to resemble bricks. The various rooms tended to slope in different directions: the wide front porch sloped forward, while the large living room sloped the other way. The whole house was set high on tapered concrete blocks. The roof was corrugated metal. It was strictly sharecropper's modern, probably circa 1948, but there were touches that indicated a conscientious homeowner. None of the screens were torn, and there was fresh white trim around the windows.

The front door was open, and through the screen door I could see a neat, well-kept home. A big, clumsy-looking brown dog came over, gave me a wary sniff, and then shuffled out of the way as Mrs. Smith came to the door. She smiled, beckoned me inside, and hurried away to fetch a glass of ice water, all without knowing what had brought me to her door. After I'd gratefully swallowed some water, she listened to my questions about Robert Johnson and promptly said, "Oh, you must mean Son Spencer." In the South, the use of "Son" as a forename designates stepchildren or children raised by grandparents. It's usually used in conjunction with the surname of the stepfather, grandparents, or whoever raised the child. Mrs. Smith smiled and said, "Sure, we knew him and his whole family."

She didn't want to say anything more until her husband returned. He'd gone down the road to borrow some tools and was due back any minute. After about five minutes, a heavy, kindly looking man came in through the back door, moved around in the kitchen for a moment, and then came into the living room. He repeated the now-familiar response: "You mean Robert Spencer." He nodded and sat down. "I can tell you about him."

Cleveland and Lula Smith talked for over a half-hour about Robert Spencer, also known as Son Spencer. They wrangled with one another over details, but their overall story was fairly consistent, and within a little while they'd added quite considerably to the information I'd gathered regarding Robert Johnson and his origins.

The Smiths had first moved into one of the sharecropper houses of the Abbay & Leatherman Plantation in 1936. At that time—to illustrate the point, Cleveland Smith led me over to the screen door to point to the place described—there was another line of houses along a road running northward. "That over there," he said, "that's the Polk place." It was much smaller than the Leatherman place, running to a thousand acres or so, with only about twenty families working on it. One of those families was that of Willie Willis, more commonly known as Dusty Willis, whose wife, Julia, and her children—apparently from an earlier marriage—were known by the surname of Spencer.

The Smiths knew the Willis/Spencer family as neighbors, but not so intimately as to understand their complete family history. The youngest of Julia's children was Robert Spencer, and there was an older brother named Leroy Spencer, and a girl, older than both boys, named Carrie. The Smiths couldn't agree as to whether or not there was another girl. In the 1930s, the Smiths recalled, none of the siblings were children; they were grown with families of their own except for Robert, who was unmarried. They guessed that he was in his twenties at the time.

I was puzzled that everyone so readily assumed that this Robert Spencer was Robert Johnson. The Smiths couldn't explain how they knew, but they were confident that it was one and the same person. "He was probably called Spencer around here because that's what the others were called," Mr. Smith guessed. "I suppose that's how it come about, but I knew his name really was Johnson. Still, I can't say how I knew."

"Well, I know how you knew," Mrs. Smith broke in. "Those records he put out, you'd look on the record there and it said 'Robert Johnson.'"

Mr. Smith disagreed, a little sharply. "No, I knew about him being a Johnson long before he put out any records."

I'd said nothing to the Smiths about any records and had not even mentioned that the man in question was a musician. This spontaneous exchange, plus a few other details that had gone by, such as his mother's name, brushed away any lingering doubts I'd had. Finally, I was listening to people with direct personal knowledge of Robert Johnson's family and his life in the Delta. The rusty old lock was beginning to turn.

According to the Smiths, Robert Spencer had moved in and out of the area during the time they'd known him. He'd come and go rather suddenly but would show up every month or two to visit family and friends. Whenever he was in the area, he'd play guitar for dances or parties or just casually for friends who dropped by the house. He usually stayed with his brother Leroy and his wife, who had a house near their mother's and stepfather's place.

Cleveland Smith went to his front door and pointed again, explaining that the building no longer stood but that it had been a house where a man named

April 27, 1970   Commerce, Miss

Cleveland — RT 1, Box 91-A, Robinsonville
Lula + Smith   Commerce, Miss

Recalls & Robert Spencer who
Sang D "Terraplane Bl" — Had a
Brother, older, than Robert Named
Leroy —

says he
Lula Died after World War II - acc to wife
—
says Robt Spencer about
Cleveland died in 1939 in Greenwood —

—

Mother was Named Julia Willis
and her husband was Willie "Dusty" Willis

Julia Willis died too

Willie "Dusty" Willis died too

— Not Polk
Plantation
which is
Julia + Willie Willis lived on Commerce Bayou by
Plantation — owned then + now by
Abby + Leatherman Co —

In 1930s Robt Spencer did it + lived with them
but was " in and out"

McCormick's notes from his interviews with
Cleveland and Lula Smith, April 27, 1970, Commerce, Mississippi.

Otis Deal ran dances and gave country suppers. Usually on Saturday nights, when he was around, Robert Spencer would play at Otis Deal's place.

Both of the Smiths remembered those occasions and they recalled, of all his songs, the "one about the Terraplane" most vividly. They started tittering as they remembered bits of the lyrics, like "Who's been driving my Terraplane for you, since I been gone?"

"Some of the people around here used to own a Terraplane," Mr. Smith explained. "That was a favorite car in that time. So then Robert got to making up this song about it, and it had such stuff in there like 'When I mash on your little starter, your spark plug oughta give me fire,' and all such as that." Mrs. Smith pulled up her apron, leaned over to hide her face, and started giggling into it as her husband blithely recited the words. "Terraplane Blues" has not been one of the songs that critics have praised. On the contrary, it's often dismissed as a rather ordinary piece of double entendre, not particularly notable for either bawdiness or wit.

The assessment from the audience for whom it was intended, however, was quite different. It was, without question, Robert Johnson's best-remembered song, not only in Robinsonville but everywhere that people spoke to me about Johnson from firsthand experience. It was particularly interesting to learn that it had been popular before the record appeared in 1937. Half a dozen people had told me that when they learned Johnson had been invited to Texas to make some recordings, they'd urged him to make certain that he included "Terraplane Blues." "I told him to make that one," Mr. Smith said, "even if he didn't do nothing else."

Not only was "Terraplane Blues" among the first few songs that Johnson recorded, but it also was one side of the first record scheduled for release, which sold better than any of the subsequent records. Yet, ironically, the Robert Johnson mystique rarely gives it any special attention (in much the same way, Woody Guthrie's devotees tend to overlook "Oklahoma Hills," the song that achieved the greatest popularity during his lifetime).

People may remember Robert Johnson's harsher, more personal songs with awe and a kind of unease, but "Terraplane Blues" was the one they quote and joke about. A fair critical assessment might be that it was probably intended as a simple source of entertainment, and that it succeeded. In the course of my time spent in and around the Abbay & Leatherman Plantation, at least ten people said that they had owned that particular record and bragged that they had played it until it was worn gray. They also talked about Johnson's other songs, but what they said was more restrained.

The Smiths said that Johnson predicted his own death in his songs, but they couldn't be more specific about just how he'd done that, and they quickly got into a disagreement about when he'd died. Lula believed he had died sometime after World War II. Cleveland shook his head, saying, "Robert Spencer died in Greenwood in the year 1939." He was right about the place, and he was only off one year about the date.

From the Smiths' house I visited several other people who told me many of the same things, sometimes elaborating or adding a few details. I walked west toward the levee, almost going from house to house. When I came out of a home two houses down from the Smiths, there was a gray sedan sitting outside with its motor running and two white men waiting for me. The car was positioned across my path, and when I walked up to it, the man behind the wheel asked me what I was doing there.

I told them they'd need to identify themselves before they got an answer. They said they were employees of the Abbay & Leatherman company and were in the habit of checking on strangers. They didn't have any guns in sight, and they hadn't done anything threatening, so I gave them the benefit of the doubt and told them why I was visiting the neighborhood. We were all conscious of the fact that at least twenty people were watching this exchange from their front porches or windows.

It turned into an amiable conversation. The men explained that they had a policy of trying to protect the families who lived on the property. They described several instances of swindlers cheating people with a burial insurance fraud or a church building fund racket. I wondered how many bunco artists worked this remote road. Ultimately, they gave me permission to go on the property and photograph things as I liked. That alone said something for the Leatherman operation. A lot of plantation operators were openly hostile to anyone photographing the dwellings they provided to their workers, which frequently brought up the legal point of whether or not a landlord could deny access to the people who lived within his domain. That wasn't quite the case here, because the houses I was visiting were sited along a public road, and I didn't enter the Leatherman property except when I walked up to one of the homes that was, strictly speaking, under the immediate jurisdiction of the landlord. The same thing had occurred a number of times before—with police or guards or overseers coming to check on me when I stopped to talk to someone—and a large consideration is that whatever trouble that comes out of it can reflect on the people who live here. Tomorrow I'd be gone, but they'd still be here to face any hard feelings left behind. It really wasn't fair to stir up trouble and then leave, so I usually tried, somewhat uncharacteristically, to make friends with all the cops and guards and watchdogs that came calling. Either make friends or play a trump card or both. In this case I asked for directions to Mr. Leatherman's place. They looked a little startled and told me he was away. We parted in a friendly fashion. They even gave me directions to one of the people I'd been told to visit.

The incident made me take a closer look at the Leatherman place. The fact that someone was watching for strangers and would send employees to check on them made an impression on me. I wondered what they were worried about. Voter registration? Perhaps the concern was that competitors would try to hire away some of their workers. Or maybe it was simply as they'd said: a standing policy to be wary of strangers. Someone told me that the same thing had happened a few days before, when a census taker—the 1970 census was in progress—had come through.

As I walked on, I noticed that most of the Leatherman houses were pretty shabby. Most were in worse shape than the Smiths' house, and some of the people seemed a bit scruffy. Still, it was far from as bad as it could get in the rural South. The kids had adequate clothes, no one looked underfed, the houses were heated, the windows were all in place, and the roofs were in good repair. As sharecroppers' places go, they ranked about in the middle of the scale. The landlords had long ago learned that they needed to treat people better if they were going to keep the workers they still needed. Not far away, I'd seen some houses where the landlord had built a string of attractive white houses with modern plumbing, butane, television antennas, and a clean, airy look about them. He'd made one terrible mistake, however: there were no porches, which are essential for country life.

A number of people had suggested that I see a man named Alex Clark, and so I made my way down to his house. He and several other men were out on his porch. Mr. Clark was sitting on the steps, wearing bib overalls and a cap. He'd only just gotten home from work, which at this time of year seemed largely concerned with maintenance and repair. He had heard about my visit and was expecting me to appear, since he'd known Robert Spencer almost as long as anyone. They'd been boyhood chums.

He greeted me and then scooted over, making a place for me on the steps. He told me that he'd been born in 1910 and that he remembered Robert Spencer as a year or so older. He said that Spencer was seven years old when he came to live with his people at the Polk Plantation—the one just across the road to the north. I wondered whether a youngster could remember such a detail accurately, and he assured me that he could because right from the start the two of them had struck up a friendship. Robert was an ordinary looking boy, Clark said, except for the fact that there was a tiny white spot in one eye and the lid of that eye dropped slightly.

As Clark talked, I could visualize the pair of friends climbing around on the levee, exploring the river bottom to hunt snakes, or making a racket around the backyard chicken coops. "You know how two boys'll get to be friends when they're the same age and growing up? Well, that's how me and Robert was," Clark said. "We was always off together. I was over at his house or he was over at mine, or we was hanging around the commissary store."

Then Clark's family moved away to Arkansas. They lived on various plantations there until 1925, when they returned to the Leatherman place. Alex didn't see Robert during those five years. "When we came back here," he said, "Robert was around fourteen then, and he was playing harmonica and getting started out on guitar."

Clark recalled that when Robert was sixteen, he started playing at a tavern at Penton, Mississippi, another plantation community about six miles northeast.

"You remember them railroad tracks you come over back at Robinson-ville?" Clark asked. "That's the Yazoo and Mississippi Valley. Or it was. Then the IC took it over." He swiveled around, pointing. "Those tracks run straight as an arrow. Next stop is Clack, and the next after that is Penton. It's just a hair over the county line, into DeSoto County."

I asked him the best way to get there by car. "Well, if *I* was going," he said, "I'd go by the levee. There's a road that runs along the top of the levee, you know? You get up on it and just stay with it, and it swings around right by Penton. It's right up against the levee." Looking off to the northeast, I could see the faint line of the levee as it curved and then straightened.

"Up there at Penton was the first place Robert started making money playing guitar," Clark continued. "Lots of times I saw him go off up there, up along the levee, him and his guitar. He'd get a ride most times, but if not, he'd walk it. Sometimes I'd go along with him, just for the company and to get acquainted up there. There was pretty nice girls up at Penton at that time." He smiled and rubbed the end of his nose.

"After that, we got off from each other. Either I was gone from here, or Robert was gone from here. I don't think it was until 1934 I got together with him again. By that time we was both grown. I was working, doing farm work, and he was playing guitar. He was making twice as much money as me. Nothing too big, but he was doing good just going around to these different plantations. Playing music at the store or at the party house or whatever, that was his game.

"Back in those days, a good musician could go on almost any plantation and make money. If the people didn't have money, then the boss man would give him some. That way the people could have their party there and didn't have to be going off someplace to frolic." Clark leaned toward me, talking softly as if passing along a confidence. "You know, back then, they'd do near anything to keep people from going up to Memphis. It's but just a few miles on up there." Clark described seeing Robert several times in the fall of 1934 around the town of Walls, Mississippi. It's in the same direction as Penton, another ten miles closer to Memphis. No one had ever told me how the town got its name, but it seems obvious when you're there: there's a big wall just beyond the town. This is where this portion of the Delta, the Yazoo Basin, comes to an end. The roads leading north or east out of Walls make a sudden hundred-foot climb, and the terrain changes from flat, muddy floodplain to green rolling pastures. The bluffs look just like a green, ivy-covered wall. Memphis is only fourteen miles from Walls.

"It used to be you could go on over there," Clark waved a thumb toward Robinsonville, "and climb up on a freight and ride on up the line as you pleased: Clack, Penton, Lake Cormorant, Walls, and it'd put you right down in Memphis. Course, Robert never did that too much. He'd try to get a ride in an automobile with somebody. He rode trains some, but not too much. He was always going up there to play for Mr. Bob Watson and Mr. Tom Tolliver. They had big places up at Walls. The last time I seen Robert was up there in 1934. Some white people was opening up a new store at Walls, and they had a celebration and got Robert to come play for it. You know, you get a musician, and he'll bring a crowd. I saw him that day, we had some drinks together, then we went off in different directions, and I never saw him again. Later, when I got back here, I learned he was dead."

I asked about other musicians, but Clark shook his head. He said that over the years he'd heard dozens of other musicians, but he never knew or cared about them. "Only reason I knew Robert was because we was friends back when we was just boys."

Other people along the road added a few more details. Some of them were contradictory or blurry, but on the whole they added up to a consistent picture of youngster known as Robert Spencer, rather ordinary except for a flaw in one eye, who'd grown up around the Abbay & Leatherman Plantation. It was initially puzzling to me how he could have grown up in the Hazlehurst area and

The bluffs rising in the background gave Walls, Mississippi, its name.
Photograph by Robert "Mack" McCormick.

grown up here as well. When people were pressed as to whether or not Robert
Spencer had spent all his time here as a youngster, they said "no" or "probably
not." One woman, who was old enough to remember the family from the time
they moved into the area, said, "Young Robert was around, but not all the time.
You know how it'll be with a family that's having hard times. They'll let some
of the young 'uns stay off with some of their kin. In a big family, the children'll
move around some, visiting here and there with their people." It therefore seemed
plausible that Robert Johnson, né Robert Spencer, spent part of his youth here
and part of it in Copiah County.

Opinions differed as to whether or not Robert's older brother, Leroy Spencer, had started him playing music or not. Some said that Leroy was the first to
take up music, and Robert followed him. Some said it was the other way around.
The point was often made that Robert was the better musician, but the common
answer to this was that "Robert learned from Leroy, at first, but then he got better
than his brother, and Leroy learned some from Robert. It went back and forth,
you see?"

Some said that Leroy Spencer played piano and guitar, but others said he
only played piano. The consensus seemed to be that he'd been best at piano but

he'd also played guitar, and then after Robert's death he'd concentrated on guitar. A man named Pete Ruffin said, "That whole family was so proud of Robert's
talent that when he passed, Leroy tried to keep it up." He told me that Leroy had
continued playing for some years afterward and had kept Robert's guitar.

One of the people I'd been talking with interrupted the conversation and
pointed, saying, "There he comes." A green Chevrolet was moving down the
road, soon turning off on a side road. When the dust settled a bit, I saw that it
had stopped in front of a house not far from where it made the turn. Someone
said, "That's Butch Long. He'll tell you all about them musicians."

The group walked with me over to Long's house, where they bombarded
him with questions and explanations. He sat everyone down on his porch and
went off to wash up. While he was away, the others explained that he'd just come
from his job at the blacksmith shop. (It was still called by its old name, but it was
now more of a garage.) No one explained why they expected Long to know about
musicians, but I guessed that he'd probably hired musicians in the past. He might
have run a party house or given country suppers.

When he returned, got settled, and understood what had brought everyone there, he proved no disappointment. He promptly rattled off an impressive
list of bluesmen and songsters: "There was Son House and Willie. They went
around together. Willie Brown. And Charley Patton. They all came through here.
Played here and played around at these different places. Over to Kirby and up at
Penton and back down at Bowdre."

The musicians he named were all familiar to me. They were well known
through the recordings they'd made in previous years. Among blues aficiona-
dos, they were more than well known. In writing about them, critics and liner
notes writers had stumbled over one another's slogans. Charley Patton had been
described as "Founder of the Delta Blues." Son House was "Father of the Folk
Blues." And Robert Johnson was "King of the Delta Blues Singers." These were all
extravagant and oversimplified labels, but they helped underscore the significance
of this particular cluster of bluesmen that Butch Long had named so casually.

In May 1930, House, Brown, and Patton had traveled to a town north of
Chicago to make some recordings for a race record company, Paramount, operated by the Wisconsin Chair Company. That occasion has often been described
as the greatest single recording session in blues history. Again the superlative
tends to oversimply and distort. The gathering preserved some of the most
revered performances of the Delta's music, but it was not the combination
of the three musicians that was in itself unusual, only the fact that they had

brought their music into a recording studio. The grouping itself was typical. As Long pointed out, the three men often traveled together. "You find one, you're liable to find the other, or maybe all three," he said.

Willie Brown and Charley Patton had been associated with one another since the 1910s, when they'd been together in Sunflower County, Mississippi. Later they'd relocated fifty miles farther north, in Tunica County, and Son House had become part of the group. For a time they were a frequent sight in the area around Robinsonville. This is not to suggest that they constituted some kind of club or clique. The three are well known today largely because of the recordings they left. One hears the names of others, some of them described as "outstanding" or "first-rate," but those who left no legacy of recordings are impossible to assess.

Nonetheless, I often heard the names of other musicians. Butch Long talked, for example, about an Enoch Williams. This was a new name to me. One of the other men sitting on the porch said he "was right up there with the best."

Another said, "No, he couldn't touch Patton, but he was next to the best."

"That Charley Patton was a devil of a guitar man," one answered.

"But I believe Enoch Williams could stay in there with him."

"You know he lives up in Memphis now."

"Who's that?"

"Enoch Williams. Lives in North Memphis. Might be on Montgomery or Thomas Street, one of those in there."

"Willie Brown's dead." Long said. "He died up at Memphis. And Son House may be dead. He's been long gone from here."

One of the men kept talking about Charley Patton. Although he had an enormous repertoire stretching from ballads through blues to hokum and novelty songs, one of things that's most remembered is his showmanship. He could toss a guitar around in the air while playing it, never missing a lick. And he could dance around his chair while playing. "But now, you take Son House," one of the men said, "he wasn't too much at all that."

"No, but he was a devil of a guitar man too. Just for straight guitar playing and all that, he was a devil."

"I believe he used to live right down the road from me."

"Who's that?"

"Son House. When I was on the Merrimac place, I believe he was just down the road." The Merrimac Plantation was the one in which Robinsonville itself sat. It was one of the region's larger operations, a full six square miles in size, with the town right in the middle.

"They never was too much at farming, them musicians," Long opined. "Some of them just seemed to barely get by with the farming, waiting for the weekend. And some of them didn't even do *any* farming. They was strictly musicians, and nothing more."

I was curious about who fit that latter category. Long thought about it for a while. "Son House, Willie Brown, Enoch Williams—they all worked on shares. I guess Charley Patton was pretty much a full-time musician." Someone disagreed, saying Patton had farmed in another part of Tunica County, but most of them agreed that after his records began selling, he depended on music for his living to a large extent.

I asked about Robert Spencer. "Oh, he came along after all them others," Long said. His wife had come out on the porch and had been listening to the talk. Here she interrupted, "You mean little Robert?" Quite suddenly, tears sprang to her eyes. "I nursed him, when he was just a little thing." She turned and hurried back into the house.

"She suffers over it, just to hear his name," Long explained. "She took care of him a lot when he was a child. Helping out his mama, you know." He called his wife, and she came back and talked a little about young Robert. He'd been a good child, easy to get along with and as friendly as he could be until people did him wrong. I carefully asked if there was any particular person who bore him ill will. She shook her head, saying, "I don't know why they killed him like that."

Long turned the conversation back to other ground. "Now you talk about musicians, that's what he was—he wasn't no kinda farmer." A couple of the men laughed and confirmed Robert's reluctance to do any kind of farm work.

When the talk had about run out, I got out the old photograph of Claud Johnson that I'd borrowed from his mother and passed it around. I asked if it looked like any of the musicians we'd been talking about. One of them said positively it was Robert Spencer. Another said it "looked like it could be him." Later when I went back by Cleveland and Lula Smith's house they both said it was Robert Spencer, but Alex Clark stared at it a long time and said, "It looks just like Robert—but it ain't him, it's just some guy that looks like him."

Robert Spencer's family history, I gathered, was complex and uncertain. A lot had happened to his people. His stepfather, Dusty Willis, had died in 1941. Afterward, Julia Willis moved to Washington, DC. Some of the people on Long's porch recalled Robert's two sisters. One was named Carrie, and the older girl was

Bessie. Bessie married a man named Granville Hines or Himes and went to live somewhere "down the country." After her husband died, she moved to Washington, DC. The brother, Leroy, died about 1961 in Tunica or Clarksdale.

Several of my Robinsonville informants told me that one or both of the sisters were still living, probably somewhere around Washington. They recalled one of them coming back at the time of Leroy's death, only nine years before. They had no idea whether she had remarried or what her current name might be. An older sister could doubtless say a great deal to flesh out Robert's portrait, but finding her in the sprawling city with its three alphabetical telephone books could take months.

There was one glimmer of hope: several of the people on Butch Long's porch believed that one day, sooner or later, Robert's sister would return to visit Robinsonville, as she had several times in the past.

● ● ●

8

LEATHERMAN

Mississippi calls them "beats." Most states call them precincts or townships. They're simply the minor political divisions into which counties are split up. In the rural South, they're usually much the same size from one county to another.

Tunica County, Mississippi, is divided into five beats. Beat 1 is the topmost section of the county. If you ignore the no-man's-land lying outside the levee, it measures something like eleven miles across and six miles from north to south. It would be a neat rectangle, except that the Mississippi River makes a bend here, and the line of the levee wobbles around, lopping off part of two sides. To the south is the rest of Tunica County, and on the north and east lies DeSoto County, which borders the Tennessee state line.

In the mid-1960s, Bernard Klatzko, a blues enthusiast from Glen Cove, Long Island, had written a breathless, compelling account of a trip he'd made into Mississippi searching for people who knew or remembered Charley Patton. Following a lead to the Dockery Plantation, he'd looked on his map and found a town by that name. He wrote, "Could a town also be a plantation, we wondered?"

Indeed it can. Where the Delta and the Yazoo Basin were concerned, more often than not, it was. A detailed map of the Delta counties shows communities that for decades remained mostly the "headquarters" of some plantation: places named Panther Burn, Dockery, Alligator Lake, and the like. Their dots look no different from the ones used to mark towns, but these were all plantations, not towns. They each have a store, a filling station, and a cotton gin.

Beat 1 of Tunica County had two incorporated towns, Robinsonville and Banks. The other communities were originally sharecroppers' settlements—Bowdre, Clack, Commerce, Green River, and Lost Lake—set in the middle of large plantations. When Robert Johnson lived there, Beat 1 was cut up into exactly twenty-one different plantations. He had a large extended family within which to move and live. He spent most of his time—but not all of it—growing up on the Leatherman Plantation and the Polk Farm. From the people still there I gained a fragmentary picture of his early life, occasionally in sharp focus for specific incidents.

The family lived in several different houses. One that they lived in for the longest was along a dogleg road on the Polk Farm near St. Peter's Church. From its wide porch, broken at one corner by a displaced foundation block, he could walk either north or to the west and come to the levee. The family also lived in another house that directly faced the levee, and Robert could step across the road and climb up to the crown. From there he could see some of the river traffic and sniff the fumes of goods and materials manufactured in Parkersburg and Davenport.

Over in the thicket were rabbit runs and bayous with catfish gliding around in the muddy water. A short way through the bottomlands was a stretch of swampy ground where water moccasins moved sluggishly among the cypress roots. A bootleg whiskey still stood nearby, maintained by a short, grumpy man who never hesitated to throw sticks at any of the neighborhood youngsters who came spying.

A walk in any other direction wasn't particularly eventful. The store and the post office at Commerce were about a mile and half to the southwest. Toward the southeast it was a two-mile walk to Robinsonville, with a cluster of houses, gasoline stations, and cotton compresses around a depot on the Yazoo and Mississippi Valley Railroad. The gravel track of Highway 61 ran alongside the railroad. Memphis was twenty-six miles away.

Robert developed an early habit of watching for people who were readying a wagon or automobile to travel somewhere. At first he would ask permission of the driver and then burst into his house to ask his mother whether he could go along to the commissary or ride into Robinsonville with a truck that was picking up freight. His mother would want to know why he needed to go along, and his answer was always veiled and shy. "Just to be going," was the most he'd usually say.

All the neighborhood boys hitched rides like this, but Robert persisted more than most. Eventually he stopped asking for permission, and whoever was looking after him had to adjust to his abrupt disappearances. There was a lot of worry one night when he didn't return, and the family had to ask around until they learned he'd gotten a ride with a man who'd gone for a visit in Coahoma County and planned to stay overnight. Robert came home the next day, looking a little sheepish when he was scolded, but a week later he stayed out overnight again. He was about ten years old at the time. A little later he showed up at the home of an older sister who lived about forty miles away. He spent two nights and then came back home, never explaining how he'd gotten back and forth. Everyone assumed he'd walked to the highway and hitched a ride. People had been shipping him around to stay with different relatives, and now he started shipping himself.

It was a musician's kind of behavior, but he developed the habit of traveling as he pleased, usually ending up at a relative's house, before he took a serious interest in music. At about the same time as he began staying away overnight, he started making up rhymes. None of them appear to have been noteworthy; at least none had stuck in anyone's mind. Neighbors recalled that Robert began making up his own verses to some church songs, adding verses or changing around some of the old ones to the familiar songs.

Robert grew more serious about religion as he got older. He often echoed some of the sentiments and phrases of Rev. Hudson, the pastor at St. Peter's. He would hang around the house of one of the elders, asking the old man questions about Bible stories and concepts. Robert developed an irritating habit of arguing with some of his friends, suddenly shouting such things as, "You're just acting through sinfulness."

One of the people who lived along State Road 304, a man a little older than Robert, remembered that this phase lasted about a year before coming to an end. "Then all of a sudden he quit talking so much about religion," the man remembered. "It was just a thing he did for a while. Like boys do."

During the 1920s, although family income was not spread evenly over the year, after the crop was in there was a lot of cash in people's hands, lasting for at least a month or two. The Robinsonville boys could make some change for themselves by doing chores or running errands for neighbors. In the early winter one year, Robert made some money this way and spent a dime on a Jew's harp he saw on a cardboard display at the commissary. Not much later he came back from a trip into Tunica with a harmonica he'd bought at a drugstore. He

A busy day outside Louis Ervin's Lunch Counter in Tunica, Mississippi.
Photograph by Robert "Mack" McCormick.

carried it everywhere for a few days, but someone managed to steal it from him. He promptly bought another one. By March he had three harmonicas in different keys.

Robert soon recruited two other boys to play with him, and they formed a little spasm band that both entertained and annoyed the community. One of the boys had a one-string guitar made from a cigar box, and the other knew several tricks for making rhythm instruments. One of the simplest was a wire stretched between the wall and the floorboards of a house. When it was drawn taunt and plucked, it would turn the entire room into a resonating instrument, emitting a deep *hwaaoo, hwaaoo*. This never lasted long, because the noisy sound would aggravate the adults, who would send the boys out of the house to play somewhere else.

There were four or five resident musicians on the Leatherman Plantation, two more on the Polk Farm, and another half dozen in the immediate vicinity. One of them was an extraordinarily fine guitar player named Willie Brown. He and Robert played together regularly later on. And there was Enoch Williams, another local musician who regularly teamed up with Robert, but that too was later on.

A number of local people played guitars and fiddles, with varying degrees of ability and interest. Some played regularly for dances and parties, while others seemed to play mostly for their own reasons, never performing in a public place or trying to supplement their income from it. There were also some who not only played for their own benefit but preferred to make up their own songs, creating blues about their personal concerns and preoccupations. Their songs mentioned lovers, friends, and enemies and talked about such close-at-hand matters as the disposition of an overseer on a particular day or the balkiness of a certain mule. Such totally personal blues are in a sense the very heart of the Delta tradition, and yet they are the ones least often heard, since they were based on rhymes made up on the spot and then usually forgotten.

As a youngster, Robert came into contact with a wide variety of music and musicians. There were guitar-playing revivalists along with three women and one man who played piano at the various churches. One neighbor played trumpet and trombone; he had been a member of a brass band that had been organized on the plantation some years before.

Robert spent some time with a man named Jim Henson, a stubby, dark fellow of around forty who played fiddle in a casual style. Robert learned several tunes from him and played them on his harmonicas. Henson was known locally for a song called "Lost Girl," and Robert eventually mastered its quick changes and fast, stride-breaking parts. Robert often showed up at a Sunday afternoon country supper to help out Henson. He would provide a bass part, usually by blowing across the mouth of a jug or a gallon bottle, producing a deep, throbbing sound that nicely backed up some of the fiddler's pieces. Occasionally Henson would let Robert take the lead, playing a number on a harmonica, contributing figures behind the fiddle, or playing a piece on his own.

Robinsonville's old-timers remembered several other things from this period. Robert was often around whenever there was a dance or any occasion with music, even though he was still a little too young to be fully welcome. He was rather aggressive about wanting to "help out" and would sometimes irritate the musicians by trying to play their instruments when they would take a break. Some of the itinerant musicians who'd come onto the plantation for a weekend were very protective of their instruments and regarded any youngster trying to learn music as a threat. They often were stingy, toughened men who were quick to turn on a youngster trying to push himself into their business. They sang blues mixed in with hokum, ragtime, party songs, and some of the older narrative ballads or those with minstrel show origins. Songs such as "Elder Green

Come to Town," "Casey Jones," and "Turn Your Lamp Down Low" were part of the mixture. Despite the knocks on the head he'd gotten for it, Robert persisted in fooling with other people's guitars. He made a pest of himself, and people remembered it because it was unlike him; in most respects he was rather shy and easygoing.

Another strong memory was of Robert playing tunes on one of his harmonicas while he sat on a neighbor's porch or simply hanging around by himself. He developed some solitary habits. It seemed to begin with his resistance to doing chores. He would be sent on an errand to fetch a tool, but an hour later he could be found sitting on a porch playing a mouth harp. Some days he disappeared entirely. He began staying out of school and took little interest even when he was there. Some his classmates remembered seeing him going off by himself when they had to hurry home to do chores. They wondered how he got away with it. He frequently did what he preferred rather than the work given to him.

The Delta is a self-conscious place. The people who run it have always been too anxious about their way of life, their traditions, their heritage. The fact is that they're often a bit short on these qualities and as soon as the land was settled they hustled around trying to whip up some traditions and heritage. The houses that came out looking like Greek temples were part of it. The ostentation that went with the horse races and polo matches on plantation grounds were another part of it. One aspect of the self-conscious was the way they tossed around the name *Old South* and the term *Delta* itself.

There's that old saw that runs, "Sir, the Delta begins in the lobby of the Peabody Hotel in Memphis and ends on Catfish Row in Vicksburg." That's colorful, but a soil chemist or geologist would balk. The Delta begins a good way upriver from the Peabody Hotel. If you happen to be driving north from Cairo, Illinois, you'll see a cotton gin and compress bearing the name of the Delta Planters Association. Just a few miles beyond you climb out of the Delta. That's the northern limit, and it runs from there to the Gulf of Mexico.

Memphis is significant not because it's in the Delta but precisely because it's out of it. The town made it because it's built on some bluffs overlooking the river, a strategic point long prized by the Chickasaw people and wrangled over for a couple of centuries by the Spanish and the French and everyone else who was trying to get a spot where they could control the river without getting wet every spring. Memphis is the only spot in several hundred miles where instead of running down the middle of the floodplain, the river runs over to one side, right up against the bluffs.

The Delta is 37,000 square miles of old inland sea that got silted in. Arkansas has the largest piece of that territory, and Louisiana has the next largest. Illinois, Tennessee, and Missouri have part of it. Only about one fifth of the Delta lies in the state of Mississippi.

Frequently when people talk about the Delta they mean only a particular part of it: the Yazoo Basin, in Mississippi. This is the choicest ground, with the most far-reaching reputation, for it was here that the old cotton culture engendered the heights of romanticism, brutality, and economic glory.

It's a bit special because it has the Mississippi on one side and another set of rivers—the Yalobusha, the Tallahatchie, and the Yazoo—curving around the other. The shape of it is an ellipsoid, but for all the corners of the land and its people sharing much in common, there are significant, overwhelming differences. The lower half was settled early, by enslavers and the enslaved. The upper half was settled later, after emancipation.

The bottom half of the Yazoo Basin floods more readily. When the Mississippi is at flood stage, those other rivers back up, creating backwaters that turn the land back into an inland sea. The upper part of the Yazoo Basin is less subject to this kind of action. During the massive of flood in 1927 there were several weeks during which the people who lived around the Leatherman Plantation could climb the levee and look west across thirty-five miles of water. It was a huge backwater that had formed on the Arkansas side where the water had run around behind the levee on that side. The same thing had happened farther south on the Mississippi side, but the upper part of the Yazoo Basin stayed relatively dry. Beat 1 of Tunica County was full of refugees from farther south.

When the United States created those cheap treaties with the Choctaw and the Chickasaw Nations in the early nineteenth century, the Delta was a hardwood forest full of sloughs, swamps, mosquitoes, and oxbow lakes. Clearing and draining the land, turning it into the flat black prairies one sees today, was a slow process that stretched over decades. The Yazoo Basin was populated only incrementally as the land was altered. The lower part of it today has an antebellum look, but much of it was not yet cleared for cotton by the time of the Civil War. The more accessible parts of the region followed along the Mississippi River or one of the tributaries. Railroads expanded the accessibility of the basin, built on treacherous roadbeds of cypress rafts laid across shifting, uncertain soil.

In 1880 a little less than one thousand African American people were living in Quitman County, in the heart of the upper Yazoo Basin. Twenty years later there were five times as many. Large parts of Sharkey, Sunflower, Tallahatchie, and Tunica Counties remained vacant until the turn of the twentieth century. Dockery Plantation, often mentioned as a gathering place for musicians, was not established until 1895.

Development thus came relatively late to this region, and the land stayed in a nearly constant state of flux. First there was the rush to populate the new farming estates, as people were coaxed to come down from the hills to work as sharecroppers while landowners pursued profits following the post–World War I economic boom. For a while the system seemed to work, but the Great Depression wiped out most of the gains. Later, mechanization stripped the land of the tenant farmers and put the landlords back in business.

The African American families who were only a generation or two away from slavery were the first to be caught up in the quickening flow of changes. In 1910 wealthy white landowners had been begging for people to come and work the Delta farms. But by 1950, most plantations were shedding their labor force, investing in new agricultural techniques and equipment. These decades flashed by, requiring everyone to learn new ways and make adjustments as the facts of cotton farming changed. For the working people, the adjustments involved moving from one part of the country to another, finding new jobs, scattering families, and coping with big-city slums.

The blues describe some of these events directly, but in a larger sense the music reflects the whole process of quickening change and adjustment. It is no accident that the greatest of the Delta blues musicians were natives of the Yazoo Basin's upper half, the region where the changes and adjustments hit hardest, compressed into the least number of years.

When I talked with people who had lived along State Road 304, there was an inescapable sense of the brevity and irregularity of life in this part of the world. People talked about the different farms where they'd worked. Many had tried their luck in a city and then returned to what was more familiar. Almost no one had remained in place for more than a generation. Most of them described their families as coming to Robinsonville from some place in the hills to the west or the south. They had moved not like pioneers seeking a new frontier but rather like passengers on a sinking ship, moving to the part still above water.

These dynamics stood out particularly clearly when I asked how Robert Spencer might have gotten the money together to buy his guitar. I hadn't really

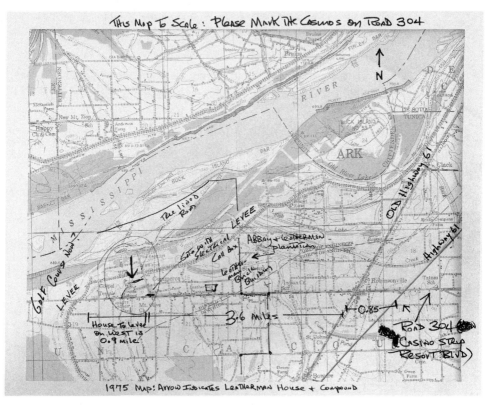

1975 Map: Arrow Indicates Leatherman House + Compound

McCormick indicated on this map various features around the
Abbay & Leatherman Plantation in Commerce, Mississippi.

expected an answer, but one of the men knew exactly how it had been done. The
owners of the Leatherman Plantation used to play polo. Out of their thousands
of acres, they set a few aside for a big green swath where the rich planters could
watch their athletic sons racing fine thoroughbreds up and down the fields after
a little ball made of willow root. The man I was speaking with described how he,
Robert, and several other boys had worked as extra stable hands on days when the
Leatherman polo matches were scheduled. Each player would use two or three
horses in the course of a game, so many boys were needed to walk the horses and
help cool them down. The boys worked for tips, and sometimes they'd get into
fights with the regular stable boys over whether or not they should divide up their
tips. Robert worked regularly for several weeks, and then one day a particularly
big tip, probably a silver dollar, gave him enough to go to the post office and buy
a money order made out to Sears, Roebuck.

The guitar Robert bought from Sears soon brought trouble. A tension developed between Johnson and his stepfather, Willie "Dusty" Willis, over Robert's refusal to take on a share of the family's farm work, except in his own erratic way. One night a cow started bellowing in the middle of the night. When Willis went to check on her, he discovered that none of the animals had been fed or watered that night.

This wasn't the only time that Robert was singled out. They were experiencing a year with too much rain and too many breakdowns in equipment, and the resulting delays were causing everyone concern. In consequence, the overseer rode by several times to check on the Willis/Spencer place. The white landowners and their overseers expected that a tenant's entire family would work, and particularly young boys. Instead, the overseer found Robert hanging around the gas station by the highway when everyone else was out chopping cotton or hoeing and pulling weeds and unwanted seedlings. The fields were full of pregnant women, little children, and old people.

"It ain't that he's lazy," Dusty said. "Something else."

"Whatever," the overseer had said. "I'd appreciate it if you'd straighten him out."

According to accounts of their relationship, Willis and his stepson never got along that well, and Robert did not hide his contempt of farm work. Julia soothed things between them, but a final clash seemed inevitable. Shortly after the conversation with the overseer, Dusty Willis said, "You put aside that guitar till we get the crop laid by."

Julia sided with Willis, and Robert had to go to the fields to work. But a week later, he slipped away and went to live with some relatives a few miles further south. Ironically, the idea of hosting relatives presumed that the guests would pitch in with the work when it got busy. So Robert had to do much the same work he had been trying to avoid at home. After a few days he left, possibly to visit with some people at Hazlehurst. The crop season and work cycles were somewhat different there. Eventually he came back home, but soon the same tensions developed again. The guitar distracted him more than the Jew's harp and harmonicas ever had, and his stepfather mentioned it several times while his mother tactfully remained silent.

Eventually, Robert began sleeping at his older brother's house. Leroy Spencer was nearly ten years older than Robert, married and raising a family, living just a few houses away from Julia and Dusty Willis. He took a prideful interest in Robert's guitar playing. Leroy played both piano and guitar, and he sometimes made some cash playing at frolics, but he wasn't particularly serious about it.

Robert lived with his brother for a while but often moved to visit one set of relatives or another: catching up, helping out a bit, and then leaving, moving from one household to another, carrying both his clothes and guitar in a long cotton picker's sack. His older sisters were married and lived in several counties in the Delta, and one lived in Memphis. There were certainly other relatives in Copiah County, possibly on both his mother's and his father's side. With cousins, aunts, uncles, grandparents, sisters, and a brother, he was able to visit relatives in many different households throughout the region. He could simply show up and see what kind of a welcome he got. One of his most frequent residences was in Memphis, where his sister Carrie and her husband lived, in the rental housing district just south of the downtown area.

Although he returned periodically to the same places, Robert never lived in any single location for a long, unbroken time. Memories of him by his friends in the Delta grew spotty, particularly as he grew older, simply because no one person saw him for any extended period. When he was a teenager he spent perhaps half his time in the Robinsonville area, but there were periods when he was away for several months at a stretch.

He always came back to the Polk Farm and the Leatherman Plantation, however, playing there, living with friends or relatives, and becoming independent enough to establish his own personal style. The Leatherman neighbors remembered him growing into a slender young man with long, tapering fingers and his head tilted a bit, saying little, but smiling, friendly and seeming at ease with the world. He weighed about 120 pounds and stood about five feet ten inches. When he smiled, a dimple appeared in his left cheek. His right eye was habitually squinted just a bit, and there was a small white mark on the cornea. Bad health and work injuries left a lot of plantation laborers marked or maimed, so Robert's flawed eye was unremarkable, but he was sensitive about it. He often tilted his head to show his dimpled side, particularly when he was getting acquainted with a new girl.

Along State Road 304, the people I met had only a vague idea of how Robert Johnson died. None of those who had been close to him liked to talk about it, partly because they know so little and had only heard about it well after it happened. Their stories were essentially rumors: He was poisoned. He was knifed. It happened because he got in with bad people. He stole someone's woman. A jealous woman did him in.

Where had it happened? Different towns were named, all in Mississippi: Greenville, Greenwood, Magnolia. Probably at one time some of them had heard better information, but Robert's family seems to have said very little about it. A lot of snapshot-like images came into focus for me: Robert Johnson as an independent young man. Robert Johnson as a kid wrangling with a simpleminded stepfather. Robert Johnson knowing he had no aptitude or expectation to live as a sharecropper. Robert Johnson playing games, earning tips, going off to fish with other boys his age, and then growing up, becoming someone else altogether different.

One snapshot came back more than it deserved. In residential sections all over the South, "Dixie Boy" hitching posts still occupied the curbs in front of many houses. These were cast iron statues of young Black boys dressed in velvet pants, red satin shirts, and white caps, their hands extended to hold the white folks' horses. They used to be both a symbol and a practical hitching post. Now they were only a symbol. They made me think about Robert Johnson working in the stables to save up for his guitar, helping tend to the Leatherman horses as the plantation owners and their guests played polo. He didn't wear the velvet pants and the red satin shirt, but he had been obliged to play the same part.

• • •

9

LISTENING AND REMEMBERING

My long search was now at an end. It had come suddenly, almost unexpectedly. After all the fumbling and the dead ends, I had found people who had known Robert Johnson. They knew him by another name, but they knew him as a neighbor and friend, had watched him grow up and drift away. They shared not isolated recollections, but a whole interlocking pile of them. There was much more than I could thoroughly digest amid my questioning, listening, making notes, ironing out inconsistencies in dates and chronology, and straining to understand those nuances that shade and color a man's nature but which are hard for all of us to articulate.

Whatever "midnight streets" Johnson had traveled, the dusty road that runs due west from Robinsonville straight to the levee was the one where he was a familiar face, a man known easily, if not deeply, with the familiarity of long association. Ironically, my painstakingly marked-up map had not helped me in the ways expected. The marks I'd made around Robinsonville and its outskirts were several in number, but they were part of a chain, largely tracing back to one source. By comparison with other towns I'd pinpointed, Robinsonville had only seldom been mentioned by independent sources, whereas places such as Helena, Arkansas, were mentioned and seconded by as many as ten different people I'd interviewed separately.

Robert Johnson himself hadn't helped any. He left no songs mentioning Tunica County, Commerce, or Hazlehurst. He had nothing to say about his home or the two major roads—Highway 51 and Highway 61—that everyone else was making songs about. He had been born and lived just off of Highway

51, and his later home was within a short walk of Highway 61, yet he mentioned neither. Johnson didn't sing about his homes, but rather about the places he passed through and knew as a brief visitor. He overthrows the notion that a blues singer can be traced by going to the places he sings about. That often works, but not always.

My map had helped primarily by illuminating the area where my search had to concentrate: the Delta just below but near Memphis. It had simply underscored what everyone had known and presumed, dramatizing the pattern so that it eventually forced me back to the Delta often enough to hit paydirt. There were fairly clear indications that Robinsonville was the right area, but even there Johnson's home base remained elusive until I went two miles in the right direction.

The next day my visit came to an appropriate finish. Everyone in the Leatherman neighborhood who had known Robert Johnson had wanted to know whether they could hear his recordings again. They had asked this repeatedly, and in return I suggested that perhaps everyone could gather at one place. They passed the idea around, and Cleveland and Lula Smith offered the use of their house and invited the rest of the community to attend. They decided to make it around dusk.

It wasn't as old and gray a gathering as I had been expecting. My months of searching had lent a feeling of antiquity to the whole process of scrounging for information about someone who had been dead for years. Part of it had to do with the rush of changes that had taken place in the Delta; Robert Johnson had lived during an era that seemed far in the past. Yet if he had been alive, he would have been a mere fifty-eight years old at the time. So the people who had known him were now in their fifties and sixties.

Cleveland Smith stood in the middle of his living room, a heavyset man with one arm set akimbo on his hip, listening for the tread of steps on his porch. When they came, he'd wait until the screen door was pulled open and the visitor hollered; then he'd shout the person inside, beckoning, talking, and pointing out chairs all at once. It was a country way of entering a house and being welcomed. If you didn't holler out when you approached a Robinsonville house, or you did something suspicious like knock on the door, a dog would bark or even be prone to attack.

Phax "Butch" Long was the oldest of the group that gathered. His wife, Sally, was the only one who seemed apprehensive, as if she wasn't certain she wanted to hear the voice of a dead man she'd known so long ago. When she arrived she explained to Lula Smith, "I had to come. See, I nursed Robert when he was young, so I had to come."

Alex Clark came with several others, arriving in stained clothes because they had come directly from work. He seemed particularly keyed up, proud of his association with Johnson. There were others who had known him, some who had known his family, and a few who came just to join in on the occasion, all active working people, looking forward to more years of life.

The room was filled with a jovial, eager feeling and a sense of expectancy. These people had known Robert Johnson—or Robert Spencer, as they spoke of him—as only a boy and young man. He was part of their collective youth. They'd watched each other grow older, but his memory and music reminded them of their youth, of their dances and frolics and their early social life in the countryside.

There was a flurry of talk among the first arrivals about the records they'd once owned. Many of them had bought Johnson's records as they had appeared in the 1930s, but over the years the discs had been broken or lost, left behind in flooded or burned-out homes. None of them had heard his voice in nearly thirty years. They found it hard, even impossible, to imagine that the old recordings were once again on sale in ordinary record stores. They watched patiently as I set up a portable phonograph, then passed around the microgroove LP album that Columbia had issued in 1961. The jacket cover was a dusky red color, with a painting of a Black guitar player hunched over a guitar. It's a high-angle view, looking down on the figure, his face hidden from view. He is wearing a shirt with vertical stripes.

One of the people took the album and rubbed his hand over the surface of it, as if to see whether the picture would come off. He shook his head and said, "I never saw him wear any such shirt as that."

Someone else disagreed. "I saw it. He had a shirt like that. Maybe not exactly like it, but close."

The shirt, of course, like the other elements in the cover, had been the product of artist Burt Goldblatt's imagination. The feeling of it was right. It was strong and evocative, but it hadn't been meant literally. The guitar was a bright orange, and Johnson's skin was a glossy pure black.

"He wasn't near that dark," one of the women said. She took the album and read it out loud, putting to rest a little of the worry that the whole enterprise was a hoax. "It sure says his name: 'Robert Johnson.'" She read on: "King of the Delta Blues Singers."

"Well, that's right enough."

"He surely was that."

"That's true. That's true."

Several others got up to inspect the album. They asked how much it cost and were staggered when they were told it was $4.98. Someone I hadn't seen before spoke up: "You selling these?" There was a little hostility in the way he said it. I told him no, and someone else answered, "I wish he was. I'd like to buy one." The man retorted, "That's too much money for one record."

A younger man came to the rescue, explaining that it was a different kind of record than the ones they were thinking of: "There ain't just two songs on this." He stopped to count a minute, flipping the jacket over, and then announced that there were sixteen songs in the album. "This is a whole different thing."

This young man was wearing an Air Force uniform, and someone told me he'd been stationed in Germany for several years and was visiting home before going to another foreign post. "He speaks a couple of the languages from over there," I was told. "Reads them, too."

I slipped outside for a minute, and by the time I'd returned they'd done some arithmetic, figuring that the new album had the same number of songs as eight of the old 78 rpm records, which had cost thirty-five cents each. It worked out to a total of $2.80 as the original price for the same amount of music.

"Twice as much. That ain't bad."

"Most things have gone up more than that. Way lots more."

"You right there," a woman laughed. "I wish I could shop at the store and not pay but twice as much as I paid back then."

They watched, still skeptical, as I slipped out the record and set it on the turntable. When the music started, breaths were sucked in and held for the eight seconds of sharp, biting introductory guitar playing. An astonishing degree of recall can be triggered by familiar things brought back like this. At the first phrase, Johnson's clenched voice singing "I went to the crossroad," half the people in the room responded. Two of them said the next word, "fell," aloud, not after the singer but with him. They finished the line with him, "fell down on my knees," and just that quickly the intervening years fell away. One man phrased the words right with the voice. Others drowned out both him and the recording, exclaiming at one another. The group erupted with comments.

Someone said that he'd owned a copy of that very record and tried to remember what had been on the other side. Another man named it—"Ramblin' on My Mind"—before the first man could think of it. One of the women noticed that the singer referred to himself as "Bob" in the song. "I always knew him as Robert," she said.

Others agreed that Robert was how they'd known him, but one of them said, "I think they called him Bob mostly over at his house." "Yeah," one of the older women remarked, "I remember to this day now, I can hear Julia Willis calling off her porch, saying, 'Bob, come on now.' She called him Bob."

They noticed the other name that came up at the end of the song: "Tell my friend, boy, Willie Brown." That brought another whoop and shout of recognition. Robert Johnson hadn't sung about the places where he was raised and lived, but he had sent a sly message back home. He'd named the local musician who was probably the largest single influence of his life in terms of craftsmanship, style, and companionship. He'd sent him a nod of recognition and thanks. "You can run, tell my friend, boy, Willie Brown, Lord, that I'm standing at the crossroad, babe, I believe I'm sinkin' down."

The name of Willie Brown brought forth another flurry of comments: How the youngster Robert had pestered Brown and other musicians, but especially Willie Brown, who was particularly sweet, gentle, and the "flat-out best guitar picker ever was around here." He had taught Robert some things and then taken him around to play music. When the record was issued, Brown had nearly burst with pride. "He was more proud of this here song than he was of his own records," one man said. Someone else said he never knew that Brown had made any records, and that triggered a round of arguing.

I had been holding the edge of the disc, letting the turntable grind away underneath it, so the next song wouldn't prematurely cut off the remarks about Willie Brown. After they'd run their course, I let the record go and the next song—partly sung, partly talked and mumbled, punctuated by snapping bass strings—brought forth cheers of recognition. It was their favorite: "Terraplane Blues."

Before it was half over, a number of the group asked me to play it again. And then they asked for it to be played a third time. Only after that did they want to hear the other songs, which met a varying reception. Some were enthusiastically greeted like old friends, but others were strange to them, pieces they'd never heard before and had never heard him sing. They decided they were likely songs he had created just for the records but had never sung anywhere else. One of the unfamiliar songs was the one most prized by many collectors, "Hellhound on My Trail," although one man recalled, "I heard

At the Smith's house party, McCormick played
a copy of the 1961 Columbia Release. Gift of Robert B.
Campbell in memory of Dorothy and William Campbell.

him do that piece a couple times, I think." They all agreed, however, that the recording of it was unfamiliar.

When "Last Fair Deal Gone Down" came along, the listeners agreed that it was a song Johnson had been singing when he had first started playing the guitar. Derived from a work song, this song is the one that mentions the "Gulfport Island Road." I asked whether anyone knew where that was. People shrugged. Someone said, "Not around here," and someone else said, "Have to be down by Gulfport, I expect." No one knew anything of Johnson's being exactly there, but they agreed that he was always going "up to Memphis" or "down the country somewhere."

"Preaching Blues" started another small dispute. One man said the recording was "different from the way I knew him to sing it," while another said he had heard Johnson sing it exactly like the recording. The first man said the song was supposed to have "something different" in it. He asked me to stop the record a minute, and then he quoted a fragment of a line he recalled: "I know my friends are blind, my enemies see right through a door." No one else recalled hearing him sing that line; it doesn't appear on any of the recordings. The dispute dissolved in some laughter regarding the last line of the song, which mentions "going to the 'stillery." The men exchanged a few remarks about the distillery that used to stand in the bottoms. The women frowned and hushed them.

It was hard to know how much to trust any particular comment. The group said that "Hellhound on My Trail" was unfamiliar, yet when I quoted a line from it, nearly all agreed that they'd heard him sing that line. And while some of the recordings were "strange," some of the selections that had lain in Columbia's vaults for twenty-five years were familiar. They knew the words to "If I Had Possession over Judgment Day." One man finished the opening verse, anticipating the singer, saying the words aloud, "then the women I'm loving wouldn't have no right to pray." Someone else answered it, "Yeah, Lord, that's it! That's the way!"

During that evening in the Smiths' house, countless memories were stirred by the old recordings. On the previous days people had talked, responding mostly to specific questions, but now they were chatting among themselves, remembering things, piling their thoughts together. Some of them seemed to recall a youngster who had never found the easing of tensions and pressures that usually comes when a boy turns into an adult. He remained "hot-blooded and full of piss." He was like a kid who risks his life on a dare: they compared him to another boy who had died taking chances with a moving freight train. Robert remained fundamentally restless, unmanageable, full of passion, and anxious about satisfying it.

Several times the same remark was made: "Robert's trouble was women, mostly." Others would nod and agree. Someone said, "He never got past being young." The picture they drew was a cliché: a Delta Romeo, blinded by passion at the age of fourteen, unstrung by tenderness and lust for his Juliette. But Robert's tragic flaw was somewhat wider and deeper; he would experience his passion and unstringing time and again, as different women and different places would attract him. It is difficult to imagine Romeo setting up conventional housekeeping with Juliette, and in the same way—except for the one time he did settle down. Although seemingly a mild, easygoing person, he was full of thoughts that provoked him.

"If you ever spent much time with Robert," one woman said, "you'd know what I mean better. I mean if you'd be with him hour after hour, for a whole day, you'd know. He'd be just as easygoing as anyone, then he'd get quiet, and didn't answer back if you talked to him. Next time you look, he'd be moving his lips, talking to himself, saying things to himself about what had happened, and the more he talked the more he got upset. Then he'd just sit and be still for a long time, thinking. Then, next, all of a sudden he'd be joshing with you, or he'd want something to eat."

Odds and ends of the memories were just details, but they added color to the picture. He dressed poorly, wore work clothes, and seldom made himself out to be the kind of well-dressed sport that musicians often were. His father had died when he was young and that disturbed him. He never accepted Dusty Willis as anything but a foolish old man his mother had taken in.

He listened to the radio a lot and would favor hanging around those houses that had a good set. He'd listen to anything: *Amos 'n' Andy*, the *Grand Ole Opry*, soap operas, news programs, or "that big dance orchestra that used to come outta a big hotel over in Hot Springs, Arkansas."

He traveled a lot, but usually not great distances, and mostly in a north–south line up and down the Delta: on the Mississippi side, on the Arkansas side, over into the Louisiana side, but not too far over. Often he would go to Memphis and occasionally up further, maybe to St. Louis. He would come back saying he'd ridden the Greyhound from Vicksburg or had caught a ride out of Clarksdale or ridden the ferry over from Helena.

When I told them that it was almost impossible to locate people in any of those towns who remembered him, Phax Long explained: "I tell you about Robert, he wasn't any *big* personality like a lot of musicians you see. Some of those guys had a sign on their hat or a sign on their guitar telling who they was, and they'd advertise themselves like, and they'd spend the evening doing things to make the people notice them. Well, Robert, he wasn't like that. That wasn't his way. His music was what he did, and he didn't do nothing else to impress himself on people.

"You know, lots of times a person might go to a place and hear the music, but he might never look at the man who's making it. The music would be off in some corner, and maybe people standing in the way might keep him from seeing. And even if he did see him, he might be busy with something else and might not get to know him—because Robert never did nothing to impress himself. He wasn't no big personality."

They described a slender young man, inconspicuous except for his guitar and his recklessly bold manner around some women, hitchhiking around the Delta, knowing dozens of different plantations, moving in and out of a few cities, moody and self-effacing, looking shyly, then more directly at a woman whose face was new, leaning over to pull her out of a crowd and saying, "You sit by me, hear?"

146

and never fazed when someone pointed out the woman's husband. He'd simply say, with the boldness of kids playing chicken on the highway, "Damn that man, girl. Damn that man. You come sit here."

Yet he would avoid violence and make a quick pretense of yielding whenever he was threatened. Then the next day, when the husband was off at work, Robert would show up at his house, slipping quickly in the kitchen door to see his latest admirer.

"It's amazing to me he lived as long as he did," one man concluded. "Considering the risks he took, and the way he was, he lived longer than he had a right to expect."

A quick reference was made to a particular incident that had happened in a house only a few doors away: "He could have got killed that time." A woman spoke up with a raw sound of jealousy, even after all the years that had gone by. "And for what? That old thing that used to live there?" She looked indignant. "Robert didn't have good sense sometimes."

An older man spoke up and cut her off: "I don't think more needs to be said about that." He shook his finger at her. "Speak no ill of the dead."

The conversation turned to lighter things. Curiously, one insignificant detail had fallen into place. One of the men there had ridden along to Hernando one time when Robert had gotten someone to drive him there to catch an Illinois Central train. They'd gone in a used Model T Ford, bought about 1927 or 1928. It was a hellish trip over unimproved roads, muddy from recent rains, and Robert would have missed the train if the train itself had not been late. The man thought Robert had gone there several times to catch the southbound train, which could put him in Hazlehurst in an hour. The group pointed out that there wouldn't have been any need to catch a northbound train, since it only went to Memphis, and he could get a Memphis train in Robinsonville.

In time the listeners' focus shifted from the surprise of hearing Johnson's old songs to enjoying them once again, and the mood changed; I could feel a kind of tension and an emotional charge. The Robinsonville neighbors made up a fair sampling of the kind of audience that the blues tradition had served. They showed no particular solemnity in the way they listened to blues. They listened closely in some spots, but at other times they nodded or shook to the music, enjoying it but making no special issue of it until a particular phrase grabbed them, when they would shout or bark "Yeah!" as if they were hearing a stirring sermon. They would say the words along with the song, or echo choice phrases just afterward. They frequently laughed with recognition or surprise as the music rolled on, even at Johnson's more brooding, dark sentiments. Even the darkest of them were listened to with a sense of exuberance—perhaps as release and an outlet for the emotions they evoked.

There's no need to take the blues too seriously when it is totally familiar. A question sometimes arises to whether the more intense of the bluesmen—Bukka White and Robert Johnson and Son House—were indeed the kind of musicians who played primarily for dances. It is not obviously dance music in the sense that many blues are. Such a question doesn't really arise in the circumstances in which they performed, or even in this re-creation of earlier listening, with people gathered round a phonograph. They listen. They hear the poetry. They observe and take note. They respond. They drink beer and they argue and they hassle among themselves and they go in back to relieve themselves and they come back to dance or ease in on some woman. The women hear and they move and they light up the shadowed rooms. They lend the music a click of jewelry and an odor of heat. They listen to the poetry. They hear the music. It flows in and it flows back out. They react. They respond. It's a total situation. A single song may gain hushed silent listening. Another may mingle with the rattle of bottles and noise of the crowd. There's no set rule. They dance. They react. They argue and talk over the music and get half-drunk and thirty years later they know the songs so well they can phrase the words right with the singer. They absorbed it all—the man himself and his music—totally, because it was theirs. For them, the blues was never meant to be taken seriously or reflectively. It was simply a force, expressing the deepest roots of their lives.

During that evening I finally caught a glimpse of Robert Johnson. The dusty red album cover by Burt Goldblatt helped. I don't know how I'd evaluate it objectively as a work of art, but it reflected considerable insight and inspiration. "Blues ain't nothing but a lowdown shaking chill," as Son House sang. Goldblatt had captured a glimpse of Johnson somehow—possibly a better glimpse than mine, because he had gotten it wholly and entirely from listening to the recordings. I had to stumble over half of Mississippi, wind up here, get all these people together, and then—maybe for the first time—really listen to Johnson's music.

I sat off to the side, one hand holding the album jacket, leaning back, absorbing, trying to hear Johnson's songs with their ears and their memories. I was staring aimlessly at the cover itself, not looking at it but *watching* it. Goldblatt had used a high angle to look down on the scene, and he had matched Robert's figure with one of his shadow, cast on the floor by his feet as if by some single hard light. And there was another shadow, not on the original painting but on the jacket, just at that moment, of a dancer moving in the same hard light. There were shadows of people hunched together, engaged with the music or engaged with themselves or their partners. There were also shadows of another guitar player, off to the side. Occasionally the two musicians would lean together and exchange a pleasurable passage. At other times the older man—heavyset, sitting more upright—would lean away from the hunched youngster in the striped shirt. "Well, now she's been sucking some other man's bull calf, oooh, in the same man's town," I could hear Johnson intone. The younger man had something shiny—a tube of metal or a bit of glass—slipped over the end of one finger, and it made a blurred place in the picture. At times his entire arm would blur during a particular passage. The voice knifed and cut the noise with no trouble. Often it was keen and knotted, sometimes a little more relaxed, deepened.

"Me and the devil were walking side by side," he sang. He paid little attention to the crowd, sometimes exchanging a word or two with the people who surrounded him but mostly maintaining a private world, shared only in part with the older musician who sat off at his side. They seemed indifferent to the way the crowd reacted. There was no sense of compulsion: listen, or don't listen, They were unaffected by the swirl of noise and distraction, and yet they commanded it. The pulse of the music could bring the whole crowd to silence. A single line could stun the room. Occasionally Johnson would let it ride, falling into some of the older songs, playing a few casual pieces, and then tightening up over the guitar and soaring, for just a moment, into a falsetto. Or he'd stun his listeners with the simplicity of a thought or the pleasure of an idea: "All I would need is my little sweet rider just to pass the time away." I saw him lift his head an inch, but not enough to see his face.

The record ended, and that broke the spell. I played it over again, but the next time the album jacket stayed as Goldblatt had designed it. I experienced no further hallucinations, although the listeners in the room remained deeply connected. I wrote furiously, jotting down what people said, trying to catch as much as I could, shuddering at the thought of the job I would have when I got back home. The Robinsonville visit had given me dozens of pages of notes and comments, and countless leads and thoughts as to how to pursue other musicians or members of Johnson's family. After a while, writer's cramp set in, and I relaxed and settled back, listening again.

This time my thoughts were more objective. I remembered what Alex Clark had said about plantations near Memphis creating the biggest problems for landowners. The closer they were to Memphis, the harder it was to keep workers on the property; the more efforts the landlord would need to make; the more entertainment he'd have to offer to compete with the allure of the city, its jobs, and its excitements. The demand for musicians and the strength of the blues tradition increased in proportion to the proximity of other temptations. The nearness of Memphis might explain why there was such a richness of music in Tunica and DeSoto Counties. Not only in the Delta but in the land to the east, the farms in the hills, but still near Memphis, near enough to make it tough to keep people from its draw. Willie Brown, Charley Patton, Son House, and Robert Johnson had all thrived here. In Beat 1. The theory doesn't fit or explain other places where musicians concentrated, but it's supported by the parallel events across the river in the Delta near Memphis. To this day Hughes, Arkansas—only twelve crow-flight miles from Robinsonville—is still such a center of taverns and music. Obviously no one factor explains anything. It only helps.

Indeed, Memphis ranked as one of America's most extraordinary centers of music in the interwar years. It supported innumerable street minstrels and party house guitar players and pianists. And there were the jug bands of Memphis, plus medicine show dancers, skiffle dancers, and the formally trained musicians who played in theater orchestras and dance bands. Few cities could claim such a heritage, and Memphis offered the young Robert Johnson a chance to hear distinctive stylists such as Furry Lewis, Robert Wilkins, Hambone Willie Newbern, Sleepy John Estes, and Frank Stokes.

It's illuminating to consider Johnson's musical education in terms of the places where he grew up. He had been born and partly raised where Tommy Johnson and his brothers lived. He had lived in Beat 1, Tunica County, with the richest of the older musicians for him to follow. He had lived both as a child and as a teenager in Memphis and heard what it had to offer. He had thus availed himself of the area's great centers of learning, although it seems to have occurred not by design, but by chance of birth and accident of residence.

This is not to suggest that clear-cut traces of these various teachers can be found in Johnson's work. The influence wasn't of that kind or shape. He shared their traditions and many of their general concepts. But essentially the older generation taught him fundamentals, gave him tools, inspired his own efforts, and set him an example to match.

Curiously enough, when he was derivative—and the recordings include some fairly obvious examples where he sings or plays imitatively—it was often something from records he had heard, by musicians he probably never knew or met. But of course he traveled in a world in which recordings by Leroy Carr, Lonnie Johnson, and Blind Lemon Jefferson were an established part of the musical spectrum. The raggedy local musicians at the crossroads store and the records wobbling around on wind-up phonographs were equal and inseparable elements in the ears of those who grew up in that generation. There were, of course, specific traits Johnson acquired from close associates: the clenched, compelling voice that Willie Brown and Charley Patton used, and the bottleneck slide guitar techniques that Son House favored, taken a step further.

Hearing Johnson's recordings in the company of people who had known him generated a number of conflicting thoughts about the man. Minor disputes started up several times during the evening. The old-timers had a kind of possessiveness about their memories, and they had to wrangle a bit to determine who was more correct or in agreement with the others. The second or third time it was played, "Kind Hearted Woman Blues" started an argument. Phax Long said the song ought to have another verse or line about "She oughta be buried alive." (It may have had such language one time; it was a commonplace phrase. Yet Johnson seems to have avoided the commonplace in the songs he recorded, so it's likely he dropped it for something more original). Long was insistent that the record "didn't have it right." But Alex Clark was equally insistent that he had heard Robert sing the song *exactly* like it was on the recording. That remark needs a grain of salt to go with. It's probably impossible for anyone to know whether it was exactly as he heard it from Robert or exactly as he heard it from the same record, thirty years ago.

Someone else said he thought the phrase in question belonged in a different song. And another person quite properly pointed out that Johnson might have used the same line in several different songs. That remark deepened the dispute. "No," Clark said, "he was careful about putting his songs together just the certain way he wanted them to go."

"Still and all, he'd have to change it around some," Long answered.

"Well, that record is right. That's just the way he sung it, and I remember him singing it over across there"—Clark paused to point his arm and mumbled some name indistinctly—"where that sugar shack used to stand."

"I don't know about that. I just heard him sing it different."

The phrases of other songs passed by, some studied and argued about, some ignored, and some anticipated before the singer actually got them out. At times there was a round of "Hush!" and a shushing of the talkers, and the whole room would concentrate on the moods of the songs and the tense, compulsive guitar that gave them such uncanny emphasis. There was some kind of reaction to almost every phrase: "Worried blues, give me your right hand." Nods of recognition and a smile. "Watch your close friend, baby, then your enemies can't do you no harm." A grunt and an exchange of glances; an incident remembered, perhaps. "I have a bird to whistle, and I have a bird to sing." Smiles of pleasure and heads turning to look at the other people. "Best come on back to Friars Point, mama, and barrelhouse all night long." Chuckles, a mixture of *huhs!*, some shushing at a bawdy remark, and a little trailing-away laughter. "She got a mortgage on my body now and a lien on my soul." A sniff of disapproval lost in something mumbled, and a grunt of agreement. "You may bury my body, oooh, down by the highway side." Another grunt. "So my old evil spirit can get a Greyhound bus and ride."

The room eventually grew still, and the lines were greeted by little more than a mumble or a nod. Occasionally there was a comment, but mostly it was a private aside. Finally someone broke into the spell. He said, "About Robert—he had a way of making up a song that makes you wonder."

A man who had known Johnson as a teenager, a man who hadn't had much to say before now, said, "He was maybe only a few months different in age from me, but you know he was always into things, moving, and going too fast."

"How do you mean?" one of the others asked.

"Well, it's there in the songs for you to hear it." He pushed a calloused thumb at the phonograph. "He was always like that. He was dying faster'n he was living."

Another dispute started. Someone argued that they had known Johnson most of his life, and he was nothing like that: "He was just an ordinary kind of guy, except he had this talent for music."

"Listen at what he's singin' there, man. Listen!"

More phrases went rushing by, and some wanted to hear certain songs over again, so the sequence was interrupted until finally the record played through again to the last song, the one they said they had never heard before. "I got to keep moving, I got to keep moving, blues falling down like hail, blues falling down like hail." The voice was now a cry, desperate and wretched. "And the day keeps on worrying me. There's a hellhound on my trail." The phrase was repeated. "Hellhound on my trail, hellhound on my trail."

The listeners shuffled about, now silent, but ready to argue some more about the man who had created such haunting songs and left them behind in these few mysterious recordings.

● ● ●

10

HINDSIGHT

In retrospect, it's plain that Robert Johnson was not quite the phantom we made of him, and the search was difficult because we persisted in looking in the wrong places. Hindsight makes everything lucid, embarrassingly obvious. It doesn't appear that he was building any mystery, only that he maintained a certain distance between himself and the songs. He was seldom autobiographical in tone. His records mention four women by name—Beatrice, Ida Belle, Betty Mae, and Willie Mae—but these are not the women who figured most significantly in his life. The mention of his friend Willie Brown seems to be the exception.

Since the 1950s at least eighteen musicians have claimed personal acquaintance with Robert Johnson in comments that have appeared in print. Close to half of them spoke about him at some length, describing traveling with him or in association with him over a period of a few weeks or intermittently over several years' time.

Yet if all these comments are studied in one sitting, they draw a curiously empty picture. While they lack detail or intimacy, it's also clear that most of the musicians are talking about the same man. There's a consistency running through most of the accounts that often centers on the similarity of the vagueness itself.

Howling Wolf said: "He never did talk about his past life . . ."

Muddy Waters said: "I don't know what kind of *work* he did. He always had a guitar with him whenever I saw him around. . . . But he didn't seem to stay in one place too long, you know, kind of restless. Think I heard he went to Helena."

And Johnny Shines, stating that he had spent two years traveling with Robert Johnson, said: "I never heard him talk even once about his family. . . . Never said nothing about his mother or father. I didn't know if he had any brothers or sisters; if he did, he never mentioned them. The only thing he was ever close to was his guitar, and he never let that go, took it with him everywhere."

Certain themes run through their comments. They mention his restlessness, sudden unannounced departures, and reticence about himself. They describe Johnson as an "ordinary guy," except for something wrong with one eye, who always kept his guitar close.

This body of material was gathered and published by people working mostly in northern cities, St. Louis and Chicago, where the musicians had migrated and established new roots, or the interviews took place in the course of a blues singer's appearance at a college campus or folk festival. The musicians would be interviewed by several people, telling them whatever they knew about Johnson in different ways, expanding and clarifying points. Vagueness, however, was the dominant theme.

Concurrently, other material that was being gathered had the same frustrating element of vagueness. A member of the Light Crust Doughboys who had been in the same studio on the morning that Johnson made his last recordings could remember nothing of that occasion, simply remarking that on "different times when we recorded, there was some colored fellows around making records."

Some of the people who claimed to have encountered Johnson reported that they'd only seen him perform from afar; others claimed to have known him well, and a few claimed to have helped him write his songs. When asked to describe Robert Johnson, many of the interviewees volunteered the fact that something was wrong with his right eye, which, given that no photographs of him publicly were available, at least seems to validate that they had seen him. The blemish was slight, but it was his most distinguishing physical characteristic and therefore an easy point to separate wheat and chaff—there being no disregard for chaff implied here, of course, since this is the stuff of imaginary retellings of stories, and legend is more significant than mere facts. It was only important to identify the facts in hope that they would lead to more intimate, firsthand knowledge of the man. It always had to be assumed that the factual story would be something of a disappointment, lacking the stature and drama of legend.

The material that came together, from all the sources, became an unmanageable, impossible maze. It piled up and obscured its own grains of fact. There was endless confusion and contradiction, and chains of apparent clues that led time and again to dead ends. Or so it appeared, standing outside this rag pile, not knowing which thread to follow. As it turned out all the most useful threads were there, in plain sight, lost only because they were threads in a rag pile.

Part of the problem was simple communication failure. In any conversation, a detail can be misunderstood or blurred by poor articulation or garbled by the attitudes or assumptions of the interviewer or interviewee. In addition, it is never easy to know when someone runs out of facts and starts filling in gaps on their own. People are mythmaking creatures, and what they don't know they'll usually provide by guesswork and imaginative, intuitive fantasy. They'll heighten the drama of story and turn the prosaic into an epic. The making of myth and legend is our most fundamental art, one subject to the harshest critical judgment of all—the simple ability to survive and perpetuate itself.

Robert Johnson long ago had grown larger than life, and into a legend—rendering it almost futile to attempt to pin down precise facts. Altogether, something like twenty-three towns had been named as the place where he'd been murdered. They ranged from Eudora, Mississippi, to San Antonio, Texas, to Cincinnati, Ohio. They included the correct one, along with twenty-two others that were wrong. Many of the accounts of his death were tangled with the equally legendary stories of Blind Lemon Jefferson freezing to death in a snowstorm. Or with the stories of Charley Patton being stabbed or Pinetop Smith being shot. They ranged from muddled stories to the kind of vivid hero-tales told of prophets and strongmen and sometimes of blues singers. All such cases require the figure to die in an appropriate manner, and—as if aware of their mythic stature—the blues singer often obliges by dying in a tangled automobile on Highway 61 or dramatically murdered just as he's about to be asked to appear at Carnegie Hall.

Certain motifs are usually adhered to in Robert Johnson's story. The image of the handsome young man dying at the hands of an evil woman is endlessly familiar. The detail of poison as the method underlines the idea of this as a woman's crime, particularly when his death occurred in an era of women poisoners inspiring several notorious trials, of the hit comedy *Arsenic and Old Lace*, and through the restirring of ancient stories of women dealing out hemlock to their lovers. He was the victim of his own lust. He was warned. He refused the warning. He was murdered. All this draws of course from the vast pool of legend that humans share. It also draws directly from what actually happened, with one significant alteration to help turn the ordinary murder into the remarkable: "It was something to do with the black arts," Johnny Shines had said. "Before he died, it was said, Robert was crawling along the ground on all fours, barking and snapping like a mad beast. That's what the poison done to him."

If one comes close to all these accounts of Robert Johnson, pushing through the contradictions and the obfuscation, there are certain personal similarities described by the men who did apparently come in prolonged contact with him. They often make the point of how little they knew him, and they ensconce this point in some vivid detail of an incident that occurred. Johnny Shines described a time in St. Louis when Johnson played "Come On In My Kitchen" very slowly and passionately, holding a roomful of people spellbound. It was one of those occasions when as the song ended no one spoke, everyone in the room was silent except for a few men and women who were crying. "Things like this often happened, and I think Robert would cry just as hard as anyone," Shines wrote in a published reminiscence. "It was things like this, it seems to me, that made Robert want to be by himself. . . . Robert would do his crying on the inside. Yes, his crying was on the inside."

The thought was echoed by a St. Louis pianist named Henry Townsend who worked with Johnson over a period of several months: "I would say he was a kind of easygoing guy; of course, this is something that's hard to tell about anybody, even if you know them for years." The people who knew him always qualify what they have to say, finally to the point of saying they hardly knew him at all. "He wasn't a flowery type of guy," Townsend continued, "he wasn't sad or depressed in his mind—not that I could see. But this could have been an inward feeling that you could only tell from a song. You know, we all kind of have the tendency to unravel our inner feelings through this kind of thing. It may have been possible that Robert was like that, but he never did show it."

It's incredible that so many people should remember Robert Johnson, describe him accurately, talk about him, tell us of weeks or months spent in his company, and yet leave us with such a vague and incomplete picture. They mentioned his concern over his guitar, his sudden departures, his inwardness, and his rash behavior over women—but they never quite showed us the man, and as the interview progressed they shook their heads, puzzled themselves at the curiously empty picture. After studying all these published interviews, the conclusion was that it just wasn't reasonable. These musicians claimed they associated with Robert Johnson not once but many times. Surely, then, they could say more.

I have had the opportunity to interview, under unhurried, almost ideal circumstances, many of the same eighteen musicians whose comments had appeared in print. They were approached with the idea of starting fresh, confident that a fuller picture of Robert Johnson could be elicited.

Robert Lockwood Jr. said: "He was a quiet type of person, and you'd never get to know him easily. Maybe you'd never get to know him at all."

Walter Horton said: "He was after my sister. He was always around here and there. I traveled up and down the line with him, but I never got to where I knew him, except to know when you wasn't watching, he'd leave."

Sunnyland Slim said: "He was just a guy. An exceptional music man but just an ordinary guy."

Roosevelt Sykes said: "We went on that trip together but I never did him no attention. He didn't want you to know him."

It was a theme endlessly repeated by musicians who associated with Robert Johnson. They talked around him, not about him. They knew little or nothing of his home, his family, whether he'd ever married or had children. They rarely ever recall any of his songs except those which appeared on record. In most instances, in fact, they seem to recall his records—"Terraplane Blues" and "I Believe I'll Dust My Broom" and "Walking Blues" in particular—better than the man himself performing.

There's reason to be skeptical of this, as to whether they knew him to the extent they claim, yet there is the same vagueness, the same elusiveness about much of what was said at Commerce by people who had known him over much of his life. It's simply that he did or said little to reveal himself: we are left to accept the idea that his shy, inward manner left few distinct traces, however incredible this seems when it's first placed aside the compelling dynamism of his songs. But this is itself a cliché, the belief that the artist and his work are often but impossible to reconcile. The revelation is in the art, not in the person.

And there are other factors. Musicians are egoists who rarely take much interest in one another beyond the immediate and apparent things shared. Blues singers may speak well of musicians who belong to an older generation, one that preceded them, but they rarely have much to say about their contemporaries. But there are traces in all these interviews of the awe in which Johnson was held as a musician, as a performer able to command himself and his instrument into a complete expression.

Another consideration to be weighed is that of the people who knew Johnson—musicians or neighbors or whoever—nearly all of them fully subscribe to the idea that one speaks only well of the dead. Almost without exception the people I spoke with have known that Johnson was dead and knew that he had died young, in some violent way. Therefore, in speaking of him they tend to look for words of praise in the obscuring tone of a eulogy. There's too often the prevailing tendency for the spokesman to sum up Johnson with some complimentary generalization. They avoid the anecdote and the specific incident that might be revealing.

Here and there they give us hints and clues—Sonny Boy Williamson said, "I believe he was just more taken with music than any other person I ever came across"—but they are too slight a structure on which to build an impression of the man.

When the opportunity came along for me to reinterview the musicians that others had talked with, they were all casual conversations—in the unlikely city of Montreal during a summerlong festival—over the period of a week or more, usually over a meal or chatting in a lounge chair and sometimes merely listening as the musicians talked and bragged among themselves. They were at ease, talking freely, but somehow where Robert Johnson was concerned each conversation reached the same limitation.

It was possible that the wrong questions were asked or the wrong person was asking them. I employed substitutes. Sunnyland Slim helped out. He asked other musicians what they knew about Robert Johnson. The responses were basically the same. Continuing the process, Dick Spottswood reinterviewed the same St. Louis pianist, Henry Townsend, taking advantage of his appearance at a festival outside Washington, DC. A tape of the conversation has the familiar pattern. Townsend gropes for words, turns back to explain and talk about himself, and says of Robert Johnson, "He may have been a little out of the ordinary. He was a quiet kind of person . . . his quietness was *unusual*. He could sit for hours if nobody said anything to him." Yet, Townsend explained, he was cordial and amiable when somebody did talk to him. He didn't gamble or hustle people. He avoided arguments and ignored overbearing people. Townsend never saw him angry. When Spottswood asked him about the themes of despair and loneliness and death and the dealings with the devil that dominate Johnson's songs, he could only speculate about himself, saying that since his own songs came out of his experience, then Johnson's songs came out of his experience, whatever it was. The answer was an inversion of the question asked: "There was something in his life that would cause him to be coming out with (those songs)."

An outline of his travels, a piece of family history, a glimpse of him smiling at a girl would contribute to the illusion of understanding him. In this regard, the interviews offered several clues and leads to follow. Johnny Shines spoke of a trip he'd made with Johnson ending up in Redwater, Texas; Walter Horton told of a time in Chicago; Sunnyland Slim told of seeing him in Helena and West Helena and Mississippi as well. Henry Townsend went home to Cairo, Illinois, several times and heard that Johnson had been there a few days before. Roosevelt Sykes made a trip from St. Louis to some Louisiana piney woods town with him. Dave Edwards knew him in Itta Bena, Mississippi, and said Johnson spoke of having been in Oklahoma. Johnny Shines expanded his account of his travels with Robert Johnson, and now New Jersey and the Dakotas were included.

But through it all there was a focus. They were all accounts of travels from and then back to the Delta. If you left him in East St. Louis, you'd meet up with him again in some Delta town. The focus was Helena and Hughes, Arkansas; and Friars Point, Tunica, and Greenwood, Mississippi.

Several interviews correctly named Robinsonville as the town where his family lived and several named Greenwood as the town where he was killed. They were mentioned along with practically every other town in that part of the Delta and got lost in the shuffle. They stand out now, looking back with hindsight.

What is clear in hindsight is Son House's testimony was not as fully appreciated as it warranted—not with respect to the specific details he tried to pass along.

Son House is a dark, deep-brown man with a courtly air and a kind of nervousness born of stress and poor health. He wears a black string tie, dresses with a kind of formality, and moves with both the grace and bearing of a man whose shoulders are stooped but who's gained some wisdom and a certain contentment. In recent years he's traveled large patches of the world performing in a style that appears to precede that of Robert Johnson: with a little finger stuck in a bottleneck or a metal tube that whines or cries over the strings of a metal-bodied guitar, underscoring the clenched, repetitious words of songs filled with sharp, nasal trembling tones, as if strained at some brink of emotion. During a performance Son House can work himself into a trancelike state with an intensity and thrust that holds, perhaps even hypnotizes an audience. On occasion the endings of his songs have met with total silence, the kind of silence that wears away only gradually and the applause coming then, slowly, as Son House himself remains stark upright in his chair, rocking tensely, still caught in the mood and presence of the song just dying away.

In 1964 Son House was living quietly in Rochester, New York, blissfully unaware of the fact that people were looking for him and that there was a small clique of people in nearby New York City who treasured the few recordings he had made for Paramount Records in 1930 and for the Library of Congress in 1941 and 1942. A group of collectors finally traced him through a search that took them to Mississippi and then back to Rochester, a successful quest that came as a climax to several years of intense searching in a period when not only blues singers but also musicians from Appalachian traditions had been sought out, recorded, and heard again.

As a result, a rather befuddled Son House found himself thrust into a world of concert halls and coffeehouses and festivals where eager young audiences listened with rapt attention, finding an affinity with this aged man from Mississippi. Part of that respect was because he had endured. He had come out of Mississippi's shacks and grown up speaking to white women only with his eyes carefully studying the ground at their feet. He had been the victim of the intolerable social order, and yet he and his music had endured, and now he had come forward as if to say the human spirit is full and the passion ceaseless. The very presence of Son House is an affirmation, and the young people with their long hair found in him a kind of reassurance, and they sat listening to this old man with a reverence born partly of a wish to taste some of what thrives outside their own suburbs, partly of compassion, and partly of the sweeping power of his songs even now, past the artist's prime.

Son House had played in the Delta from 1927 onward, traveling with other musicians and drinking buddies to plantations typically in the vicinity of where he lived. He remained a working man and described himself as "a Saturday night music man" to distinguish himself from those ramblers who held no day job and did nothing but play music.

He remembers Robert Johnson coming around to these frolics to listen and watch. Son House makes no particular claim to teaching Robert Johnson, but the relationship appears self-evident: "All that was up in Tunica County, you see, where I'd go to play . . . this boy Robert would come. There at Banks, Mississippi, and there to those other places. One place out there was called the Kirby Plantation and another was the Murphy. He'd come to them." All the places he named are in Beat 1.

Son House often told the story about young Robert Johnson coming around, listening, pestering him, trying to play his guitar. "He couldn't do nothing then. Nothing hardly but just bang on it," he said. "But a little later he come back. A few months it was, and I hadn't seen him, and he come back and challenged me. He said, 'I want you to listen here.'"

Recalling the story in 1965, the details still seemed fresh in his mind. He leaned forward with his left hand chopping at the air, trying to describe the crowded party house and the youngster pestering him, until he finally gave in and let him have his guitar. "He picked it up and he started in and he scared me. He could play so much, and he'd gotten it in just that little bit of time."

Son House's explanation of this was supernatural: "He was better than most that's been music people their whole life. You see, there wasn't no normal way he could have done that. He just came back and he had this power of music in him." He paused before going on. "What I believe is, he must have got it from the devil."

That story, or parts of it, have been published several times as Son House told it to different interviewers—he told Pete Welding that Johnson must have "sold his soul to the devil in exchange for learning to play like that"—and the published accounts all agree substantially on this event.

The story of this Faustian transaction tended to overshadow what else Son House had to say about Robert Johnson. He said that Johnson had left home after an argument with his stepfather, and he went on to name the plantation. Some of his interviewers, however, had trouble understanding and transcribing his accent. In one instance an interviewer named the plantation "Lellman," and in another it was "Letter-man."

So, now, looking back on what Son House told us we are faced with certain details he offered about Robert Johnson. The mention of the stepfather is a good index to the nearness, the accuracy, and the near-accuracy of Son House's information. He said that Johnson had been known as "Saunders." He was wrong, but close. He'd simply confused one common name for another, remembering "Saunders" instead of "Spencer."

Son House offered every clue needed to lead directly to the Leatherman Plantation. It needed no long journey or years of quest and questions. It could have been as simple as asking the long-distance operator for information for Tunica, Mississippi, and then requesting the number of a "Lellman" or "Letter-man," slurring it a bit so the operator would have to decide what the precise name was. That alone would have done it. In the tiny Tunica directory the only names that could possibly sound like those are a Mrs. William Leatherman at Robinsonville and an S. R. Leatherman at Commerce, Mississippi.

It probably needn't go that far. A local operator would have known immediately. Leatherman is a well-known name in that part of the world. And that of course is one reason that men like Son House are often not understood by

162

outsiders. When they travel, they bring their world with them, its music and its important names. When Son House talks to you, he expects *you* to know who a Leatherman is, much the same as a New Yorker expects you to know a Rocke-feller. So the failure is sometimes because it's hard for outsiders to get into Son House's world.

Looking back with chagrin and apology, it's plain that Son House did his damnedest to tell us about Robert Johnson's home and where his family lived. Where and how he died remained another mystery entirely.

• • •

II

GREENWOOD

Towns in the Delta look alike. They're built to the same plan, stretching along the four-foot hump of a railroad, the shops all facing the tracks, sometimes on both sides, often on only one side. Cleveland and Belzoni and Come and Itta Bena are all like this. They're simply loading depots for the plantations, a point from where cotton is shipped and where tractor parts and fertilizers are sold.

Just as the towns look alike, the land too is all the same. The fields are flat, leveled as if by a carpenter's plane, and as you drive through it suggests a maze of well-groomed, well-attended tabletops. Cotton needs a lot of room—an unexceptional plantation runs to a thousand acres—but even while diversified now to include soybeans and alfalfa, it still hews to the original design. Somewhere near the center of each of these plantations is a "headquarters"—the complex of a gin, sheds, workshop, office, and the compound of "big houses" for the owner and overseers. A bit away from the headquarters there's a row of identical shacks, built for sharecroppers and deserted now that mechanization rules the land. At one end, probably at the end nearest the highway or good road where it can pick up some additional trade, there's a plantation store, and not far away a church. Away from the church and away from most everything else except another row of shacks, you will find a jukehouse or party house. It's bigger than the other shacks with a barbecue pit in back and a big, cleared room large enough for dancing. The man who lives here runs the party house and sees to the social life of the workers.

The information I had indicated that Robert Johnson had died somewhere in Leflore County (area: 592 square miles), somewhere outside the corporate limits of Greenwood itself. Since 1961 I had tracked rumors placing Robert Johnson's death in at least thirteen different towns, from San Antonio to Bogalusa, Louisiana, but by 1969 all signs were pointing to LeFlore. I ordered the death certificates of many "Robert Johnsons" along the way and now held a copy of what I believed to be the correct one, filed in the county on August 18th, 1938.

A broad, cool river makes several looping bends as it runs through Leflore County, practically turning back on itself. It's called the Tallahatchie River where it runs along the northern edge of Greenwood, but then after another loop that brings it back through the heart of town it's mysteriously renamed the Yazoo River. Greenwood is bigger than most of the Delta towns; it's well away from Memphis and is a market center for its own piece of the middle Delta. Mississippi's largest cotton exchange is here, and several blocks along Front Street are given over to cotton factories and brokers whose office windows overlook the Yazoo River.

It was dark when I got to town and turned off Highway 82 to go bumping around over railroad tracks in the quiet darkened streets. After a while I found a motel and checked in, telling them I didn't know how long I'd be staying.

A lean man of indeterminate age brought some ice to the room, and after a little small talk he confirmed that he had been living here in 1938. He said he'd never heard of a musician named Robert Johnson. I had the idea he was lying, but I decided I was simply over anxious to get into it and frustrated by the fact that it was too late at night to start.

I crawled in bed and pulled the phone book out of a bedside drawer. I opened it to the yellow pages and stared at the listings under "planters." I wondered which one I was looking for.

In the morning, after breakfast, I decided to start with the funeral parlors to see if any of them had had any part in burying him. It was possible that a mortician would have an idea of the cause of death, which the death certificate itself had significantly omitted. There were four Black funeral parlors in town. I visited each of them in turn and found remarkable the theater that the morticians were required to keep up to assure concerned white locals that the town's corpses remained segregated. The facilities of some of the funeral parlors indeed were entirely separate, but in others a funeral parlor in a converted house simply advertised two different names, with two different entrances and morticians, while sharing the same facilities for the preparation and storage of the dead.

The Black morticians were all helpful and pulled out dusty old ledgers to check and search their files. One man called several retired morticians who in turned checked the records they'd kept. Still it came to nothing, and I gave up on this line of inquiry altogether. One of the men I'd met was so helpful and interested that when I thanked him and mentioned that I was going to go take a look at the town, he insisted on joining. "I'll drive and you'll get a better look," he said, motioning me toward his car.

It was a rather strange tour, a Black mortician driving around and enthusiastically pointing out to me large southern mansions. It didn't seem strange to him. He shrugged and said, "It's my town." He turned out to be a history buff and told me the place had been named for a leader of the Choctaw Nation named Greenwood Leflore. Lefore became unhappy with the town and started another, competitive cotton market farther upstream on the river. "That was back in the days when cotton left out of here by riverboat, of course." He showed me Front Street and said there used to be seventeen saloons there, all in a row, but they were gone now. We crossed the Yazoo bridge, and he showed me the Provine mansion and talked about how it had featured recently as a setting for a film adaptation of William Faulkner's *The Reivers*. To make the place look like 1905, he recalled, they covered TV antennas with branches and the street with sand to hide the pavement. "I never knew it was such a lot of work," he commented. He pointed to where actors drove up and down the street in a yellow Winton Flyer while people were playing croquet on the house's front lawn.

After that he drove me on Grand Boulevard to the edge of town and showed me a bridge that crossed the river. It was a streamlined concrete span with nothing extraordinary about it. The mortician told me it was the bridge made famous by Bobbie Gentry's hit song "Ode to Billie Joe." We talked some about it—he told me where the Carroll County picture show was, but he wasn't sure about the location of Choctaw Ridge.

Gradually I coaxed him into taking me back into the center of town, and we parked on Johnson Street facing the railroad tracks. We sat there awhile, and he introduced me to some people who came along and then left for an appointment. I walked back to the funeral home, got my car, and came back to Johnson Street, parked there, and let the rear door hang open. Some of the same men were still hanging around, and gradually I worked the conversation around to what I wanted to know.

The part of Johnson Street we were on is a row of old wooden two-story buildings built right at the edge of the broad sidewalk. There's some cafes and pool halls mixed in with rooming houses. Every few feet along the sidewalk edge there's a wooden box or a chair or high concrete stop where people sit, chatting

The Tallahatchie Bottoms near Greenwood, Mississippi.
Photograph by Robert "Mack" McCormick.

with one another or passers-by. I knew I was in the right place when one man who I'd asked nothing more than whether he'd ever heard of a musician named Robert Johnson, suddenly backed off and said, "I don't know nothing about that stuff." What stuff?

Even though at first I didn't mention a killing or anything of the kind, several men who stopped to talk clearly interpreted the question that way.

At one point there were two men sitting in the back seat of my car, passing around a bag-wrapped bottle I'd provided, and talking about different musicians they'd heard over the years. One of them turned to me, asking, "That fellow you mentioned, he made records didn't he?"

I nodded.

"They killed him, didn't they?"

I nodded again.

"Sure they did," he said. "They killed him out at Star of the West."

"Where's that?" I asked him.

He waved a hand vaguely and said, "Just a place. Place you call Star of the West." The name rang a bell with me because only the night before I'd read myself

Parking by the tracks on Johnson Street, Greenwood, Mississippi.
Photograph by Robert "Mack" McCormick.

to sleep with a local guidebook that described an old steamship named *Star of the West*. The mortician had mentioned it as well. It was a two-deck, oceangoing sidewheeler built by Cornelius Vanderbilt in 1852 and eventually chartered by the federal government. The ship drew the first shots fired in the Civil War on January 9, 1861, when it had attempted to carry supplies and reinforcements to Fort Sumter. A few months later, in a dazzling bluff carried off by three cavalrymen off the Texas coast, the Confederates captured the vessel and used it for a time as a hospital ship. Then in 1863, when General Grant had tried to get through Yazoo Pass and come at Vicksburg through the back door, the Confederates brought *Star of the West* up the Yazoo River to Greenwood, and then up the Tallahatchie to a point above town, where they sunk it across the river to block Grant's ships. *Star of the West* nearly was the history of the Civil War, but what did it have to do with Robert Johnson?

"It happened to him years back," the man continued. "Out to Star of the West. Someone gave him bad whiskey." He took a sip from the bottle and passed it. "It was over some woman."

He leaned out of the car and called to someone walking by, "Hey, Lucas!" The man stopped, walked over, and joined the group. The man who'd called him

168

over introduced him as someone who had been present the night it had happened. Lucas asked, "When what had happened?" "You know," the man replied, "back when that guitar player got poisoned."

Lucas said, "You mean over there across the river?"

"That's what I'm talking about. Years back."

"Sure I was—" Lucas stopped. "Well, I know about it, but I wasn't there."

"Now, goddamn, Lucas, you always said you was right there."

"Not me," Lucas countered. "I wasn't there and I'll tell you why I wasn't there. I'm never any place where such as that goes on. You can bet on it. And if I am there, I'm blind. If I was there and if I talk about it, I might be the next one drinking something poisoned. So I wasn't there, you understand me?"

Lucas and his friend both eased out of the car and walked on after bidding me goodbye with traces of a sly grin. After they'd walked away a few steps, Lucas's friend hurried back just for a moment. "He was there," he said.

Within another half-hour or so a few more people gathered around the car, talking. One of these men wasn't as guarded as Lucas. On the contrary, he bragged that he had been no more than twenty feet away when it had happened. He'd seen the man who'd done it and everything. "The guy warned him, you see, he'd said to him 'Don't touch my woman,' but this was one of those real nice-looking guitar players and he couldn't leave women alone. So the guy killed him. Gave him a drink with something in it."

In the next hour I heard the same story twice more from people who knew of it, and once from another man who'd been an eyewitness. They all agreed the motive was jealousy and that the woman involved had aggravated the situation in every way she could. The familiar element came up in most of the stories.

"The man told him," the eyewitness said, "'stop messing with her,' but this musician wasn't going to take that. The man told him, 'I'm going to kill you,' but the guy doesn't leave off. See, the man was sneaky about it. The guitar player probably was watching out for a gun or a knife, but the man didn't do that. He took advantage of Robert's nature. You know he was like all musicians when they get to playing and drinking, and he'd be too lit up to pay attention to everything that happened. The man killed him as easy as you please."

After a while I had enough of this to give me a fairly complete picture of exactly what had happened. I began to see the textures of the room and the crowd itself. But I drove away without learning the location. I telephoned the helpful mortician and asked about Star of the West.

"It's a ship they sunk in a bend of the river."

"What about a *place* with the same name?" I asked.

"Oh, yes. Right there where they sunk the boat, the plantation that's in the bend of the river there is called 'Star of the West.' The 'Wade Place,' it's called, too. Run by L. W. Wade."

I looked in the phone book again and saw the name listed. That was the place I wanted. "You were looking right at it a while ago," the mortician said. "You just go right over the Tallahatchie bridge and soon as you get across, make a left turn, and follow the road along the river. That's it."

As I drove across the arch of the high concrete span I got a quick look at a spread of wet fields hemmed in by a loop of the river. I turned onto the river road and drove along it for a mile or so, passing a yard where half a dozen vast red wire cotton wagons were stored before reaching the headquarters. The gin was in

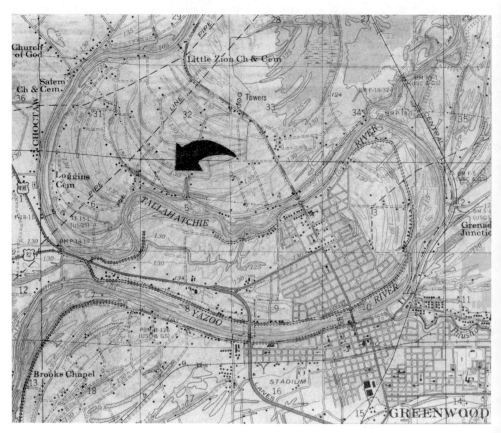

McCormick's arrow on this topography map indicates
the location of the Star of the West plantation.

170

Jimmy Edward's home, with the L. W. Wade gin in the background.
Photograph by Robert "Mack" McCormick.

a red brick building with giant ducts off to the side. It was quiet and deserted. The place seemed extraordinarily neat and well-tended. I drove back and stopped at a house, where the people inside directed me to another house nearby with a screened-in porch. The mailbox outside had the number 393 and the name James Jones on it. The man I found there, however, introduced himself as Jimmy Edwards and said he lived in what until recently had been the party house.

I asked about Robert Johnson. "That was the name of that guitar player that died down at Tush Hog's house," he said. "He was a stranger among us."

Jimmy Edwards and some neighbors helped fill in the story, at least a bald outline of it. Some years ago a guitar player had come here and stayed with Tush Hog, a local musician who lived on the Wade place. He'd fallen sick one night and was ill for a week or longer. Maybe two or three weeks. People had carried him into Greenwood to see a doctor and then brought him back out here. A little while later he'd died.

I asked about someone named Jim Moore. His name had appeared on the death certificate as the informant, which usually is the closest relative available. There'd been a sharecropper named Jim Moore on the Wade place years ago, and then—after they talked about it for a while—some of the people agreed that when the guitar player had first showed up, he stayed at Tush Hog's house, but then after he got sick he might have stayed with Jim Moore. They thought they could have been related, maybe first cousins.

When I asked how he'd died, there wasn't much response. Here, where it had happened, there was hesitance to pursue the subject.

One of the people said, "I don't think any of us know exactly except that at that time there was a party house here run by a man named 'Smokey Hamber,' and that was where all the music and women hung around in those days. Used to be lots more people on the place back then."

"Anyhow, this guitar player was there one night playing music and he stood up all of a sudden, grabbed his belly and said, 'I'm poisoned,' and then fell over.

"Well, the people carried him out of there and he just stayed sick, sinking down, until he was gone."

He told me the building itself was gone. "Tornado carried it off a few years later. Had to rebuild all this."

The house where he died is gone too, they explained, saying it was over in a section known as the Deadening.

The word was new to me, and I found out that it came from a method of clearing land used years ago, where trees were killed by girdling the trunks and letting them die slowly and then rot. It was a labor-saving method for someone who could wait a few years to clear extra land. They used this method to clear the bottoms along the river at the west side of the property.

It's all clean and cleared land now, but the name stuck. As they were telling me about this I watched a white El Dorado inching along the road toward where we were standing. One of the people waved and the car crawled to a stop. I went over and introduced myself to Luther Wade, owner of Star of the West. He's a thick-necked man who sees the world through spectacles with heavy lenses. He looked to be in poor health. Tiny veins in his face seemed distressed.

He was puzzled at my interest but cooperative. He said he couldn't recall a musician who had died there but admitted that he didn't pay much attention to that sort of thing. He remembered Tush Hog and enjoyed listening to him play, but like the other people, he couldn't remember his real name. "Some people, you know, never have anything but a nickname. That's all you ever hear."

Luther Wade is still preoccupied with the central problem of a Delta land-lord. "These days it's all this damn hourly-wage stuff," he complained. "Got to pay a man for every hour he works." He waved to some of the houses along the

172

Little Zion Missionary Baptist Church, Leflore County, Mississippi.
Photograph by Robert "Mack" McCormick.

road, "This used to be a good place for a man to come with his family and share-crop for me. Now it's all tractors and that hourly-wage stuff."

He told me to go ahead and ask around as much as I wished, and the Cadillac went inching off down the road as Mr. Wade looked over his well-shrubbed estate. People had backed away, sensing a slight tension building up as I talked with Luther Wade. But when he left it eased off, and the people came back over to offer me additional memories. Two people admitted they'd been present when Robert Johnson had "gotten sick," but unlike the men on Johnson Street, they were much more cautious about describing it as homicide. They started exchanging glances with one another, so I backed off the subject.

They told me he had been buried at the Little Zion Church cemetery and pointed out the road that would take me there. It was a couple of miles away, just north of the Wade place and near the river. I drove to it and found a cemetery in a grove of bare trees. The trees had their trunks whitewashed about two feet high. It was in disrepair, and most of the graves were unmarked. I looked at the wet lumpy earth and the tangle of weeds and got back in my car. There was nothing for me here.

On Tuesday morning I decided to take a look at the official Leflore County records. People around Greenwood seemed to treasure history and it was possible that some of this reverence would be reflected in the local bureaucracy. I anticipated finding dusty but neatly kept ledgers full of official transactions as I climbed in the car that morning.

The Leflore County Courthouse is a pile of gray stones on the banks of the Yazoo River. The halls are high echoing tunnels where footsteps have the clattering sound of rain on a tin roof. In these halls county employees asserted the various legal powers that had to do with death and taxation. I was charmed by the name on the sign for the Chancery Clerk's office: Noel L. McCool. I tried his office first.

There was a small, gray-haired lady there who came over to where I was standing and asked if she could help me. I showed the death certificate and asked if she could direct me to any additional records bearing on the event. She bent to peer at the document and after studying it long enough to digest the essentials, exclaimed "Goodness!" She shook her head vigorously. "This isn't at all proper." She had one of those pleasant, soothing southern accents.

We agreed that the document was a travesty. The purpose of a death certificate is, by law, to make a public record of the fact, the circumstances, and the cause of death. In this case the machinery had gone through the motions, but only to produce a document that satisfied little more than its own bureaucratic need to fill out forms. Robert Johnson's death certificate gives no hint of what brought death to a man in his middle twenties. Across the right side of the sheet, the side reserved for the medical details, someone had written "No Doctor" and let it go at that.

"Of course," the lady said, "It was thirty-one years ago. That's a long time."

I agreed that it was.

"Still, it isn't proper to treat things that way."

She suggested I go across the hall to the Circuit Clerk's office, where the records of inquests pertaining to unusual deaths would be kept. I took another look around trying to spot Noel L. McCool, then thanked her and took her advice. Across the hall the people were friendly and helpful. After some peering and stooping to read the labels on old file drawers, they found the right one and learned there had been no inquest on a Robert Johnson, nor on any Johnson, during the month of August 1938. They looked in several other places, with the same results. A young lady who'd taken her time studying the record seemed a bit intrigued by the fact that the dead man was listed as a musician. "Back then they weren't always too concerned about how people died," she said handing the paper back. "It's been a long time, you know."

"I know."

A man in the office came up alongside her and in a tone of voice that meant that he was just giving an opinion, speculated on what might have happened. "It looks like he died and his people just buried him and that was all there was to it." He pointed out that that was pretty common at the time.

If that truly was the case, I wondered how a death certificate came to be filed at all.

"Probably someone here at the courthouse got word of it and got the next-of-kin to come in and fill out the form, and that was all there was to it."

He continued to offer his opinion. I told him I'd tried to locate the Jim Moore who was listed as the informant, and the best anyone could tell me is that he died too, about ten or fifteen years ago.

"About the only person left is the one who signed the document as registrar. Cornelia J. Jordan."

He shook his head. "I'm not sure she's left either. I've never heard of her."

"Let's assume you're right about the way it was handled," I said. "What office would have been responsible for filing the document?"

He told me it would be the county health department, which now was located in an annex across the street. It was a newer building and the people there seemed less inclined to help me out. A tall waspish lady glanced up from her typewriter, pursed her lips, and said I'd be better off to write a letter to the proper department in the state capital in Jackson.

I explained that I already had all that the state office could provide and that I wanted to find their local records, and particularly some supplemental information.

"Well, I wasn't working here that long ago," the lady explained. She waved at some coworkers. "None of us were."

"But you do keep records?"

She said that they sent everything to Jackson. It was hard to believe that they wouldn't even keep a copy for their own records, but that's what she maintained. About half of the things in the world are hard to believe, however, so I shrugged and asked for the name of the county coroner in 1938.

"That's something else you'd best write Jackson for," she told me. I stared at her to see if she was trying to give me a hard time. I decided she was simply one of those government bureaucrats who refer every inquiry to some other place.

I asked her to get in touch with the present coroner and ask if he knew who had the job in 1938. After some hunting of telephone numbers, she got a hold of James Hankins at one of the local funeral parlors. She handed me the phone, and Hankins confirmed that he had no idea of who was coroner that long ago. I asked if there was any possibility that someone kept supplemental notes or records pertaining to this death.

"Not that I can imagine," the coroner said, "Unless maybe the clerk who made the record kept something."

The office workers talked it over among themselves and decided they didn't know anything about Cornelia J. Jordan either. One of them said, "I've heard the name, but I don't think you'll find her now." She shrugged as if to suggest that even if I did find her there wasn't much hope that she would remember anything about filing this form. She concluded, "It looks to me that no one ever found out what happened to this young man."

"No one in the *courthouse* may have learned," I said. "It's generally agreed around town that he was murdered."

They looked a little startled at that. Then the tall waspish one in front said, "If it was a case of a suspicious death, then that's the sheriff's business." She looked pleased now that she'd found somewhere else to send me.

I went back across the street and found the sheriff's office. There was a loud conversation in the doorway of the office, a deputy arguing with a state highway patrol officer. The deputy turned to me impatiently, and I introduced myself. He nodded, and I started to explain what I needed. When he got the gist of it, he interrupted, "When was that?"

I told him.

"Christ, I wasn't here then. That's over thirty years ago."

"Yes, I know."

I asked him if there were any records of investigations conducted then.

"I don't know," he said. After I asked him to check, he went off to look inside some file cabinets and talk to another deputy. They both came back. "We can't find anything that far back. Nothing."

I thanked him and asked if I could see the sheriff.

They told me he was out of town. I left the office and walked out of the building. I stood outside for a while, staring at the water of the Yazoo River, and decided to let it go for now. I checked out of the motel and left town.

Over the next several months I continued running things down. I learned a lot about the three Equen brothers, for example: Earle, Standard, and Murdock.

One was a doctor in Atlanta, and another ran the big plantation at Winter City now owned by his daughter. Earle Equen had worked as an insurance agent except for four years, from 1936 through 1939, when he had served as sheriff of Leflore County. It was a reasonable assumption that the sheriff at the time, even if it had not become a matter of record, knew about the incident at Star of the West. But his widow told me that Earle Equen had died in 1953.

The next spring I drove back to Greenwood, partly to follow some leads I'd developed by mail and telephone, and partly to confirm the story I'd heard before. Testimony about any event, particularly an event over thirty years in the past, is altered and shaded by each person's memory. Away from Greenwood the stories had a legendary quality that hinged on the supernatural. Here where it had happened, the story was more prosaic, and it was fleshed out by certain recurring details.

After some digging and the long careful listening that a stranger has to do to set people at ease, once again I heard essentially the same story. It was not, after all, an unknown event. Robert Johnson had stood up in a dance hall filled with over a hundred people, clutched his body and called out, "I'm poisoned." Plenty of people had witnessed the event and talked about it. After he had died, it remained intensely talked about it, albeit guardedly.

What I'd learned put me in a curious position. Having knowledge of an apparent crime, I was obliged to report it. I didn't expect they'd do anything about it, but there's no statute of limitations on murder. After another day of talking and listening to people in and around Greenwood, I drove back to the big dark stone courthouse and walked down the corridor to the sheriff's department, where I asked to see Sheriff Arterbury. While waiting, I studied the usual collection of FBI circulars, a hardware store calendar, some public notices, and the filing cabinets that apparently contained nothing of Leflore County's history beyond a few recent years.

"You can go in now," a deputy told me.

I walked through a door and shook hands with Sheriff John Arterbury. He seemed to be a bland, easygoing sort of man, nothing like the stereotype of the fat redneck southern sheriff. He asked what he could do to help me.

Once again I handed over the death certificate, and asked him to study it. I noticed the photostat was getting a little worn looking from all the public officials who'd been handling it. He finished with it and looked up at me inquiringly.

"For some time I've been following rumors that a man named Robert Johnson was murdered," I told him. "The rumors led to that death certificate and that led me here to Leflore County."

The sheriff nodded, waiting for me to go on.

"Since I've been here I've been frustrated trying to understand what the official procedures might have been back in 1938." The sheriff looked a little surprised when I mentioned the year. He glanced down at the death certificate.

"Of course, I wasn't the sheriff back then, but I'll try to help."

"The facts seem to be simply this: a man was poisoned, he died, then people boxed him up and buried him. Yet nowhere in the whole courthouse can I find anything about the incident or what official interest it might have aroused."

He looked at me for a moment with that blank stare that even part-time lawmen acquire. "Where you'd get your information?"

I told him that one particular eyewitness account had checked out thoroughly. Two other people confirmed a portion of the story, agreeing in substance. I talked to over a dozen people who either were present or had some general knowledge of the incident. "In short," I said, "among people of the right age group, it's common knowledge."

"I see."

"My question is, has your office done anything about it?"

He hesitated and said, "I'll check on it, of course." He paused. "Of course, there's no way I can explain what went on back then. I expect things were done a lot differently around here thirty years ago, especially where some people were concerned."

I described my previous visit and asked if he would double-check his files. He left and returned after a few minutes, shaking his head. "That's about it," he said. I asked if there was anyone in the sheriff's department who'd been here at the time Sheriff Equen had the job. Again he shook his head. "I'm sorry we can't help you."

"No, you've helped me a great deal."

"How's that?"

"Now I know how it feels to report a murder."

He looked at me for a while, then smiled amiably. "Of course, you could make out a complaint, if you're a witness." He paused. "Or you could give us a deposition giving us the names of witnesses."

"No names," I said. "I'm sure you're perfectly capable of locating your own witnesses. A Black deputy could do it just by talking to old-timers along Johnson Street."

"Let me think about it a little," he said.

The thing that bothered me was the indifference that colored everything here. No one had said "So what?" or "Who cares?" On the contrary, they had been patient and polite and utterly indifferent. Sheriff Arterbury simply was waiting for me to leave. He could have at least made a note of the facts I'd described or had a copy made of the death certificate I'd shown him. The difficulty with law-and-order people is that they're so selective in the application. This murder was too old to pursue, yet there's men at Parchman still serving prison sentences for crimes that are thirty years old.

"The last time I heard of Leflore County, it had to do with the same kind of thing."

"What's that?" the sheriff asked.

"Another murder where nothing was done."

Sheriff Arterbury shifted and sat upright in his chair. "Emmett Till?" He asked me. "That the one you're thinking of?"

Leflore County had produced an international furor back in 1955 when a Black fourteen-year-old boy was accused of making some overtures toward a white woman tending a country store at Money, Mississippi. The incident had occurred just seven miles north of Star of the West plantation. A few nights later two men had abducted the boy, and subsequently his gunshot, maimed body turned up in the Tallahatchie River. The woman's husband and his half-brother were tried for the murder in the adjacent town, where the actual killing had occurred. That jury refused to convict, and subsequently a Leflore County grand jury had refused to indict them for the kidnapping itself.

A tight, strained smile crossed the sheriff's face.

I stood up and thanked him for his time. "I think I've been picking on you, sheriff. I hope you'll forgive me."

He came around the desk and walked me to the door. "I hope you find whatever it is that you're after," he said.

"I will. All I want is a little glimpse of what happened." I stopped and turned back to face him. "In other parts of the world, it is thought that we Americans are innocent people. Places like Mississippi and men like Robert Johnson tend to alter that a fraction."

The sheriff gave me a hard look, then retrieved his smile, and stood there as I walked out the door.

It was a late Friday night in July and a hotbox room pushed full of working people and their sweat and their music.

In the kitchen a woman was selling pork sandwiches and bottles of soda water. Behind the house, just off the path leading to the privies, a scarred man was selling mugs of Choctaw beer for a dime and small unlabeled bottles of whiskey for a quarter. Inside the house everything was tinted blue by the thick smoke haze.

The guitar player was a stranger who'd been in the area a couple of weeks. He was known to a few of the people because of some records he'd made, but during the early evening he had played for the dancers, not so much the songs on his records, but snapping, straightforward dance music and some poor-me blues that necessarily were part of his repertoire. There had been another musician, a local farmer, playing with him part of the time. They had alternated, or occasionally helped one another out with a bass line and then gotten together on a breakdown or some piece of hokum.

He sat against one wall with some crowded table jammed at one side of him. On the other a cleared part of the floor was filled with people dancing close and moving their bodies against each other. There were some men who danced alone in an exhibition style. They ignored the other dancers and appropriated the space they needed. Around the edges of the room was a lot of movement, people drifting in and out of other rooms, threading their way out to buy food or drinks. The guitar player was in a straight-backed chair that sat on two soda bottle cases that had been overturned to make a small platform. Behind him a guitar case lay open with some square packets of extra strings at the ready. Underneath the chair there were some bottles and mugs. From time to time he reached down to lift one up to his lips. He was a drinker, but it didn't affect him a great deal. There was an open window nearby where people outside stopped to listen, chat, or pass in a drink for the guitar player.

Women in the edges of the crowd watched him, eyes measuring him and hunting his face, studying him as if to learn something. When the mood of the evening had shifted, he'd started singing his own songs more often, and he'd done some things to startle the listeners. Some of the songs had an accelerating frenzy that left people in his part of the room ringing around him and attentive. The rest of the room's crowd was farther away, concerned with other things. The singer would look directly at a woman close to him as he sang a song of invitation, and then at the end of it he'd lean toward her and say, "You know what I'm talking about now, baby?" It was not just a performer's device but something almost too direct and too personal, but he got away with it because it was late enough and the crowd was numbed.

The other guitar player was outside, playing for people dancing on the porch. The building was surrounded by people who'd moved outside for the cool air. There were young boys hanging around to hear the music and to spy on some of the couples moving in the shadows. People outside came up to the windows to watch and listen, feeling the waves of heat pressing out through the opening. They'd call out things to the musician or watch the woman who went over to him, bending over to whisper in his ear. The guitar player reached under his chair for another drink. He spilled more than he drank because the bottles would overturn as someone reached and groped for them. There was a little puddle on the floor that had run down from where a bottle overturned. It was customary to see that the musician always had a drink. The man who ran the house or the bootlegger outside would refill it, or someone in the crowd would press a fresh bottle on him. People are always putting money in a musician's pocket or giving him booze. In the blur of the evening the gifts and courtesies are a parade.

There was a contradiction between the singer and his songs. They were bold and extravagant. He was shy and inward, a smiling, amiable, remote figure who knew that women were watching him and who never pushed himself at them, but let them seek him out by coming over and whispering in his ear. Along the sides of the room a man was edging through the crowd, working his way through people he knew until he managed a position alongside the singer's chair. In a moment of excitement as the crowd and music reached a peak, he leaned in and placed a fresh bottle under the chair. There was nothing furtive about it. He just did it, and then the crowd shouldered him aside, and then the singer was reaching for the fresh bottle, sipping from it, hardly aware in the blur of the evening with its overpowering heat and excitement, and with the underlayer of whiskey he'd already drunk, what he was tasting. Bootleg whiskey is harsh stuff that varies from one batch to the next. It is all pop skull and red eye and white lightning. It bites and wrinkles the mouth and gags the throat.

Outside the young boys were listening, waiting for the music and savoring the adult things, watching as the crowd swelled and the night moved on, and the singer reached from time to time to drink from his bottle, setting it down more carefully so it wouldn't tip over like the last one.

• • •

AFTERWORD
John W. Troutman

Mack McCormick wrote this version of *Biography of a Phantom* in the early to mid-1970s. It is marked by evocative descriptions of landscapes, people, and conversations. It carries a self-effacing wit, as well as the heft of someone who pored over song lyrics, road maps, and small-town phone books, who trod up and down paved and dirt roads for hundreds of hours, who knocked on countless doors. Moments in the book command great suspense; others convey extraordinary beauty. Some convey humility and self-reflection; others are laced with a sense of superiority and disdain. McCormick wrote and rewrote the book several times over the course of the following forty years, but he never submitted it for publication.

The Robert "Mack" McCormick archive, now housed at the Smithsonian's National Museum of American History, enables researchers to study this work and to learn much more about his career and life than he likely ever would have allowed if he were alive today. Of course, this potentially is the case when any person's collection of deeply personal things—diaries, letters, poetry, emails, photographs—is gathered and dispersed when they pass away, or in some cases, when those things are delivered to a research institution for public study and scrutiny. McCormick had always assumed his archive would be collected by an institution, and he continued to explore and add to it, even in his final days. But he also seems never to have taken the time, even at the end, to prune it of documents that we assume he would have preferred not to share. Or perhaps he believed he had nothing to hide. What follows, drawn from the documents and notes found in the McCormick Collection, is an archivally driven reconstruction of the brutal aftermath—the bad dealings and tragedies that occurred in the wake of McCormick's research and writing of the manuscript. The manner by which we have chosen to detail and explore the tragedies exposed in the archive will represent just one of the dilemmas that this work has posed.

But this is nothing compared to the dilemmas that Carrie Thompson faced after McCormick found her. In the spring of 1972, McCormick had located her and Robert Johnson's other sister, Bessie Hines, living near one another in Maryland. He found them by searching phone books in the Washington, DC, metro area after learning from acquaintances in Mississippi that they had moved to the area decades before. They spoke by phone, and McCormick shared his interest in interviewing them for his book. In July 1972 he knocked on their doors, and after meeting them, he recorded hours of conversation in their homes. Thompson and Hines signed agreements with McCormick to provide stories for his book, which they hoped in turn would "call attention" to themselves as the rightful heirs to Johnson's estate.

McCormick, however, did not attempt to reconnect with her again until well over a year later. By then, according to Mrs. Annye Anderson, Carrie Thompson was experiencing added stress in her life: her son was not doing well, and she had become the caretaker for her sister Bessie Hines, who would soon pass away. In the midst of these challenges, Thompson had no idea what had happened in regard to McCormick's book or to some cherished family photographs that she and her sister had let him borrow after he promised to return them. She had been once hopeful that he could assist her in seeking royalties from Johnson's recordings, but now she was frustrated after McCormick seemed to have disappeared with her and her sister's property.

Unfortunately for Thompson, in June 1973 a second blues hunter, Steve LaVere, had located her. He visited her about a year into those sixteen months of waiting on a call from McCormick. She grew to trust LaVere, and she shared with him another photograph she had recently rediscovered in her things, from Memphis's Hooks Brothers Studio—a Black-owned business serving its local community—of Johnson wearing a pinstripe suit, holding his guitar. She loaned it to LaVere to make a copy of it at a nearby mall. He returned the photograph but kept the copy, interviewed her, and made plans to come back with an agreement in hand. When McCormick finally called her a few months later and learned of Thompson's visitor, he pleaded with her not to allow LaVere to scoop her story from him, arguing that she had signed an exclusive agreement.

Thompson was unconvinced by McCormick and was no longer willing to trust him. Meanwhile, Thompson had located yet *another* photograph, this one of Johnson in a photo booth with guitar in hand, a cigarette dangling from his mouth. As Mrs. Annye Anderson recounts in her book, LaVere pitched a book and, eventually, a new, comprehensive release of Johnson's music with the inclusion of these photographs and Carrie Thompson's stories to John Hammond, then vice president of Columbia Records. In November 1974, Thompson signed to LaVere all her rights to Johnson's recordings, photographs, and other materials in return for LaVere's presumably splitting all future royalties with her. Though she remained cautious about trusting LaVere, at least he was backed by a major record label. If even just a portion of the royalties were directed to Johnson's legal heir, which she assumed would be recognized as her, then her family finally would begin to receive the royalties that her brother himself never lived to collect.

McCormick was devastated by this turn of events. Up until this point, he had maintained stability and remained productive over the previous couple of years—perhaps too productive: on top of making significant progress on the book, he was sought after by the Smithsonian and other organizations to bring "the folk" to perform at their folklife festivals. Work was lining up for him, he had recently become a father, and under normal circumstances it should not have seemed at this juncture that his career and welfare—or even the success or failure of this book—would hinge on whether Thompson shared her story with someone else.

Yet, he plummeted into darkness—a place where he occasionally dwelled, as is amply documented in his archive. He carefully kept up and pruned his literal "enemies list," and at times throughout his life he would scribble down fantasies to play out in his mind. Sometimes they detailed plans to take someone down—often, someone close to him—who he believed had betrayed him. Phone call scripts appear in the archive, scrawled on loose paper. One script seems to depict an anonymous recovering heroin addict in San Benito, Texas, calling to tip off police about his pusher driving across the state for New Orleans in a Rambler with California tag BAF 10. It is next to a letter McCormick wrote to California-based Arhoolie Records owner Chris Strachwitz, demanding satisfaction over what McCormick deemed was a double-cross. Decades later, in a screed written but never delivered to Peter Guralnick and a handful of other unnamed people whom McCormick believed had betrayed him, he wrote, "In my fading years should I go from town to town hiring bone-breakers to put you fellows in rehab for 2 years? OR should you start thinking of ways toward redemption before my sentimental journey reaches your village? Wasn't it clear to you that I'm already in line to meet my maker with blood on my hands?"

These were McCormick's fantasies, built upon his delusions, often expressed eloquently, but never acted upon, as far as we know. Regardless, McCormick's first reaction following his learning about Thompson's cooperation with LaVere—and before he knew anything about a record release—was to return to his darkness. He scripted phone calls. In one, he impersonated a reverend in Baltimore, claiming to have a mutual friend who heard that Thompson was "double-dealing" and commanding her, "Purge yourself." In another menacing call script, he impersonated a police lieutenant from Texas, informing her that he had just released a suspect who said he had been offered $200 to drive to Maryland and burn down her house unless she kept "faith with the man from Texas." The lieutenant asked, "Frame House? Burn easily?" The script ended, "Let us know if your house is set afire."

There is no evidence that he carried out such phone calls, but then again, it did not really matter—the damage had been done by McCormick and LaVere in other ways. The stress and anxiety over having to deal with these two white men, takers, was affecting Thompson's health, including her sleep. In her book, Mrs. Annye Anderson shared a letter written a couple of years later from her sister Carrie Thompson, in which she described a disturbing dream:

> [Two] white men [near] my house, they got out and went behind their truck, one twirled a rope and it went around a man's neck, [he] fell to the ground . . . the truck pulled up a little and backed over the man. . . . I was in my drive way, saw it happened, tried to get the tag n[umber] . . . and ran back in the house thinking if he saw me that he might come back and kill me . . . when I got in side, they was a lot of hippys in here, and they were taking thangs out. Robert [Carrie's grandson] was here. . . . They had almost stripped the house but it didn't look like my house inside, they was shelves all around more like a store. . . . These guys were putting what they took out of the house in these cars. Funny, I didn't seam mad, I said to Robert, "they took just about every thang."

According to Anderson, Thompson in the letter then turned to LaVere: "I wish I had never got into it at all. . . . Just feel hopeless now, hate for the white man getting the benefit of what I should have, although according to God's word the unjust won't prosper."

THE LETTERS

In the years that followed, no one prospered. McCormick made sure of it. In April 1975, John Hammond cheerfully relayed to him the news of their impending June

1975 three-volume release of Johnson's music, "complete with his picture on the cover and extensive biographical information." Upon learning of this and feeling entitled to claim a greater right of ownership to Carrie Thompson's stories than anyone else, Mack quickly determined that he needed to shut it down. He argued that he had an agreement with Thompson (and Hines, who subsequently had passed away) before LaVere's agreement with Thompson and that it included what amounted to an exclusive first publication license for all information, documents, photographs, and other materials related to Thompson's Robert Johnson–related collection. This news bought him time and sent chills through Columbia's legal office as they scrambled to study the situation.

Then things began to get strange. McCormick would describe his agreements with Thompson and Hines but not share them. Columbia's legal team tracked down and called McCormick's phone number, but no one would pick up. On November 10, McCormick sent Hammond a five-page letter, arguing that his extensive research on Johnson preceded that of LaVere, as did his agreement with Thompson and Hines—and that he was feeling "a bit ripped-off here." Hammond responded that they felt confident moving forward, that Thompson did not feel that McCormick had a binding agreement for exclusive rights, and that the record release should be "a great help to your book" in terms of publicity—the latter a reasonable prediction.

One week later, McCormick pivoted to another argument. Rather than push the angle that he had an exclusive agreement with Thompson and Hines, he suggested that many people whom McCormick met along the way had a preemptive claim as heir to Johnson's estate. McCormick described encountering several unnamed family members with greater claims to heirship status, including more than one child of Johnson's. He told Hammond that he planned to create an agreement with each of the relatives he interviewed in order to cut them into the book's royalties, secured by an advance payment, and encouraged Columbia Records to pursue a similar avenue.

A few days later, McCormick sent a four-page letter coming from a different direction, claiming his exclusive rights to Thompson's stories because he had created a "pipeline" for getting relatives in Mississippi in touch with Thompson for the first time in years, thus enabling LaVere to find Thompson. It is not clear whether these manic efforts to sink the Columbia release, including undermining Thompson's credibility as an heir, was erupting from McCormick's mental illness or from a place of moral turpitude, but in either case, McCormick was in decline.

Hammond and others at Columbia began receiving correspondence from associates of McCormick in Houston, including Patricia Scott, McCormick's secretary, and a representative, Norris Stonecipher, who shared excerpts of agreement language between McCormick and Thompson. Columbia Records' legal team was rightly perplexed. In addition to the confusing array of defenses and excerpted but unsent agreements, his archive would later reveal that McCormick had invented and regularly communicated through each of these personas and more. At the time, however, McCormick created enough confusion for the legal team to see risk in moving forward with the release until questions could be answered. By 1976, Hammond had retired, but he continued to plead with McCormick to reconsider his position, arguing that without his doing so the exciting new release of Robert Johnson's music would never get into the hands of the public, and "we will all suffer."

As Mrs. Annye Anderson previously has documented, Carrie Thompson indeed was suffering while fighting multiple battles throughout the remainder of her life—battles that did not exist until those two white men knocked on her door. As the drama with McCormick and Columbia Records unfolded, she also grew to feel less compelled to help LaVere, and soon she was working with an attorney to revoke their agreement, and separately to demand the return from McCormick of her and Bessie Hines's photographs. One of the photographs featured Robert Johnson posing with his nephew, Carrie's son, Lewis Harris. Both are looking dapper: Harris is wearing his Navy uniform, on leave from Norfolk, visiting family in Memphis. Johnson is wearing that same pinstripe suit that he wore in the photograph with his guitar—both were taken during the same sitting, at Memphis's Hooks Brothers Studio. In addition to Thompson's photograph of Johnson and her son, Bessie Hines lent to McCormick two mounted pages full of family photographs, which included photographs of Johnson's mother; his brother Charles Leroy Spencer and his wife; Bessie Hines's husband, Granville Hines; and several other photographs of family and acquaintances. Thompson's attorney sent letters to McCormick, demanding their return. He never complied, arguing that he purchased them from her through a detailed agreement. She died in 1983 without seeing them again.

In parallel with Thompson's efforts, and then, after her death, continuing through the 1990s, LaVere demanded that McCormick turn the photograph of Johnson and Harris over to *him*, as he claimed the rights to license all photographs of Johnson that had belonged to Thompson. McCormick continued to ward off his enemies. By 1976 he was sharing with Columbia Records excerpts of a detailed, two-page agreement made with Carrie Thompson, which indicated that McCormick had paid Carrie Thompson five hundred dollars for, among other things, the:

> transfer of all rights, including right to secure copyright, use, possession and title to all photographs, physical, documents, manuscript, family materials or memorabilia or similar matter in the possession of Carrie Thompson which relates to Robert Johnson himself, his parents, Carrie Thompson herself, or other members of his family or close personal friends which the author judges pertinent and valuable to a biography of Robert Johnson.

Hines and Thompson, the archive confirms, never consented to any such agreement. McCormick left a paper trail of evidence in his archive that reveals his fabrication and forgery of this longer agreement (the short agreement they had signed only provided for his use of their interviews for the book). Meanwhile, as he became increasingly paranoid that the photographs would be stolen from his house or successfully won by LaVere in court, in the years following he claimed in correspondence, depositions, and interviews that the Johnson/Harris photograph variously was stolen from him in a house robbery shortly after LaVere was made aware of its existence; that he sold it in 1978 to a German television production company and never heard anything from them again; or that, if he had it, it was in his storage facility in Mexico (which never existed).

For fifteen years, the release remained held up by McCormick alone. In 1990, Columbia Records' legal team finally decided to release the collection as a box set, regardless of McCormick's claims. It ended up selling more than a million units, an astounding volume for a box set, let alone one made up of a repackaging of songs recorded more than fifty years earlier. The new enjoyment of Johnson's music, and the success of the box set's marketing, was enhanced using Thompson's photographs and stories of her brother Robert Johnson's life. Thompson was gone by then, but it would not have mattered. Half of the take went to LaVere, while the other half was placed in escrow until the courts ruled on the rightful heir to the Johnson estate.

In 2000 the Mississippi Supreme Court decreed Claud Johnson the sole heir to his father's estate. The *New York Times* reported the verdict on its front page, alongside one of the photographs of Robert Johnson that had been licensed from Carrie Thompson by LaVere and a photograph of Claud Johnson and his mother, Virgie Mae Cain, both beaming with excitement and relief. The article noted that Claud Johnson would receive over one million dollars, based largely upon sales of the box set during the ten years prior.

That was a very far cry from what Johnson himself earned in his lifetime. John Hammond observed in a 1972 letter to McCormick that during the late 1930s and early 1940s he "knew everybody at American Record Company from the president down to the lowliest secretary. I knew the factory at Bridgeport from top to bottom and I was (like you) a record and blues freak. I've never been able to find any contracts bearing Johnson's name—not even contracts for his tunes. Nobody made any money—least of all the American Record Company because it is estimated that none of his records sold over 2,000. . . . Knowing the way ARC worked in those days, I doubt if Johnson ever got more than $5 a side. The only thing that is strange is that nobody bothered to copyright his tunes and collect royalties. . . . It's one of the few times in the history of the record companies where everybody got screwed—including the company."

THE PHANTOMS, THE HELLHOUNDS, AND THE CRIME SCENE

While McCormick had always struggled to manage the relentlessly looming specters of depression and paranoia, of spirals and drifts toward fabrication, fantasy, and occasional criminal behavior, he had successfully kept them at bay for most of the 1960s while pursuing remarkably agile and creative fieldwork investigations, pulling off complex folk festival work, and writing at a prolific pace. Sometime around or shortly after 1973, when Thompson decided to dismiss McCormick and deal with LaVere, his condition deteriorated. There is no coincidence as to why his earliest polished drafts of *Biography of a Phantom* hold up as his strongest: they seem the least undermined by internal terrors, harmful decisions and actions to himself and others, and manic twists of logic that color his later drafts and Robert Johnson–related research pursuits.

McCormick's stories continued to spiral and expand over the decades— about his knowledge of Robert Johnson's killer, for example. He pursued several leads in this matter and eventually interviewed in 1975 a man whom he had long suspected, Jimmie Lee "Smokey" Hamber, whose assumed guilt was due simply to his after-hours occupation of running frolic houses on various plantations in the area of the Star of the West during that period. It turned out that Hamber was not around at the time, however. McCormick never succeeded in tracking down the family of Tush Hog, the man who cared for Johnson when he turned deathly ill and whose family McCormick felt was the best bet for providing the information he was seeking on Johnson's final days. Of course, even as he encountered and spoke with people familiar with the circumstances of Johnson's death, such as Robert and Izena Edwards, it is doubtful that any of those willing to speak with him would be inclined to throw in accusations of murder to a white stranger, even if they harbored such suspicions for one of their neighbors. By the 1980s McCormick began fabricating stories about his knowledge of the killer, or of his agreement not to reveal the killer's name until after the killer died. McCormick's archive bears no trace of his collecting compelling evidence against a suspect responsible for the death of Robert Johnson.

The archive does reveal, however, that many more stories would overtake McCormick's imagination. When Claud Johnson and Steve LaVere filed suit against him in 1998, seeking, among other things, for him to turn over the family photographs lent him nearly thirty years earlier by Carrie Thompson and a photograph of Claud as a young man, lent to McCormick by his mother, Virgie Mae Cain, McCormick generated hundreds of pages of at times baffling notes for his attorney. Within them, he questioned whether Thompson's brother Robert, while a musician, was the Robert Johnson who recorded those sides in San Antonio and Dallas, and he provided research notes on no fewer than thirty-one individuals whom McCormick argued may have produced those recordings.

In one of his last long-form biographical interviews, published just a year before his death, he seems to have narrowed down the list considerably, providing elaborate descriptions of his research on six possible Robert Johnsons, whom he had nicknamed "Claud's father, Little Robert, Little Dusty, San Antonio visitor, Oklahoma, [and] a man called Slate." "Oklahoma," it turns out, was a code name for the father of man named George Gibbs whom McCormick extensively describes in his archive, including Gibbs's 2:00 a.m. no-show when McCormick arranged a clandestine meeting one night to examine some of his corroborating documents. In the end, however, research into McCormick's archive yields two conclusions on these matters: one, that much of what McCormick described about his research on these men was fabricated (including the entire persona of George Gibbs); and two, that throughout the years, as evidenced in notes to himself, it seems McCormick came to believe a number of these stories and assertions as *truths*.

This book, then, ultimately is less about the life of Robert Johnson than it is about the human hellhounds and psychological phantoms that affected everyone involved. Their impact and reverberations seem interconnected and boundless, beginning with the lynchings and other racially motivated violence that terrorized and jeopardized Johnson's family as well as Black communities throughout Mississippi during the early 1900s. They extend to the ineffable consequences of entombing Johnson's humanity in a mythology that ascribed his musical brilliance literally to the doings of the devil, rather than to recognizing the labor of his craft, and the allusions and allegory in the poetic wellspring of Black songwriters that Johnson was drawing from and replenishing. They manifest in the historical plunder and exploitation of Black music and musicians by the record industry, and the toll weighed on Johnson's family members as they endured decades of litigation over Johnson's recordings and likeness. They manifest in the condition that both fueled McCormick's manic research production and vast assembly of knowledge, and that also relentlessly tormented him, constraining his ability to make good choices, and then expanding the suffering of all those around him when his choices were bad. It is a story of tragedy, suffered by all, where mental health plays a role, but so does racism, greed, and the instruments of white supremacy in the legal system and corporate structure, in which the concerns of Carrie Thompson were so easily and consistently dismissed.

McCormick's archive, as well, contains the multitudes of American music. It tracks his painstaking chronicling, often by knocking on doors, of not just Robert Johnson but hundreds of early to mid-twentieth-century southern vernacular musicians. It is infused with hundreds of tapes of field recordings, thousands of photographs, reams of correspondence from folklorists and blues fiends, dozens of his unpublished manuscripts on the meaning of it all, and crime scenes. It documents how, for a while, a small group of white male enthusiasts assumed an extraordinarily outsized impact on national, even global conversations about Black music. It documents the weight by which their interpretations—at times drifting to explanations of the blues as rooted in racial, sociological, or libidinous pathologies—impacted how the art of Black men and women was characterized and promoted by the music industry and the media. It exposes in fine detail how the tension generated by the access that their claims to authority and possession provided them could lead to dispossession and trauma, always shouldered by the Black men and women whose music they loved.

The dispossessions continue even today, when the blues continues to generate revenue for some, not only in the sale of recordings but also within local tourism economies. Blues scholar Brian Foster, for instance, explores the thoughts of hundreds of Black residents of the Mississippi Delta on the persistent inequities of the distribution of blues wealth in their communities. He writes of one Mississippi blues epicenter, "While Black Clarksdalians freely acknowledge the (economic) potential of the town's blues development agenda, they question when, or if, it will tangibly benefit the livelihoods of local Black folks. The folks I spoke with had yet to see the proof."

THE MONSTER

Mack McCormick's daughter, Susannah Nix, hated the Monster. It was the name McCormick gave to the archive that slowly consumed their family's house and lives. His incessant typing in his office was relentlessly painful to hear—she could not stand the sound and its associations. Although she saved every part of his archive, she got rid of the typewriters.

After her father passed and she moved the archive to a secure storage unit (not in Mexico as rumored), she deliberately took time to think about its future. She recognized the value of the archive and the stories it contains about so many musicians, stories that should be preserved and available not just for researchers like McCormick to study but also for the families of those whose doors McCormick knocked on so long ago. She also hoped to see at least some of her father's writings, including *Biography of a Phantom*, see the light of day—a hope that McCormick held as well, but grew increasingly challenged to realize. She also knew that questions and secrets lingered in the archive, but the volume of the Monster made it virtually inaccessible without having access to the resources required to organize and process it to make it legible for study. Susannah's goal, however, was to make it available for others to help reconcile all that she knew and didn't know about her father and his work and dealings.

When conversations began with the Smithsonian, she made it clear that she did not know all that was in the Monster or what secrets it held. She did know that inside were thousands of photographs. Mack had told her years before that he had lost the photograph of Robert Johnson and Lewis Harris. Given the size of the Monster, she believed him—maybe he had. But as she and her husband packed up the archive the weekend after he died, there it was, in a file marked "Johnson photo."

The photograph was located near copies of multiple contracts with very different terms, each set signed by Bessie Hines and Carrie Thompson. Folders seemingly connected to the photographs were scattered endlessly throughout the archive and were difficult to see as a whole. Meanwhile, she fielded dozens of calls and emails from strangers coming out of the woodwork offering unsolicited advice or requests, as well as hateful comments on online blues forums from people assuming she would cast it all into a dumpster (she hated the Monster, but she certainly cared about it, too). While the statute of limitations seemed to have placed all of those old photographs in McCormick's legal ownership, the ethical considerations, of course, could raise questions of an entirely different matter. When Susannah made the decision to donate the archive to the care of the Smithsonian, she made it clear, and in complete agreement with the Institution's position, that she desired the museum to study such questions when they processed the collection and "do the right thing" if bad dealings were evidenced in the files.

The museum's archivists, led by Vanessa Broussard Simmons, tamed the Monster, developing a two-hundred-plus-page finding aid in the process. Understanding the history of the Thompson and Hines photographs was a top priority and a significant undertaking, given that the rights to licensing their other photographs had been litigated in court over the years, involving multiple, opposing parties within Johnson's family. If the museum found issues with McCormick's previous claims to ownership of any objects in the archive, it had to take painstaking care to determine, as best as it could, the rightful heirs of those objects.

The story of the photographs was much clearer by the spring of 2020, particularly as the longer agreements were confirmed to be fraudulent and forged, and the museum began to lay plans for their transfer, initiating the process through the necessary internal channels, oversight, and review to clear the way. Remarkably, Mrs. Annye Anderson's book was published later that summer. It was like putting two puzzle pieces together. The museum's findings fundamentally corroborated her narrative regarding her family's dealings with McCormick and LaVere, providing additional evidence to boot. The internal process remained slow but deliberate, hindered by reduced access to the collection because of COVID-19 restrictions. When the final internal reviews were cleared the following year, the museum began reaching out to the heirs of the individuals who lent photographs to McCormick in order to return them to the families. Along with the return of those photographs, Mrs. Anderson requested that the Smithsonian transfer McCormick's interviews of her sisters Carrie Thompson and Bessie Hines to the control of her family as well. For Anderson, what McCormick and LaVere took from her sisters—not simply through the financial losses accrued through legal costs, but also the years of stress, anxiety, sadness, nightmares, and trauma—delegitimizes any signed agreement between them and McCormick. In respect for her wishes, we expunged the stories her sisters provided to McCormick from this publication and have restricted public access to them.

THE FUTURE

But is that enough? While McCormick's book languished, many of the same stories Thompson had shared with him she later shared with Steve LaVere. They found their way into the liner notes for the 1990 Columbia box set, while McCormick shared some of the stories with other writers. By the end, neither McCormick nor Thompson profited from their agreements or encounters. McCormick, of course, gained claims to authority within and beyond the Blues Mafia by virtue of his deep well of research on Johnson, but the effects of his mental illness effectively short-circuited his career or any ability to financially capitalize on it. In total, he managed to publish only one piece on Robert Johnson in his lifetime—a half-page inset essay in a bimonthly, short-lived magazine, published in the summer of 1988. Even then, the piece relied not upon any of Thompson's or Hines's stories, but rather on McCormick's claim that he had met and interviewed Johnson's murderer, a claim that the archive reveals to us as false. This magazine, *American Visions: The Magazine of Afro-American Culture*, in fact was published by none other than the Smithsonian's National Museum of American History—the same museum where his archive now resides.

The Smithsonian, of course, has been implicated in McCormick's story since the late 1960s. McCormick used pay from his contracted work for the Smithsonian's Folklife Festival to subsidize his fieldwork on Robert Johnson. In addition, he brandished the name of the Smithsonian while pursuing his Johnson research when the Smithsonian had not authorized him to do so. His archive reveals, for example, that he sometimes used Smithsonian letterhead or claimed to be calling from the Smithsonian when he spoke to people who knew Johnson. Now, in addition to his archive's being housed at the Smithsonian, his book is seeing the light of day, fifty years later, under a Smithsonian imprint. It has been edited by a white, male musician and historian who, while learning to play guitar thirty-five years ago in his childhood bedroom, still remembers feeling a jolt of excitement at fifteen after bringing home and first listening to the 1961 Columbia LP of Johnson's songs and who was mesmerized by the subsequent release, two years later, of Columbia's box set—the same box set that, unbeknownst to the kid in the bedroom, McCormick's hollow threats had held back since 1975—and who now as a Smithsonian curator collects music stories and objects on behalf of the

Institution. It raises the question of how much truly has changed and how much has remained the same. It also, importantly, speaks to the powerful hold that Robert Johnson's collected works of poetic and technical profundity can continue to engender and inspire, close to a century after he recorded them.

Much of the story of *Biography of a Phantom* feels unresolved. The structure and organization of this edition of the book, its framing of the multiple layers of storytelling, the elimination of Thompson's and Hines's stories—these decisions provide but a few of the quandaries apparent in our presentation of it. Looking ahead, how do we ensure throughout any deliberations of Johnson's work that he and his family's interests remain at the core, rather than in a phantom periphery? How might archives and museums best support and redress the wrongs of people represented in collections by virtue of unethical dispossessions? These are important questions that deeply implicate how researchers, writers, and institutions engage historical materials while acknowledging—even attempting to address—disparities of power. The Smithsonian is joining in the chorus of calls for museums to reevaluate their practices on these and related matters.

Likewise, we might ask, in conclusion: To whom does this book belong? Who owns its stories, and who decides? A specific rationale drove our decision to edit, frame, and publish McCormick's book in this manner: we imagined that his true life's work might ultimately come down not as much to his interpretive revelations on Robert Johnson or the blues, but rather to his role in amplifying the critical, ongoing conversations and dilemmas that churn around these questions. *Biography of a Phantom* is on the one hand a testament to Mack McCormick's extraordinary reach and tenacity as a researcher and writer, and on the other it is a disturbing cautionary tale on the profoundly complex, at times harrowing, and sometimes haunting practice of telling (or selling) others' stories. Emerged from a vast archive filled with evidence to support either contention, it is both things, in ceaseless entanglement, surrounded by hellhounds and phantoms.

• • •

NOTES

John W. Troutman

EDITOR'S PREFACE

vii: "His work is a tribute": The epigraphs are from Michael Hall, "Mack McCormick Still Has the Blues," *Texas Monthly*, April 2002, and Annye C. Anderson and Preston Lauterbach, *Brother Robert: Growing Up with Robert Johnson* (New York: Hachette Books, 2020), 119.

vii: "McCormick was 'the most enigmatic blues mafia figure of them all'": On McCormick's status in the Blues Mafia, see Daphne Brooks, *Liner Notes for the Revolution: The Intellectual Life of Black Feminist Sound* (Cambridge, MA: Belknap Press of Harvard University Press, 2021), 298. Brooks engages the perspectives of many Black women over the last century whose milestone Black feminist intellectual music explorations, archival work, and contributions to literature and scholarship have remained ignored not only by the Blues Mafia, but by many of today's leading critics, journalists, and scholars. She also critically assesses the works of several white writers and blues collectors, as well as ruminates on Mack McCormick and his archive.

ix: "seeking transformative social change was not their driving impulse": For the best discussion of the "Blues Mafia" generally, see Marybeth Hamilton, *In Search of the Blues* (New York: Basic Books, 2009), 201–246, esp. 220, for the origins of the name. Hamilton notes that white blues writer Samuel Charters was exceptional within the Blues Mafia as an outspoken advocate of studying the blues to expose entrenched social inequalities and encourage support of the Civil Rights Movement. See also Amanda Petrusich, *Do Not Sell at Any Price: The Wild, Obsessive Hunt for the World's Rarest 78 RPM Records* (New York: Scribner, 2014), esp. 116–132.

ix: "Lomax rarely acknowledged Work's involvement in the research project": The research of Work, Jones, and Adams was at last published in their *Lost Delta Found*, edited by Robert Gordon and Bruce Nemerov (Nashville, TN: Vanderbilt University Press, 2005). On Lomax's reluctance to credit their work in his publications, see 23–26. Clyde Woods characterized the work of the Harlem Renaissance writers and poets through the work of Baraka as forming the "Blues Epistemology" that largely was ignored by the Blues Mafia. Woods, *Development Arrested: The Blues and Plantation Power in the Mississippi Delta* (New York: Verso Books, 2017), 16–21.

x: "of the Black artists whose music obsessed, if not haunted them": See Hamilton, *In Search of the Blues*, 230. Regarding this phenomenon, Elijah Wald writes, "As white urbanites discovered the 'Race records' of the 1920s and 1930s, they reshaped the music to fit their own tastes and desires, creating a rich mythology that often bears little resemblance to the reality of the musicians they admired. Popular entertainers were reborn as primitive voices from the dark and demonic Delta, and a music notable for its professionalism and humor was recast as the heart-cry of a suffering people." Wald, *Escaping the Delta: Robert Johnson and the Invention of the Blues* (New York: Amistad, 2004), 3.

x: "His own stepfather, Charles Dodds Spencer": For details of Spencer's escape, see Anderson and Lauterbach, *Brother Robert*, 14–17.

x: "until Mack McCormick knocked on their doors": For the lucrative nature of the Robert Johnson cottage industry of criticism, see Steve Cushing, *Pioneers of the Blues Revival*, 2nd ed. (Urbana: University of Illinois Press, 2014), xvi.

xi: "he moved at least twenty times during his first sixteen years": Files on McCormick's involvement with the Smithsonian are found in his archive in the National Museum of American History's Archives Center, as well as in the archives of the Smithsonian Institution's Center for Folklife and Cultural Heritage, and the Smithsonian Institution's former Division of Performing Arts. See McCormick's list of residences in the Robert "Mack" McCormick Collection, Archives Center, National Museum of American History (referred to in the remainder of the notes as "McCormick Collection"), box 23, folder 24. For his tenth-grade essay award, see McCormick Collection, box 25, folder 7. For McCormick's early years, see Cushing, *Pioneers*, 374–380, and Hall, "Mack McCormick Still Has the Blues."

xiii: "began work as a press agent for the Buddy Ryland Orchestra": For McCormick's list of jobs, dates, and locations, see McCormick Collection, box 23, folder 24. For *Down Beat* and the Buddy Ryland Orchestra, see box 23, folder 17. For his correspondence with discographers in 1947, see box 23, folder 36.

xiii: "I had several things that might have worked out": For details of McCormick's arrest, see the newspaper clipping in McCormick Collection, box 28, folder 13. For his correspondence to Effie Mae Crowder after his arrest, see box 24, folder 1. See also box 23, folder 37.

xiv: "she did as best as a mother could to acknowledge his successes": For the *Down Beat* congratulations, see McCormick Collection, box 24, folder 1. For examples of McCormick's mother's struggles, see box 23, folder 31.

xiv: "Jail would not slow down his pursuit": For McCormick's letter to Thornhill and correspondence with Dick Martin, see McCormick Collection, box 24, folder 1. Dick Martin's popular show was called "Moonglow with Martin." Martin wrote many long letters to McCormick while he was in jail about music and also, in revealing passages, about the Jim Crow conditions facing Black musicians who would play New Orleans while on tour.

xiv: "Have just gotten your letter": For his correspondence with the probation officer, see McCormick Collection, box 28, folder 13. For his letter to Oliver, see Box 77, folder 3.

xvi: "In between his fares, he knocked on doors": For McCormick's time in California and correspondence with his mother, see McCormick Collection, box 24, folder 2. For some of his cab licenses, see box 25, folder 16.

xvii: "Mack went beyond the facts": McCormick's work with Hopkins and Lipscomb is extensively documented in multiple locations throughout the McCormick Archive. The archive also features drafts, proofs, and original artwork for the Almanac label. For Guralnick's quote, see Hall, "Mack McCormick Still Has the Blues."

xvii: "Notions of 'field work' versus 'fieldwork' held very different meanings for all involved": McCormick used the Houston Folklore Group's newsletters to ask the membership for leads on finding artists or their families. Using this method in the fall of 1960, he found Carrie B. Jefferson, the sister of Lemon Henry "Blind Lemon" Jefferson. McCormick had even written FBI Director J. Edgar Hoover for leads on Jefferson's family, under the auspices of the Houston Folklore Group. See McCormick Collection, box 73, folder 2. For McCormick's interesting description of Sam Hopkins's first three concerts before a "folk" audience at the Alley Theater's "Hootenanny in the Round," see box 71, folder 1 and box 76, folder 5. For copies of some of the Houston Hootenanny programs, see box 27, folder 1. McCormick visited and recorded incarcerated people at several Texas prisons, including the Clements State Farm, Wynne State Penal Farm, and the Ellis State Penal Farm. The latter two were in Huntsville. One of the Mexican American bands he recorded at Wynne was Los Norteños, featuring Joe Guevara and Rene Huerta on vocals. See box 146, folder 2.

xviii: "Folklore bona fides": see McCormick Collection, box 146, folder 2, and Cushing, *Pioneers*, 397.

xix: "reliant upon Mack's ability to locate and establish rapport": Alan Govenar, along with Kip Loring, edited Paul Oliver's set of the manuscript notes, beginning in 2011, with Oliver's blessing. McCormick seemed furious that Texas A&M Press was publishing the manuscript without his permission and was writing letters to the press to that effect in the year of his death. For some of his writings on the subject, see McCormick Collection, box 27, folders 12 and 14. Entitled *Blues Comes to Texas: Paul Oliver and Mack McCormick's Unfinished Book*, the edited volume was published in 2019 and has garnered much praise among blues researchers, who welcomed the publication as long overdue.

xix: "many ended up willing to speak with him": Gayle Dean Wardlow provided an account of the early days of "knocking on doors" to acquire rare blues records from Black families in his essay "Knocking on Doors for 78s: Buying Race Records in the South," *Victrola and 78 Journal* 9 (1996): 9–14. According to Ted Gioia, Wardlow "even took a job as an exterminator in a black neighborhood with the hope that it would gain him entrée into households where these treasures [recordings and information on musicians] might be uncovered." Gioia, *Delta Blues: The Life and Times of the Mississippi Masters Who Revolutionized American Music* (New York: Norton, 2008), 153.

xx: "Are there any singers in your family?": McCormick's research notes (including those he withheld from Oliver), photographs, historical documents, recordings, and manuscript drafts that he produced and accrued while working on the Texas blues project are included in McCormick's sprawling archive, which is housed in the National Museum of American History's Archives Center. Oliver's set of manuscript drafts and notes have been catalogued at Oxford Brookes University. On McCormick's "grid system" description, see Cushing, *Pioneers*, 385–386; on McCormick's census work and the relationship that it spawned between McCormick and Edward "Buster" Pickens, see 389. McCormick provided advice to Oliver during their early correspondence on what to expect and on how to succeed in the "hunt" when knocking on doors. The correspondence reveals his strategies of self-presentation (including the sometimes use of, as he described it, the "Negro variety of English") and his other sometimes racist assumptions about some of the people he would encounter when knocking on doors. The correspondence also provides descriptions of times when he was accosted by local police, not only in the South but also in Los Angeles, for spending time in Black neighborhoods or in the company of Black musicians. See the letter from McCormick to Paul Oliver, May 18, 1960, McCormick Collection, box 76, folder 5, p. 174, 176.

xx: "sustainability remained a problem": In one interview McCormick recounted, for example, that in 1964, soon after he married Mary Badeaux, the sister of his frequent collaborator Ed Badeaux, they briefly moved to Paracho in Michoacán, Mexico—for centuries a global epicenter for the crafting of fine guitars—where Mack was "searching for an income" by investigating the export of the instruments to take advantage of the "folk music craze" of the time. Cushing, *Pioneers*, 394.

xxi: "The magazine published McCormick's research notes": John Jeremiah Sullivan, "The Ballad of Geeshie and Elvie," *New York Times Magazine*, April 13, 2014. Sullivan or the *Times* hired a research assistant to work with McCormick in his home, ostensibly on McCormick's behalf. The assistant shared with Sullivan photographs of some of McCormick's research notes after McCormick asked her not to return to his home. Sullivan noted in the essay, "I admired the bravery of her act of quasi theft, feeling strongly that it was the right thing to do. You're not allowed to sit on these things for half a century, not when the culture has decided they matter. I know he didn't want to sit on them—he was trapped with them. I give us both a pass." McCormick documented his hoaxes—essentially as "notes to self"—throughout the archive, so that he could attempt to keep track of whatever fantasies he had spun. This is helpful documentation for researchers interested in lining up the research materials collected by McCormick with the materials shared to Oliver. It is also clear that McCormick withheld a great deal of research from Oliver, as such material is strewn throughout the McCormick Archive. For some of the hoax documentation, see McCormick Collection, box 26, folder 5; box 152, folder 27; box 79, folder 5; and box 84, folder 1. For letters written by McCormick in the last year of his life, vigorously protesting the impending publication of his and Oliver's book, see McCormick Collection, box 27, folder 14.

xxiii: "Hammond was trying to recruit Johnson to perform": For Hammond's early writings on Johnson and his recollections to McCormick of the December 23, 1938, "From Spirituals to Swing" concert in New York, see McCormick Collection, box 94, folder 12, and box 29, folder 9. As to when he first learned of Johnson's death, Hammond recalled to McCormick in a letter dated November 7, 1972, "It was Don Law who gave me the bad news sometime in June of 1938, before the trip that Goddard Lieberson and I made to the South to find talent for the concert. The trip, where we picked up Mitchell's Christian Singers, Sonny Terry, and Bill Broonzy, as a substitute for Robert Johnson, proved interesting."

xxiii: "giving millions of people their first taste of Johnson's songs": For Hammond's comment about the Columbia series, see the letter from Hammond to McCormick, November 7, 1972, in McCormick Collection, box 29, folder 9. For the Clapton quote, see Kimberly Mack, *Fictional Blues: Narrative Self-Invention from Bessie Smith to Jack White* (Amherst: University of Massachusetts Press, 2020), 115. Mack compares Clapton's comment on hearing Johnson's music for the first time with one provided by Bob Dylan: "the stabbing sounds from the guitar could almost break a window. When Johnson started singing, he seemed like a guy who could have sprung from the head of Zeus in full armor." Mack adds, "these contemporary autobiographical renderings not only show the enduring power of Johnson's mythos but also effectively tell the larger story—the biography—of transatlantic white engagement with the blues from the Southern United States."

xxvi: "he wrote *Biography of a Phantom* as a crime thriller": For one of McCormick's descriptions of the book's concept, including his reference to *In Cold Blood*, see his letter to John Hammond, November 10, 1975, in McCormick Collection, box 29, folder 9. For notes to himself on how to present his character ("Know how to do things," "be positive, knowledgeable," "some physical labor—I fix rattles in car—change a tire & sweat dropping from my nose," "need emotional interchange with people," "I get nasty with people," "Irritated by drivers," etc.), see McCormick Collection, box 118, folder 1.

xxviii: "those two terms can convey different meanings": These editorial decisions are imperfect and subject to debate, particularly when they involve the ever-evolving, rich discussions on how to identify the country's many diverse communities and identity groups most respectfully and accurately. For some of McCormick's deliberations on the use of the word "Negro" in the late 1970s, see McCormick Collection, box 118, folder 1.

xxviii: "we decided to remove those passages from the book": According to her publicly stated preference, the author of *Brother Robert* is addressed here as "Mrs. Anderson" or sometimes as "Mrs. Annye Anderson."

xxix: "arguments and assertions about Johnson that have unfolded over the past half-century": The list of writings about Robert Johnson's life and music is vast. The most exceptional is Anderson and Lauterbach, *Brother Robert*. Bruce Conforth and Gayle Dean Wardlow's *Up Jumped the Devil: The Real Life of Robert Johnson* (Chicago: Chicago Review Press, 2019) introduces new and comprehensive research into Johnson's life and travels, but it is tainted by assertions of Johnson's "womanizing" and speculates without substantiation on the factors influencing a variety of his decisions. On page 113, for example, they write, with no evidence of support, that Johnson was "uninterested in anything or anyone other than his music and his Memphis family," and that it was this alleged disinterest in the welfare of other people that led to the breakup of his marriage with Callie Craft. The authors cite conversations with McCormick as the source of some of their claims. Kimberly Mack's *Fictional Blues* innovatively engages the mythmaking surrounding Robert Johnson. Elijah Wald's *Escaping the Delta* remains an exceptional foray into Johnson's music and influences and to the listening habits of his contemporaries, as well as on how Johnson came to hold such cultural sway in the decades that followed. Peter Guralnick's pithy but impactful *Searching for Robert Johnson* (New York: Plume, 1998) benefited from McCormick's sharing of some of his research. In addition to dozens of articles published in enthusiast periodicals such as *Living Blues* and *Blues Unlimited*, a selection of additional books published from the 1970s through the present that focus on Johnson include Samuel Charters, *Robert Johnson* (New York: Oak Publications, 1973); Robert Palmer, *Deep Blues* (New York: Penguin Books, 1986); Greil Marcus, *Mystery Train: Images of America in Rock 'n' Roll Music*, 6th ed. (New York: Plume, 2015); Tom Graves, *Crossroads: The Life and Afterlife of Blues Legend Robert Johnson* (Memphis, TN: Devault-Graves Agency, 2017); Alan Greenberg, *Love in Vain: A Vision of Robert Johnson* (Minneapolis: University of Minnesota Press, 2012); Edward Komara, *The Road to Robert Johnson: The Genesis and Evolution of Blues in the Delta from the Late 1800s through 1938* (Milwaukee, WI: Hal Leonard, 2007); Gioia, *Delta Blues*; Barry Lee Pearson and Bill McCulloch, *Robert Johnson: Lost and Found* (Urbana: University of Illinois Press, 2003); and Patricia R. Schroeder, *Robert Johnson: Mythmaking and Contemporary American Culture* (Urbana: University of Illinois Press, 2004). For a recent assessment of how scholars have speculated on the power dynamics at play during Johnson's recording sessions with Don Law in San Antonio and Dallas, see Brian Ward and Patrick Huber, *A&R Pioneers: Architects of American Roots Music on Record* (Nashville, TN: Vanderbilt University Press and the Country Music Foundation Press, 2018), 161–170.

INTRODUCTION

2: "Best come on back to Friars Point, mama": These lyrics are excerpted from Robert Johnson's composition "Traveling Riverside Blues," recorded on June 20, 1937, in Dallas.

2: "It was in this era that a very few people began the search": Those unreleased songs from the "company files" were made available for the first time on the 1961 Columbia Records release *Robert Johnson: King of the Delta Blues Singers*.

3: "The Dallas branch office passed the request to a salesman in Memphis": Though Johnson first recorded for American Record Corporation in November 1936, his first releases were sold in January 1937. "Race Records" was a music industry term often applied to the recorded music of Black recording artists working in the 1920s–1940s. The category gained ground in the industry, if not originated, when in 1922 Okeh Records established and marketed racially segregated record catalogs of southern musicians recording on their label. See Karl Hagstrom Miller, *Segregating Sound: Inventing Folk and Pop Music in the Age of Jim Crow* (Durham, NC: Duke University Press, 2010), 187–214.

4: "someone else went into the Delta and reported talking with Johnson's mother": In research notes from 1941, Alan Lomax described his encounter with the woman he identified as Robert

Johnson's mother: "July 17—South from Memphis we found Son House at Robinsonville,— handsome and sensitive man. We went with him to see Robert Johnson's mother. She told us of her son, spoke of God, her great master; got happy as we left—prophysying [sic] in the dusty yard. Later we recorded Son House's magnificent deep song—his blues—about as fine and impassioned as I've heard. Had a run-in with the manager of the plantation Son rents on. He was extremely insulting and hostile." Library of Congress, Alan Lomax Collection, Manuscripts, Mississippi, Tennessee and Arkansas, 1941–1942, www.loc.gov/item/afc2004004.ms070309/.

4: "a slender young man with a mark in one eye": The condition or event that created the appearance of a dot or mark in one of Johnson's eyes is unconfirmed.

I. THE TOWN

5: "The town is a shadow of itself": McCormick first visited Friars Point in late 1969 or early 1970. See McCormick Collection, box 108, folder 13.

6: "markedly similar to some of the African art that I had seen": McCormick provides no further specification of the art he has seen that reminds him of this stick, other than "African art."

10: "Perhaps he intended them to go together?": Robert Johnson's "Traveling Riverside Blues" and "Honeymoon Blues" were recorded back-to-back in Dallas on June 20, 1937.

10: "I found his house": McCormick also provided in this paragraph the description of a "squalid one room home with a naked, fat bellied child standing in the doorway, staring dully at the world"—a description that performs little work in this paragraph other than to resuscitate commonly circulated stereotypes from the period of people living in impoverished circumstances.

2. THE SEARCH

14: "My enemies have betrayed me": "Me and the devil was walking side by side" is from Johnson's "Me and the Devil Blues." "I got stones in my passway, and my road seems dark at night" and "My enemies have betrayed me" are from his "Stones in My Passway."

15: "Baby, you know what I'm talking about": This lyric is from Johnson's "Traveling Riverside Blues." Johnson added the spoken line in the second take of the recording. Wald identifies several songs recorded in the period that contain similar "lemon" lines: Bo Carter's "Let Me Roll Your Lemon," Tampa Red's "Juicy Lemon Blues," Blind Boy Fuller's "Let Me Squeeze Your Lemon," and Bumble Bee Slim's "Lemon Squeezing Blues." See Elijah Wald, *Escaping the Delta: Robert Johnson and the Invention of the Blues* (New York: Amistad, 2004), 182.

15 "The words 'blues falling down like hail'": Johnson's line "Blues falling down like hail" may have been inspired by the line "Blues falling like drops of rain" in Lonnie Johnson's 1925 recording "Falling Rain Blues."

15: "They were making a loud, pounding blues": McCormick's association of the crafting of Chicago blues with the "lifestyles of the urban ghetto" evokes the romanticization of poverty that some white blues writers of this period would ascribe to the living conditions of impoverished people. These conditions had been determined by racist practices such as redlining, which built segregated Black and brown neighborhoods upon an ever-crumbling foundation of inequitable resources and infrastructure. Note that McCormick acknowledges the racist practices behind the "Jim Crow tenant and ghetto worlds designed to segregate Black people" later in this chapter.

15: "The pacesetters in Chicago": Johnson was covered early on by artists recording both in Chicago and in Mississippi. Arthur "Big Boy" Crudup recorded his "Dust My Broom" on March 10, 1949, in Chicago. Elmore James, having met Robert Johnson in the 1930s, recorded a well-known version of "Dust My Broom" as "Elmo James" for Trumpet Records of Jackson, Mississippi, in 1951. By that point versions of Johnson's "Sweet Home Chicago" had already been recorded by Mississippi's Tommy McClennan ("Baby Don't You Want to Go," 1939, recorded in Chicago) and Walter Davis ("Don't You Want to Go," 1941, also recorded in Chicago). These two songs of Johnson's were among the most popular to be covered by the Chicago blues musician community in the mid–twentieth century, and they established the foundation for his continued influence among blues musicians after his death. Johnson drew his lyrical inspiration for the songs from the earlier works of a number of artists. For examples, see Wald, *Escaping the Delta*, 134–139.

16: "within the ranks of Columbia Records itself were several key people": Frank Driggs and George Avakian were jazz enthusiasts who worked as producers at Columbia Records when John Hammond, also at Columbia, was one of the earliest advocates, if not the *first* advocate, for the production and release of the 1961 album.

17: "Ebony would work in a reference": For the quotation, see Clayton Riley, "The Creative Black Man: Artists Struggle to Overcome Limiting Concepts of Art," *Ebony* (August 1972), 138.

18: "They verge on superlatives, sometimes to an almost evangelistic excess": For "the most titanic artist," see Greil Marcus, "He Sold His Soul to Play That Way," *New York Times*, November 22, 1970. The quote from the "interview with a musician" was attributed to Johnny Shines, first published in 1966 from an interview conducted by Pete Welding. For a reading on this and other similar quotes from Shines, see Barry Lee Pearson and Bill McCulloch, *Robert Johnson: Lost and Found* (Urbana: University of Illinois Press, 2003), 96.

18: "I was not the first to make the trip to absurd places like Friars Point": The comment "absurd places" could read as a slight to the people of Friars Point, but McCormick also could have been referencing the absurdity of his obsession to travel to unfamiliar towns and raise troublesome questions to strangers.

20: "they accepted few of Mister Charlie's dictates": "Mister Charlie" was a commonly used derogatory term for oppressive and bigoted white men. For a literary example of its use, see James Baldwin's 1964 play *Blues for Mister Charlie*. Lightnin' Hopkins also incorporated a piece called "Mister Charlie" into his performances. McCormick's assertions of the role of blues artists' "egos" allude to stereotypes circulated by white blues writers that are steeped in essentialist notions of a blues "authenticity" of poverty and of the libidinous proclivities of its practitioners—racist ideas couched in clinical observations rendered by these writers for a "type" of people. For studies of the relationship between the blues and Jim Crow segregation, see R. A. Lawson, *Jim Crow's Counterculture: The Blues and Black Southerners, 1890–1945* (Baton Rouge: Louisiana State University Press, 2010), and Adam Gussow, *Seems Like Murder Here: Southern Violence and the Blues Tradition* (Chicago: University of Chicago Press, 2002).

20: "They went by names like Johnson and Thomas and Williams and Smith and Jones": Eddie Jones recorded in the 1950s under the name "Guitar Slim." James Sherrill recorded four sides in 1937 under the name, "Peanut the Kidnapper." William Bunch recorded under the name of Peetie Wheatstraw, who was also known as "The High Sheriff from Hell." Kimberly Mack considers such self-styled monikers the "the myth of the bad man" within a broader tradition of African American tall tales and storytelling. See Kimberly Mack, *Fictional Blues: Narrative Self-Invention from Bessie Smith to Jack White* (Amherst: University of Massachusetts Press, 2020), 25–66.

20: "to doubt that his quarry exists": McCormick's use of the imagery of hunts and quarry manifests in literary expression a quite accurate dynamic at play. It also invokes alliterations disturbingly close to lynching. See also his use of "hunting" people in description of his fieldwork to Paul Oliver, McCormick Collection, box 76, folder 5.

3. THE MAP

23: "You could run the bill up with a magnificent gumbo or crawfish bisque": For McCormick's notes on the restaurant, see McCormick Collection, box 108, folder 13. DiDee's had gained some renown beyond Louisiana by the 1970s. See Calvin Trillin, "The Definitive History of DiDee's Restaurant, So Far," *The New Yorker*, April 17, 1978.

26: "The news that year had been full of all three countries": Elijah Wald notes that Johnson's line referencing China may have been drawn from a similar line in Kokomo Arnold's 1935 recording, "Sissy Man Blues," while Johnson's next line, combining references to "Philippine's Island" and Ethiopia, was "the most geographically flamboyant verse of his career." Wald, *Escaping the Delta: Robert Johnson and the Invention of the Blues* (New York: Amistad, 2004), 135–136.

27: "I got womens in Vicksburg": For the verses, see Robert Johnson, "Traveling Riverside Blues."

29: "It retains the structure and the flavor and the cadence of the work song": McCormick is referring to Alan Lomax's 1947 recording of Benny Will "22" Richardson and group singing "It Makes a Long Time Man Feel Bad," which was made while they were incarcerated at the Lambert Camp at the Mississippi State Penitentiary (better known as Parchman Farm). The recording later was released on a 1958 LP, *Negro Prison Songs*. For a recording, see https://archive

.culturalequity.org/field-work/parchman-farm-1947-and-1948/parchman-1247/it-makes-long
-time-man-feel-bad. Wald believes that Johnson "sang ['Last Fair Deal Gone Down'] on the
streets to amuse white listeners, providing them with an upbeat exaggeration of the levee
work songs. He sings lines like, 'My captain's so mean to me' with a good deal more humor
than anger, and though the verses look pained on paper, the whole effect is broadly theatrical
rather than deep or personal." *Escaping the Delta*, 161.

4. BACK TO THE DELTA

33: "There was nothing unusual in this": For nineteenth- and twentieth-century histories of
Chinese immigration to and Chinese American communities developing within the Mississippi Delta, see James Loewen, *The Mississippi Chinese: Between Black and White*, 2nd ed. (Long
Grove, IL: Waveland Press, 1998), and John Jung, *Chopsticks in the Land of Cotton: Lives of Mississippi Delta Chinese Grocers* (Long Beach, CA: Yin & Yang Press, 2018).

37: "Nowhere else in the country was the present day more closely wed to its history":
McCormick's sweeping characterizations of people living in the Delta in this period connect
both to his observational insight as well as to his assumptions of their lack of worldly knowledge and intellectual curiosity.

37: "The others are merely wretched": Once again, McCormick in this passage combined
insight with insult.

39: "Helena was the home of *King Biscuit Time*": McCormick seems to have visited Max
Moore to discuss the *King Biscuit Time* program in late 1969. In December of that year, Moore
mailed him ephemera related to the programming and samples of scripts and schedules.
See McCormick Collection, box 153, folder 38, and box 123, folder 22.

40: "a man who claimed Johnson was his stepfather": McCormick is referring to Robert
Lockwood Jr.

41: "their principal customers were Black sharecroppers": Their success in paying these bills,
of course, were subject to the risks of unfavorable weather, insect infestations, bad dealings
by landowners and various blights.

42: "The back of the postcard had a brief message": Max Moore later provided McCormick a
copy of this postcard. See McCormick Collection, box 153, folder 38.

43: "continued to identify himself as 'Robert Junior'": Lockwood had been known as "Junior"
since his birth, because his father's name was Robert. He was frustrated that people assumed
the "junior" was in reference to Robert Johnson. Bruce Conforth and Gayle Dean Wardlow,
Up Jumped the Devil: The Real Life of Robert Johnson (Chicago: Chicago Review Press, 2019),
137. For McCormick's notes on his August 17, 1971, interview with Lockwood, see McCormick
Collection, box 154, folder 22. In the interview, Lockwood told McCormick that after Robert
Johnson died, Robert Johnson's brother (remembered by Lockwood as "Lonnie," though he

presumably was referring to Leroy Johnson), had shown Johnson's Kalamazoo-brand guitar to Lockwood in Memphis, after Johnson had died. McCormick also interviewed by phone Lockwood's mother, Estella Coleman; the recording of the conversation is in the archive, as are notes of the interview in box 154, folder 22.

45: "The stops were only four to eight miles apart": Max Moore sent McCormick this particular itinerary from a September 6, 1952, tour circuit as an example of the typical Saturday schedules from the period. See McCormick Collection, box 153, folder 38.

49: "this was remarkably steady work": A photocopy of this itinerary, typed on a printed Interstate Grocery Company notepad, is in McCormick Collection, box 123, folder 22.

5. COPIAH COUNTY

49: "There were also some letters": McCormick's archive indeed includes many such files on then-deceased individuals or prison records of people who seemed to fit McCormick's criteria for being persons who interested him.

50: "It was a death certificate for a Robert Johnson": The manuscript provides a date of 1953 for this birth certificate, so we changed this to 1938. It is unclear why McCormick provided the year of 1953 for this death certificate. If indeed he is referring to the death certificate of Robert L. Johnson, who it indicates was born in Hazlehurst to Julia Major and Noah Johnson, as the passage indicates, then the year provided on the certificate is 1938. Note that the correct last name for his mother is Majors, not Major. Having only the spelling on the death certificate to work from, however, McCormick continued to pursue information about the "Major" family until he was corrected by Carrie Thompson and Bessie Hines when he met them in 1972. We preserved the error in the main text, since McCormick references the word in relation to others whom he later meets, prompting additional confusion and misdirection during his search.

51: "A Mexican at the next table": We assume that McCormick did not inquire as to the Latino individual's background and nationality, including determining whether he was born in the United States. For the latter population, in particular, the term has a history as a slur and as a means to render them as an othered, foreign population who do not belong.

53: "a sign for a restaurant named after a Johnson": McCormick kept a page from the June 1969 Hazlehurst phone directory that lists the address for "Johnson Restaurant" at 104 W. Gallatin. See McCormick Collection, box 123, folder 22.

58: "some of the old double-entendre lines": The line in Johnson's "Terraplane Blues" is "I'm goin' to heist your hood, mama, I'm bound to check your oil."

59: "Virgie Mae Cain had been just seventeen": McCormick first met and interviewed Virgie Mae Cain on April 2, 1970, and returned to tape an interview with her on the following day. See McCormick Collection, box 102, folder 4. Virgie Mae Cain is also known in various vital documents, court cases, and publications as Virgie Jane Cain, Virgie Jane Smith Cain, and

Virgie Jane Smith. McCormick referred to her by the latter name, but we changed it to Virgie Mae Cain, which seems to be the most common usage.

60: "It was at this party where Virgie met Robert Johnson": Others suggest that Cain and Johnson met in March 1931. See Bruce Conforth and Gayle Dean Wardlow, *Up Jumped the Devil: The Real Life of Robert Johnson* (Chicago: Chicago Review Press, 2019), 108.

60: "They stayed together about nine months": Conforth and Wardlow conjecture that turmoil existed between Cain and Johnson at the time because "he was playing the devil's music," and they speculate that he married Callie Craft that May, "perhaps as a reaction to being rebuffed by Virgie." See Conforth and Wardlow, *Up Jumped the Devil*, 110.

61: "he couldn't read and write": It is clear that Johnson could read and write due to testimony from McCormick's and other researchers' interviews with Johnson's acquaintances and family, and by Annye C. Anderson in her book with Peter Lauterbach, *Brother Robert: Growing Up with Robert Johnson* (New York: Hachette Books, 2020).

63: "It was a photo of a young man sitting slumped and relaxed": This is a photograph that McCormick borrowed from Virgie Mae Cain with a promise to return it. He never did. Both Cain and, later, Claud, requested the return of this original photograph. Confusing notes in the archive suggest that McCormick may have sent Cain an enlarged copy of the photograph (through the Smithsonian, which he claims exhibited the photograph at one point), but there is no confirmation that Cain received a copy or that the Smithsonian ever had access to the photograph. See McCormick Collection, box 29, folder 5, and box 102, folders 4 and 5. In 1998, Claud Johnson attempted to retrieve the photograph of himself from McCormick through a court action. See box 30, folder 5. The original photograph was found in the archive and as of this writing is being processed to return to Claud's heirs.

64: "He was curious and excited": McCormick first interviewed Claud Johnson in April 1970, after he met Claud's mother. See McCormick Collection, box 102, folder 4. It seems that McCormick left a copy of the 1961 *Robert Johnson: King of the Delta Blues Singers* record with Cain; the record got her son Claud thinking about the estate. Claud Johnson hired an attorney, who contacted McCormick on January 6, 1972, to ask for his assistance in pursuing Claud's claim of Robert Johnson's estate. Notes near this letter indicate that for a while McCormick was pondering how he might create a contract for Claud to sign, granting McCormick rights to Johnson's estate, just as Steve LaVere drafted a contract for Carrie Thompson to sign that had granted LaVere rights to the estate. See box 29, folder 8. Claud Johnson and McCormick continued to speak, at least through 1974, about Johnson's pursuit of the estate. See box 102, folder 5. For a profile of Claud Johnson after he was declared the heir to the Johnson estate, see Ellen Barry, "Bluesman's Son Gets His Due," *Los Angeles Times*, June 2, 2004.

64: "standing in front of the Gallman Chapel AME Zion Church": The chapel is located above Crystal Springs, Mississippi, which is just north of Hazlehurst. The road is also referred to as "County Line Road."

65: "a gifted but tortured blues singer who died of women and youth": McCormick plays into a misogynistic trope here, blaming "women" for a young man's demise.

68: "a rack of leaflets for the Southern National Party": This quotation from the SNP flyer is also found in critical reporting of it in Millsaps College's student newspaper, *The Purple & White*, in the column "The Midnight Skulker," on January 16, 1970.

68: "He had won 59 percent of the vote in 1968": McCormick was referring to the Copiah County popular vote in 1968.

69: "between wherever they'd started and some city": For a detailed political, social, and economic history of the Delta during this period, see Clyde Woods, *Development Arrested: The Blues and Plantation Power in the Mississippi Delta*, 2nd ed. (London: Verso, 2017), 88–154.

71: "It was a book by Leroi Jones": The quote that the blues are "the fullest expression of the Negro's individuality" was excerpted from a review of LeRoi Jones (later known as Amiri Baraka), *Blues People*, in *Ebony* 19, no. 2 (December 1963): 24. This reference demonstrates that McCormick at least was familiar with Baraka's work, although his archive indicates that he does not seem to have engaged him in correspondence.

71: "That was 1967": On May 11, 1967, a truck driver and civil rights activist, Benjamin Brown, was shot in the back by local law enforcement officers while a bystander at a student protest. He died the following day. See Jerry Mitchell, "No Marker Recognizes Ben Brown's Killing on JSU Campus," *Clarion Ledger*, May 12, 2014, www.clarionledger.com/story/journeytojustice/2014/05/12/benbrownkilling/8991361/. Almost three years later to the date, two more campus killings by law enforcement officers took place, when Jackson State junior Phillip L. Gibbs and local high school senior James Earl Green were shot and killed during another moment of intense protest and agitation. See Whitney Blair Wyckoff, "Jackson State: A Tragedy Widely Forgotten," NPR.org, May 3, 2010, www.npr.org/templates/story/story.php?storyId=126426361.

73: "rambling along about anything and everything": McCormick's unfortunate characterization (if not operating assumption) of Brown as unworldly is typical in his writings and those of other folklorists of the era who believed such descriptions would lend colloquial authority and rustic authenticity to their "informants."

74: "Her name was Minerva Cain": The 1940 US Census lists a Minerva Cain as married to Edgar Cain, working as a teacher in Copiah County, and living at a residence on Highway 51. She died in January 1979.

75: "She'd tried to teach him to read and write": It may be the case that Johnson enrolled in Ms. Cain's class for a few months while visiting his father. Conforth and Wardlow, however, assert that Johnson did not visit Noah Johnson during his youth and did not search for him until 1930. See Conforth and Wardlow, *Up Jumped the Devil*, 94–96.

75: "she'd had a raft of children": The assertion that Julia Majors had many children with Noah Johnson is incorrect. Robert was the youngest of Julia Majors's children, but her only child with Noah Johnson. Regarding Madison Majors, he indeed was an uncle to Julia Majors. For a genealogy of the Majors family, see Conforth and Wardlow, *Up Jumped the Devil*, 273. Note that McCormick switches from "Major" to "Majors" for the next few paragraphs. It is unclear whether Minerva Cain was providing the correct name of "Majors" when describing Julia's family, or whether McCormick inadvertently self-corrected his use to "Majors" during this section of the chapter.

75: "Another of the Majors girls": Mrs. Annye Anderson writes that her "mother's sister, Aunt Mary, lived around us in Memphis, too." See Anderson and Lauterbach, *Brother Robert*, 24.

79: "I got a sweet Black angel": Lucille Bogan wrote and recorded "Black Angel Blues" in 1930. It was subsequently recorded by several Delta artists, including Tampa Red (1934) and Robert Nighthawk (1949), with a hit variation by B. B. King ("Sweet Little Angel," 1956). Houston Stackhouse may have performed the song early in his career, but his recording of it was not released until 1994, many years after he had passed away.

79: "Houston Stackhouse started playing guitar": McCormick's notes from a July 1, 1970, interview with Stackhouse, in Washington, DC, are in McCormick Collection, box 39, folder 4. McCormick's archive suggests that he worked with Stackhouse during the 1970 and 1972 Smithsonian Folklife Festivals in Washington and during the 1971 Festival of American Folklife in Montreal.

82: "Robert Johnson's first record had been issued in January 1937": The budget label Perfect Records appears to have released "Kind Hearted Woman Blues," backed with "Terraplane Blues," on January 4, 1937. Oriole Records and Romeo Records followed suit, selling the records for twenty-five cents apiece in select dime stores and department stores. Vocalion waited to release the record through its March 1937 catalog. Conforth and Wardlow, *Up Jumped the Devil*, 150–151, 185.

85: "There were three Majors listed in that phone book": At this time McCormick was still searching for a "Julia Major"—the name provided as Johnson's mother on his death certificate, rather than her correctly spelled name, "Julia Majors."

6. OTHER JOHNSONS

90: "He did tell me my daddy had a brother up in the Delta": Before meeting Robert Johnson's sisters, who quelled the theory, McCormick spent a lot of time investigating whether musicians Robert Johnson and Tommy Johnson were closely related. They were not. Claud may have been told instead about Robert's musician brother, Charles Leroy Johnson, or Smith may have provided entirely incorrect information to Claud.

91: "Mager and his brothers": Notes on one of McCormick's interviews with Mager Johnson are in McCormick Collection, box 102, folder 14.

93: "Now don'cha hear me talkin'": The lyrics are quoted from Tommy Johnson, "Big Road Blues" (Victor, 1928).

96: "the general family understanding that they were somehow related": All of these theories, McCormick would later learn, were untrue.

96: "A dead end": Hudson clearly had no interest in speaking with this white stranger who knocked on his door. His tactics of refusal led McCormick to provide an ungenerous description of him.

97: "I gritted my teeth and went away": Another tactic of refusal to speak to white strangers about such matters was to claim that one's religious beliefs or church forbade discussing their past life working in secular music (especially the blues). For some, of course, this was a deeply held conviction rather than a tactic. See also McCormick Collection, box 76, folder 5, p. 176, where McCormick describes how people would react to him and his strategies.

97: "When a Charley Patton song was played": Patton's first name in some documents and publications is spelled Charlie.

98: "But he'd never heard 'Hellhound on My Trail'": Although the original records spelled this as "Hell Hound," most sources seem to use "Hellhound."

7. MISSISSIPPI 304

102: "The handful of people I'd encountered were cranky and uncommunicative": Many of Robinsonville's African American residents had left town for brighter futures and economic prospects by 1970. Those who remained faced bleak prospects for employment and severe economic challenges in the years that McCormick was conducting his research. That the people McCormick summarily dismissed in this passage saw little to gain in entertaining this stranger's line of questioning should not have come as a surprise.

102: "found the clue": In 1964 Blues Mafia founding member Nick Perls, along with Dick Waterman and Phil Spiro, discovered the whereabouts of Son House, who was living in Rochester, New York. See Daniel Beaumont, *Preachin' the Blues: The Life & Times of Son House* (New York: Oxford University Press, 2011), 1–6.

104: "Was there one named Johnson?": Chris Strachwicz, who traveled in Texas with McCormick in the early 1960s, has described McCormick's mannerisms and questioning strategies when approaching locals as akin to that of a police officer. See "Conversation with the Blues (1965): Its Significance and Legacy" webinar, February 24, 2022, https://brookes.cloud .panopto.eu/Panopto/Pages/Viewer.aspx?id=6fafc6a5-1a23-4ef7-a877-ae47008c6c98.

110: "went up to talk with Jack Hudson": McCormick met Jack Hudson in April 1970. See photographs of Hudson and his bus in McCormick Collection, box 18, folder F-223.

114: "Cleveland and Lula Smith talked for over a half-hour": McCormick interviewed Cleveland and Lula Smith on April 27, 1970. He reported from the interview that Robert Spencer was also known as "Son Spencer," yet "Son" seems instead to have been the nickname for Charles Leroy Spencer. In the same interview, however, the Smiths distinguish Robert from Charles Leroy Spencer. The interview notes are found in McCormick Collection, box 104, folder 16.

117: "the Robert Johnson mystique rarely gives it any special attention": McCormick recorded a fascinating phone interview with Virginia Heisley, who was a record buyer for two locations of the "J. R. Reed Music. Co." which had locations in Texas. She recalled ordering 250 copies of "Terraplane Blues" for one record store in Houston. McCormick pushed back on those high numbers, but she was certain. She provided numbers for purchases of other Johnson records, as well. See the recording in McCormick Collection, 1485.25. Bruce Conforth and Gayle Dean Wardlow estimate the sales of "Terraplane Blues" were "in the thousands." See *Up Jumped the Devil: The Real Life of Robert Johnson* (Chicago: Chicago Review Press, 2019), 151.

119: "They'd been boyhood chums": McCormick interviewed Clark on April 27, 1970. The interview notes are found in McCormick Collection, box 104, folder 16.

123: "and had kept Robert's guitar": McCormick interviewed Ruffin on April 27, 1970. The interview notes are found in McCormick Collection, box 104, folder 16. Pete Ruffin (1903–1981), according to the 1930 US Census was farming in Beat 1, Tunica, Mississippi. In 1940 he was farming in Walls, Mississippi. He was buried in Robinsonville.

123: "That's Butch Long": McCormick was using the name "Butch Long" to refer to a man living in the area most typically referenced in public records as "Phax Long." He also refers to the name "Phax Long" later in the manuscript. See McCormick Collection, box 104, folder 16. An eleven-year-old Phax Long is recorded in the 1920 US Census as living in Beat 1 of Tunica County, Mississippi. He lived then in a household that included his grandfather, Phax Phillips. In the 1930 US Census, a "Fox Long," recorded as being twenty-five years old, was married and working as a farmer in the same beat. The World War II draft card for Phax Long indicates his birthdate as September 13, 1904. At that time he was married to Jennie Long from Memphis, Tennessee. His employer was listed as S. R. Leatherman, Robinsonville, Mississippi. His name was listed in the Robinsonville telephone book through 1997.

125: "I asked about Robert Spencer": For an alternative version of the chapters on meeting Cleveland and Lula Smith, Alex Clark, and Phax Long, see McCormick Collection, box 125, folder 17.

126: "The brother, Leroy, died about 1961": Charles Leroy Melvin Spencer died in 1961 and is buried in Tunica County, Mississippi. Annye C. Anderson and Preston Lauterbach, *Brother Robert: Growing Up with Robert Johnson* (New York: Hachette Books, 2020), 100. The two sisters they recalled were Carrie Thompson and Bessie Hines.

8. LEATHERMAN

127: "Could a town also be a plantation, we wondered?": The quote is found in the booklet written by Bernard Klatzko in *The Immortal Charlie Patton, 1887–1934*, vol. 2 (Original Jazz Library, OJL-7, 1964).

128: "From the people still there I gained a fragmentary picture": The archive does not clarify this, but the pages that follow seem to represent a composite of comments Mack McCormick heard from people he met near or on the Leatherman and Polk plantations.

130: "they formed a little spasm band": A spasm band is characterized by playing instruments not originally intended as such—a washtub, for instance, or the guitar made from a cigar box that McCormick mentions. The term dates to 1895, first encountered in the name of a popular proto-jazz ensemble, the Razzy Dazzy Spasm Band.

131: "Henson was known locally for a song called 'Lost Girl'": The 1930 US Census records a fifty-five-year-old man named Jim Henson working as a farmer in Beat 4 of Tunica County, Mississippi.

132: "the Delta begins in the lobby of the Peabody Hotel": The quote McCormick provided was, "Suh, the Delta begins in the lobby of the Peabody Hotel in Memphis and runs clear to the Gulf of Mexico," but it seems that he meant to refer to a quote from author David Cohn in *Where I Was Born and Raised* (New York: Houghton Mifflin, 1948).

133: "it was here that the old cotton culture": McCormick is correct on these points: the enslavement of Black families that was core to the Delta's emerging "cotton culture" followed the brutal, forced removal of most of the Choctaws, Chickasaws, and other Native peoples from their lands. This enslavement, followed by the coerced labor of incarcerated Black men through Mississippi's notorious convict lease system, and later the development of exploitative labor practices through sharecropping, occurred through the brutality and human rights abuses perpetrated upon Black families in the "cotton culture" and enabled the economic glory achieved by white enslavers and landowners. From the late nineteenth through the mid-twentieth centuries, this cotton culture was romanticized through the "plantation songs" of Blackface minstrelsy, genteel literary depictions of the "Old South" and slavery as righteous and morally sound, and other cultural expressions that worked to legitimize and rationalize both slavery and the Jim Crow status quo.

134: "coping with big-city slums": McCormick is describing, through the use of the phrase "big-city slums," the segregated, red-lined working-class neighborhoods in cities throughout the country that suffered from inequitable resource allocations. Many African American families fled the racial violence and economic limitations of the Delta and surrounding areas decades prior to mechanization.

135: "enough to go to the post office and buy a money order": Bruce Conforth and Gayle Dean Wardlow provide a different story regarding Johnson's first acquisition of a guitar. See *Up Jumped the Devil: The Real Life of Robert Johnson* (Chicago: Chicago Review Press, 2019), 62. Mrs. Annye Anderson reports that it was her father who taught Johnson to play guitar, when

Johnson was seven years old. See Annye C. Anderson and Preston Lauterbach, *Brother Robert: Growing Up with Robert Johnson* (New York: Hachette Books, 2020), 24.

9. LISTENING AND REMEMBERING

141: "Alex Clark came with several others": For notes on McCormick's conversations with Alex Clark, Phax Long, and Cleveland and Lula Smith, see McCormick Collection, box 125, folder 17, and box 104, folder 16.

145: "he was full of thoughts that provoked him": McCormick added, "none of the Robinson-ville people here can think of Robert Spencer as settled and responsible. They remember only the young man who grew older but no more at ease. His teenager's recklessness stayed with him as he aged, and grew more inward." These judgments seem more conjectural on McCormick's part than rooted in direct comments from those who spoke with him, and they also feed unnecessarily into the cliché he was acknowledging—a one-dimensional portrait of a Delta blues singer rooted in mythologies spun by white writers.

146: "He dressed poorly": Other accounts depict Johnson as a sharp-dressed man; some of these memories may refer to Johnson when he was younger, before he had earned enough money to buy suits. It is unknown when his biological father Noah Johnson died, nor how well Robert came to know him. Dusty Willis was younger than Robert's mother, Julia. For McCormick's research leads in his quest to discover more information about Noah Johnson, see McCormick Collection, box 102, folder 9.

148: "Blues ain't nothing but a lowdown shaking chill": McCormick is referring to a line in Son House's "Walking Blues," recorded by Alan Lomax in 1942 on behalf of the Library of Congress, and distributed commercially beginning in the early 1970s. See Alan Lomax and Son House, *Walking Blues* (Washington, DC: American Folklife Center, US Library of Congress, 1942).

149: "I could hear Johnson intone": McCormick's line about the "other man's bull calf" is derived from the lyrics of Johnson's recording from June 20, 1937, entitled "Milkcow's Calf Blues."

150: "the more entertainment he'd have to offer": McCormick added, "It followed that the demand for whores, bootleggers, gamblers, and musicians increased nearer to Memphis." This claim asserts a generalization without substantiation that sharecroppers working near Memphis demanded access to illicit trades.

10. HINDSIGHT

154: "His records mention four women by name": McCormick provided the name "Bertie Mae" instead of "Betty Mae," who figures in Johnson's "Honeymoon Blues."

154: "He never did talk about his past life": Quoted from Pete Welding, "I Sing for the People: An Interview with Howlin' Wolf," *Down Beat* 34, no. 25 (December 14, 1967): 20–23.

154: "Think I heard he went to Helena": Quoted in Paul Oliver, *Conversation with the Blues* (New York: Horizon Press, 1965), 67.

155: "I never heard him talk even once about his family": The Johnny Shines quotes come from Pete Welding, "Ramblin' Johnny Shines," *Living Blues* 22 (July–August 1975): 23–32, and 23 (September–October 1975): 22–29. The veracity of Johnny Shines's and other musical contemporaries' claims of knowing and traveling with Robert Johnson are disputed by some, including members of Robert Johnson's family, who believe that some artists attempted to respond positively to white writers' and critics' interests in Robert Johnson without actually having spent much time with the man, if any time at all. Mrs. Annye Anderson writes, for example, "I met Johnny Shines, a musician who'd told many stories about traveling and performing with Brother Robert. I know Johnny Shines knew Robert Johnson, but not as well as he claimed. But if you want to get a little money, and tell white folks what they want to hear, they'll give you a few dimes." See Annye C. Anderson and Peter Lauterbach, *Brother Robert: Growing Up with Robert Johnson* (New York: Hachette Books, 2020), 125–126. If Mrs. Anderson's assertion is correct, this would explain why some contemporaries interviewed extensively on their knowledge of Johnson seemed never able to answer fundamental questions about Johnson's family and background, even after having claimed to have traveled extensively with him. The impression left in consequence is one that Johnson cared little about his family or loved ones, while *Brother Robert* paints an entirely different, and much more human, picture of him.

157: "Robert would do his crying on the inside": Quoted from Johnny Shines, "The Robert Johnson I Knew," *American Folk Music Occasional* 2 (1970): 30–32.

157: "he never did show it": Quoted in Pete Welding, "The Robert Johnson I Knew: An Interview with Henry Townsend," *Down Beat* 35, no. 22 (October 31, 1968): 18, 32.

157: "Surely, then, they could say more": In regard to Pete Welding's interview with Henry Townsend, Barry Lee Pearson and Bill McCulloch note in *Robert Johnson: Lost and Found* (Urbana: University of Illinois Press, 2003), "Reading this remark, one gets the sense that Welding was fishing for testimony that would support his own portrait of Johnson as doomed and demon driven. Townsend's respectful response—maybe he felt depressed, but he never showed it—could have been an example of the way older blues musicians often deflected leading questions from white interviewers. Whether it was or it wasn't, the response nonetheless delicately disputed any dark suggestions from Welding about Johnson's psyche. Overall the critics' view is so much at odds with the impressions of people who knew Johnson and who heard him perform that we have to challenge most, if not all, of the latter-day analyses. One begins to suspect that it is Robert who sits impassively in the chair, while [Giles] Oakley, [Samuel] Carters, [Pete] Welding, and company lie on the couch and pour out their obsessions" (42).

159: "in the unlikely city of Montreal": McCormick is referring to the 1971 Festival of American Folklife in Montreal.

159: "He asked other musicians what they knew about Robert Johnson": Oddly, McCormick left out of his manuscript the recollections of some of Johnson's peers whom he interviewed, including those of guitarist and one-time member of the Beale Street Jug Band, Willie Morris. While interviewing Morris on July 4, 1972, during the Smithsonian's Folklife Festival in Washington, DC, Morris recalled seeing Johnson play in two Memphis clubs: King's Palace on Beale and Third Street and at the Memphis Star on Beale and Fourth Street. He recalled that Johnson sometimes played with his brother in Memphis, and recounted memories of Johnson's mother, stories about Johnson from around Robinsonville, and the success of "Terraplane Blues." See the digitized interview in McCormick Collection, 1485.18.

160: "Son House's testimony was not as fully appreciated as it warranted": For a biographical treatment of Son House's musical life, see Daniel Beaumont, *Preachin' the Blues: The Life & Times of Son House* (New York: Oxford University Press, 2011).

161: "Son House makes no particular claim to teaching Robert Johnson": Beaumont provides an assessment of how Johnson came to know Son House and takes the examples of his "Walking Blues" and "My Black Mama" to argue that Johnson was influenced by seeing Son House perform in person. *Preachin' the Blues*, 88–91.

162: "the published accounts all agree substantially on this event": Assertions of association between Robert Johnson and the devil have long fascinated white blues writers, who often prompted Johnson's contemporaries to speak on the plausibility of such a relationship. Wald argues that the mythology of Johnson making a deal with the devil tells "us less about the realities of Johnson's music than about the romantic leanings of his later, urban white listeners," while Pearson and McCulloch consider the writers who trade in this mythology as "Hellhound Conspirators." They argue, "after all the tedious fly-specking of the song texts, all the interviews, and all the thousands of words that have been written and spoken on the subject, there is no verifiable link between Robert Johnson and the devil. The historical evidence is tainted by hearsay, dubious research, compromised methodology, and questionable reporting. Even the folkloric evidence is too threadbare to stand up under close scrutiny. Most significantly of all, a majority of the musicians who were close to Johnson are on record as saying the story is a crock." See Elijah Wald, *Escaping the Delta: Robert Johnson and the Invention of the Blues* (New York: Amistad, 2004), 266, and Pearson and McCulloch, *Lost and Found*, 38 and 102. Ted Gioia assessed those comments and protests the idea that they were driven by the interests of the writers: "This story, in all its lurid details, sprang up decades before [the 1960s], and in all probability came from the musician himself." See Gioia, *Delta Blues: The Life and Times of the Mississippi Masters Who Revolutionized American Music* (New York: Norton, 2008), 164. Kimberly Mack, meanwhile, suggests that all of these writers are missing the forest for the trees: "what [Pearson and McCulloch] are actually interrogating is how the African American folk tradition that eventually morphs into the African American blues tradition is brought to bear on Johnson's legend. Essentially, Johnson's mythos is built on the fictional autobiographical and biographical narratives that continue to fuel the tellings and retellings of his life and legend in popular culture, and in expressive art of all kinds. Ultimately, Pearson's and McCulloch's findings—after reading through scholarly and journalistic works about Johnson by Stephen

Calt and Gayle Dean Wardlow, Peter Guralnick, Mack McCormick, Samuel Charters, Paul Oliver, and others, and discovering that the likely origin of the crossroads tale is a single interview with Son House by Pete Welding in *Down Beat*—confirm the importance of stories and storytelling in the blues tradition, whether those tales originate with the blues makers, fans, or scholars and journalists." Mack, *Fictional Blues: Narrative Self-Invention from Bessie Smith to Jack White* (Amherst: University of Massachusetts Press, 2020), 112.

162: "an interviewer named the plantation 'Lellman'": For "Lellman," see Julius Lester, "I Can Make My Own Songs—An Interview with Son House," *Sing Out!* 15, no. 3 (July 1965) 38–47.

II. GREENWOOD

165 "rumors placing Robert Johnson's death in at least thirteen different towns": McCormick wrote that before 1969 he had investigated possible locations for Robert Johnson's death in Hot Springs and West Helena, Arkansas; Eudora, Gulfport, Friars Point, Minter City, McComb, Leland, Tunica, Greenwood, and Clarksdale, Mississippi; and Chicago and Cairo, Illinois. The copy he received of the death certificate from Leflore County included only the front of the certificate. Years later, Gayle Dean Wardlow discovered that critical information on his death was provided after a later inquiry on the back of the certificate. For the story, see Wardlow, "Robert Johnson: New Details on the Death of a Bluesman," in *Chasin' That Devil Music* (San Francisco: Backbeat Books, 2001), 91–93.

166: "enthusiastically pointing out to me large southern mansions": Most of Greenwood's mansions, including Provine House, were built in the early twentieth century.

171: "A little while later he'd died": Chronology is difficult to verify when reconciling notes in the archive with this chapter of McCormick's manuscript. Some of the conversations in this chapter seem to date to 1969, and by 1970 at the latest McCormick had become familiar with several details, including the involvement in the story of the man known locally as "Tush Hog." Two of Jimmy Edwards's neighbors who filled in details of Johnson's last days were Robert and Izena Edwards. McCormick recorded an interview with them on October 28, 1975, the same day that he interviewed planter Luther Wade. However, in the audio recording of the interview with Robert and Izena, they recall McCormick visiting them several years earlier, asking the same questions. McCormick therefore likely first interviewed the Edwards in 1969 or 1970, and then returned in 1975 to record an interview with them and to collect additional details. Izena Edwards died in 1977, less than two years after McCormick recorded an interview with her. She is buried in Little Zion M.B. Church Cemetery, the same cemetery as was laid Robert Johnson after he passed away. For the Wade, Jimmy (Jimmie) Edwards, and Robert and Izena Edwards notes, see box 109, folder 13, with additional manuscript versions and quotations provided in box 127, folder 4. Barry Lee Pearson and Bill McCulloch note that "Tush Hog is a common nickname in Alabama and Mississippi, where it identifies a tough guy or fighter." See their *Robert Johnson: Lost and Found* (Urbana: University of Illinois Press, 2003), 116n15.

172: "They thought they could have been related": According to Bruce Conforth and Gayle Dean Wardlow, in 1938 Jim Moore was living next door to a relative of Robert Johnson's named Jessie Dodds. Their proximity may suggest why Jim Moore was listed as an informant on Johnson's death certificate. See *Up Jumped the Devil: The Real Life of Robert Johnson* (Chicago: Chicago Review Press, 2019), 258.

172: "a man named 'Smokey Hamber'": For a while, McCormick pursued information on Jimmie "Smokey" Hamber, believing that he may have had something to do with Johnson's death. He eventually interviewed Hamber (likely in October 1975); see the notes in McCormick Collection, box 111, folder 3. Hamber indicated that he was not living in the area at the time of Johnson's death, and did not know him. Robert and Izena Edwards corroborated that Hamber was not living in the area when Johnson was killed. They reported that Johnson, in the two months or so that he was in the area before he died, primarily played at Gib May's and Tush Hog's frolic houses, and was spending a lot of time with a single woman named Lilian Gaitor (spelling not confirmed). Izena Edwards said the "gossip" was that he died "unnaturally," perhaps by poison, perhaps over his involvement with a local woman. See McCormick Collection, box 109, folder 13. Gib May is represented in official records in Leflore County. There are several people with names that have spellings similar to "Lilian Gaitor" found in Mississippi records.

172: "Luther Wade is still preoccupied": McCormick drew from a number of quotations in his October 28, 1975, interview with Wade, including Wade's complaint about the "damn hourly-wage stuff." It is unclear, however, when McCormick first met Wade. See McCormick Collection, box 109, folder 13.

174: "Across the right side of the sheet": In the 1990s, Gayle Wardlow discovered a note that summarized a later investigation of Johnson's death, which had been typed onto the back of Johnson's death certificate. The note read, "I talked with the white man on whose place this negro died and I also talked with a negro woman on the place. The plantation owner said this negro man, seemingly about 26 years old, came from Tunica two or three weeks before he died to play a banjo at a negro dance given there on the plantation. He staid [*sic*] in the house with some of the negroes saying he wanted to pick cotton. The white man did not have a doctor for this negro as he had not worked for him. He was buried in a homemade coffin furnished by the county. The plantation owner said it was his opinion that the negro died of syphilis." The back of the certificate also revealed that Carrie Harris (Thompson), Johnson's sister, had ordered a copy of the death certificate on September 14, 1938. Since the front of the certificate indicates that "no doctor" was present to examine Johnson's condition when alive, or to examine his body, after he died, it is impossible to know how he died, nor why his death was attributed, one month later, to "syphilis." See Wardlow, "Robert Johnson: New Details on the Death of a Bluesman," 91–92.

174: "That's a long time": This quote suggests that this courthouse encounter took place in 1969.

177: "Earle Equen had died in 1953": McCormick recorded a phone interview with Equen's widow in November 1973. See McCormick Collection, 1485.23.a.

179: "a Leflore County grand jury had refused to indict them": Till was kidnapped, tortured, and killed by Roy Bryant, the husband of the woman in the store, Carolyn Bryant, and by Roy Bryant's half-brother, J. W. Milam.

179: "The sheriff gave me a hard look": We removed a section that follows, where McCormick describes encountering a woman who had an intimate relationship with Johnson. We found no substantiation of the interview in the archive and reasoned that it might be a fictional, conjectural addition by McCormick.

AFTERWORD

182: "the tragedies exposed in the archives": The archive is extraordinarily wide-ranging, as were McCormick's research interests, and the documents pertaining to Robert Johnson comprise only around 30 boxes out of a total of 165. The research that supported the publication of this edition of *Biography of a Phantom* exposed the many layers of the archive, but those layers and the dilemmas and revelations that follow them extend to every corner of the archive.

183: "now she was frustrated": For some of Thompson's challenges and her frustrations with McCormick during this period, see Annye C. Anderson and Peter Lauterbach, *Brother Robert: Growing Up with Robert Johnson* (New York: Hachette Books, 2020), 73, 106–107, 110–111, 113, 115.

183: "as the rightful heirs to Johnson's estate": See Thompson's original agreement, dated July 8, 1972, in McCormick Collection, box 30, folder 1. See Hines's original agreement in box 19, folder F-329.

184: "Though she remained cautious about trusting LaVere": For Thompson's agreements with LaVere and her growing distrust of him, see Anderson and Lauterbach, *Brother Robert*, 109–113. See also a timeline and description of Thompson's agreements with LaVere in *Anderson v. Stephen C. LaVere, Delta Haze Corp.*, Supreme Court of Mississippi, February 20, 2014, 136 So3d 404.

184: "he plummeted into darkness": For the heroin letter, see McCormick Collection, box 29, folder 2. In an April 20, 2022, interview for Smithsonian Folkways, while recalling his road trips from California to Texas during this period, Chris Strachwicz did not recall driving a Rambler. For Guralnick, see box 116, folder 8.

185: "In another menacing call script": For the scripted threats to Thompson, see McCormick Collection, box 30, folder 2.

185: "Just feel hopeless now": For the letter about the dream, see Anderson and Lauterbach, *Brother Robert*, 121–122.

185: "In the years that followed, no one prospered": For the quotation from Hammond's April 30, 1975, letter to McCormick, see McCormick Collection, box 29, folder 9. For the voluminous exchanges between various Columbia Records executives and attorneys and McCormick, see box 29, folder 9, and box 95, folder 14.

186: "McCormick sent Hammond a five-page letter": See McCormick to Hammond, November 10, 1975, in McCormick Collection, box 29, folder 9.

186: "McCormick was in decline": For this frantic, back-to-back set of correspondence from McCormick, see McCormick Collection, box 29, folder 9.

187: "he continued to plead with McCormick": Hammond indicated to McCormick that Columbia Records had only found out about the pictures and biographical information in May 1974, but other sources indicate that Hammond was presented with LaVere's pitch in the summer of 1973, soon after LaVere's first meeting with Thompson. See *Anderson v. Stephen C. LaVere, Delta Haze Corp.*, Supreme Court of Mississippi, February 20, 2014, 136 So3d 404. For McCormick's learning of the Columbia Records deal from LaVere, see Robert Gordon, "The Devil's Work: The Plundering of Robert Johnson," *LA Weekly*, July 5–11, 1991. For examples of correspondence to and from or notes regarding McCormick's personas of Stonecipher and Scott, as well as two others—D. N. Anthony and J. D. Horn—see McCormick Collection, box 110, folder 18; box 99, folder 22; box 29, folder 9; and box 23, folder 12.

187: "sent letters to McCormick": In documents and publications, Lewis is sometimes spelled Louis. For letters from Thompson's attorneys to McCormick in 1981, see McCormick Collection, box 30, folder 2.

188: "McCormick left a paper trail of evidence": McCormick's notes to himself that seem associated with the fraudulent two-page agreements with Thompson and Hines include the phrase "use signature as is—or trace. This does not allow coming up with an original." In addition, both the shorter and longer documents were dated the same day each for Carrie Thompson and Bessie Hines. Yet the longer document is on legal paper with a different watermark and is from a typewriter using a different typeface. For correspondence referring to excerpts from the fabricated and forged, two-page agreement, and evidence suggesting the inauthenticity of the latter, see McCormick Collection, box 30, folder 1, and box 30, folder 2. For McCormick's submission of excerpts of the fraudulent agreement and the increasing dismay of Columbia Record's legal team, see box 95, folder 14. For the unsubstantiated stories about a burglary in his home, German television producers, and a warehouse in Mexico, see box 23, folder 14; box 29, folder 5; and box 29, folder 2.

189: "That was a very far cry from what Johnson himself earned in his lifetime": See Rick Bragg, "Court Rules Father of the Blues Has a Son," *New York Times*, June 17, 2000. In the article, Claud Johnson's mother is identified as Virgie Jane Smith Cain. On litigation that extended beyond this case, see Associated Press, "Snapshots of Bluesman Robert Johnson Lead to Family Tug-of-War Headed to Mississippi Supreme Court." See also Hammond to McCormick, November 7, 1972, in McCormick Collection, box 29, folder 9. Hammond meant to refer to American Record Corporation, which administered the recording and release of Johnson's records, and not American Record Company, which was a different company. Johnson's producer for both recording sessions, Don Law, speculated that Johnson may have been paid $25 per side. See Brian Ward and Patrick Huber, *A&R Pioneers: Architects of American Roots Music on Record* (Nashville, TN: Vanderbilt University Press and the Country Music Foundation Press, 2018), 161–170.

190: "a suspect responsible for the death of Robert Johnson": McCormick's most detailed notes on Johnson's death are associated with his interviews with Robert and Izena Edwards. See McCormick Collection, box 109, folder 13. For his interview notes with Jimmie Hamber, see box 152, folder 4. In *Up Jumped the Devil: The Real Life of Robert Johnson* (Chicago: Chicago Review Press, 2019), Bruce Conforth and Gayle Dean Wardlow report that McCormick told them the name of the wife of the killer was Beatrice Davis. Conforth and Wardlow then identify her husband as R. D. "Ralph" Davis and suggest that he did not intend to kill Johnson when he mixed mothballs into a jar of corn liquor. The passage is uncited, save for the indication that McCormick revealed to them the name of Beatrice Davis. However, the Davis couple does not seem to appear in McCormick's archive—either in his hundreds of research files or even in one of his many "hoax notes."

190: "McCormick came to believe a number of these stories and assertions": McCormick seems to have latched onto the fact, for example, that Carrie Thompson's brother Robert was identified on the back of his death certificate as a *banjo* player and not a guitar player. Most attribute this as an unsurprising mistake made by the disinterested informant—according to the document, the "white man on whose place this negro died," likely Luther Wade—who was questioned by the LeFlore County Registrar when Johnson's sister Carrie demanded an investigation one month following his death. For the thirty-one Robert Johnsons, see McCormick's notes to his attorney in 1999 in McCormick Collection, box 99, folder 8. For the descriptions of six of them, provided by McCormick near the end of his life, see Steve Cushing, *Pioneers of the Blues Revival*, 2nd ed. (Urbana: University of Illinois Press, 2014), 414–418. McCormick was deposed for a suit filed by Claud Johnson and Steve LaVere to yield to them the photograph of Robert Johnson and Lewis Harris Jr. believed to have been in McCormick's possession and a photograph of Claud Johnson provided to McCormick in 1970 by Virgie Mae Cain (who expected its return). In addition, the filing requested that McCormick provide copies to the court of any Robert Johnson-related objects in his possession. LaVere believed that his own agreement with Carrie Thompson granted him the license to exploit any photographs ever found of her brother Robert. McCormick indicated that the photographs may have been misplaced, lost, or stolen, and the suit seems to have fizzled.

191: "the persistent inequities of the distribution of blues wealth": For an assessment of some of these tropes, see Marybeth Hamilton, *In Search of the Blues* (New York: Basic Books, 2009), 241. For the study of Clarksdale, Mississippi, residents' views on local blues tourism, see B. Brian Foster, *I Don't Like the Blues: Race, Place & the Backbeat of Black Life* (Chapel Hill: University of North Carolina Press, 2020). See also Chris Thomas King, *The Blues: The Authentic Narrative of My Music and Culture* (Chicago: Chicago Review Press, 2021), and Adam Gussow, *Whose Blues? Facing Up to Race and the Future of the Music* (Chapel Hill: University of North

Carolina Press, 2020), each of which explores the racial politics and questions of cultural appropriation in blues history as well as in the contemporary blues world.

193: "When Susannah made the decision to donate the archive": Susannah Nix also donated to the Music Maker Foundation her advances for the publication of this book, as well as for the 2023 release of McCormick's field recordings on Smithsonian Folkways.

194: "In respect for her wishes": Mrs. Annye Anderson is co-heir and executrix of both Carrie Thompson's and Bessie Hines's estates. The "return" of interviews to the control of only one party in two-party interviews, with signed agreements in place, raises a range of issues compounded by questions surrounding the ownership of McCormick's own notes, manuscripts, or other written recollections of those interviews. At the same time, Mrs. Anderson's request proved simple and compelling to not only the Smithsonian team working on the archive, but also to Susannah Nix. Sorting through the implications and logistical execution of the request is taking time, but in the meantime the museum has restricted public access of these materials.

194: "he managed to publish only one piece": For McCormick's one published work on Johnson, see Robert Burton McCormick, "The Search for Robert Johnson," *American Visions: The Magazine of Afro-American Culture*, June 1988. Copies of the essay, drafts, and notes about its publication are found in McCormick Collection, box 68, folder 19, and box 101, folder 22. In *American Visions*, McCormick wrote, "I took advantage of the frequent travel required by my job as a writer, a record producer, and cultural historian attached to the Smithsonian Institution to continue the search." McCormick shared some of his research with Peter Guralnick, which resulted in the publication of an essay by Guralnick and eventually his book *Searching for Robert Johnson* (New York: Plume, 1998).

195: "calls for museums to reevaluate their practices": For a useful framework when considering the proper "looking after" of early blues artists, see Daphne Brooks's *Liner Notes for the Revolution: The Intellectual Life of Black Feminist Sound* (Cambridge, MA: Belknap Press of Harvard University Press, 2021), and in particular her ruminations on blues scholarship and criticism on pages 271–309. She deploys Kara Keeling's notion of "looking after" as a "form of radical Black queer praxis" when considering how we might move to engage the archive of blues women such as L.V. Thomas and Geeshie Wiley (307). The Smithsonian has been reckoning with questions of ethical ownership since at least the 1970s, as indigenous people's voices grew more prominent in protest of the institution's collections of their ancestor's remains. The 1989, Public Law 101-185, 101st Congress National Museum of the American Indian (NMAI) Act required the Smithsonian Institution to survey and instigate the return of American Indian and Native Hawaiian human remains and funerary objects. The 1996, Public Law 104-278, 104th Congress amendment to the NMAI Act expanded and clarified this work to require the Smithsonian "to return, upon request, human remains, funerary objects, sacred objects and objects of cultural patrimony to culturally affiliated federal recognized Indian tribes," as well as to qualified Native Hawaiian organizations (https://americanindian.si.edu/explore/repatriation). Work toward the transfer of the Thompson and Hines photographs began in earnest in the spring of 2020. It was a unique project for the Smithsonian, falling beyond the confines of repatriation legislation, and gained the support of the Secretary's Office. In 2021 the National Museum of American History launched the Center for Restorative History (CRH), which "redresses exclusions in our national story using the principles of restorative justice. The CRH uses these principles to center the knowledge and expertise of communities, working in partnership with them to address and document historical harms, current needs, and obligations in an effort to make history more accurate and inclusive" (https://americanhistory.si.edu/restorative-history). Also in 2021, the Smithsonian organized the Working Group for Ethical Returns to develop policy for transfers of objects beyond the 1996 NMAIA legislation. As a result of that work, the Smithsonian announced a policy on Ethical Returns on May 3, 2022 (www.si.edu/newsdesk/releases/smithsonian-adopts-policy-ethical-returns). With increased urgency, the ethics of museum practices and policies regarding collections, audience, and interpretation are being reevaluated and reimagined.

ACKNOWLEDGMENTS

Several colleagues, family, and friends old and new were responsible for seeing through this component of a sprawling set of work involving the Robert "Mack" McCormick Collection. Susannah and David Nix, along with Bill Kroger, placed trust in our Smithsonian team to organize and steward Susannah's father's papers, photographs, and recordings. All three of them have been remarkably generous and patient collaborators in this process. I could not have imagined a better or more thoughtful partner to work with than Susannah—her deep commitment to seeing her father's book in print and his archive opened to the public was matched only by her resolve to ensure that the challenging truths about her father's complicated life were made visible in the process.

From the beginning, several Smithsonian staff played critical roles in this work. Bob Horton, former head of the National Museum of American History's Archives Center, shepherded the acquisition process for the collection and did some of his own knocking on doors with me as we worked to locate heirs for photographs that needed to be transferred from the collection. Craig Blackwell of the Smithsonian Institution's Office of General Counsel provided critical guidance from the beginning. Craig Orr and Cathy Keen of the museum's Archives Center, along with myself and Jeff Place from Smithsonian Folkways, packed up the collection over a few hot August days in Houston. Vanessa Broussard Simmons led the museum's Archives Center team to organize and process the collection and has continued to serve in a critical role for museum projects related to the collection. The Archives Center's Alison Oswald, Kay Peterson, and Franklin Robinson also provided key work to process the collection and render it accessible. I was provided steadfast support by my curatorial division's chairperson, Stacey Kluck, by our Deputy Director of Public History, Benjamin Filene, and by the Elizabeth MacMillan Director of our museum, Anthea Hartig.

Carolyn Gleason of Smithsonian Books believed in our approach to the book from the beginning and provided excellent guidance and editorial advice. I greatly enjoyed working with her team, made up of Jaime Schwender, Matt Litts, Sarah Fannon, and Julie Huggins, as well as our copyeditors, Duke Johns and Gregory McNamee. Thanks to Scott Baretta and Preston Lauterbach for providing some key support along the way. Mrs. Annye Anderson's wisdom, insight, and life experiences, as shared in her essential book, *Brother Robert*, profoundly affected my approach to the manuscript. I would like to extend a special thanks to James Ellis Thomas, Vanessa Broussard Simmons, and Malinda Maynor Lowery for reading drafts of my editor's preface and afterword as well as for providing some important interventions.

Finally, I would like to express my endless gratitude to my partner, Sara, and our son Jack for their love and support. Thanks also, as always, to Ron Ritchey, Lynne Baursfeld, Mag Ritchey, Dolores Vaughn, and Malisa and Chris Dorn.

• • •

INDEX

Note: Illustrations are indicated by page numbers in *italics*.

Abbay & Leatherman Plantation. *See* Leath-
  erman Plantation
Adams, Samuel, ix
African American, use of term, *xxviii*
Almanac Records, xvi, 199
American Record Company, 189, 220
American Record Corporation, 220
Amico, Robert, 74
Anderson, Annye, vii, xxviii, xxix–xxx,
  183–87, 193, 201, 208, 210, 215, 222
Arhoolie Records, 184
Arnold, Kokomo, 205
Arterbury, John, 177–79
Avakian, George, 16, 204

Badeaux, Ed, xiii, xvii, 200
Badeaux, Mary, 200
Baraka, Amiri, ix, 197, 209
Berry, Chuck, xxiii
"Big Road Blues," 65, 211
Black, use of term, *xxviii*
"Black Angel Blues," 210
Bloom, Willie, 39
Bloomfield, Mike, xviii
blues, xviii–xxi
  country, ix–x, xx, xxiii, 14
  Delta, x, 44, 69, 134
  exploitation of, 185, 191–92
  urban, ix–x, 15
Blues Mafia, viii–x, x, 194, 197, 211
Blues People: Negro Music in White America
  (Jones). *See* Baraka, Amiri
Bogan, Lucille, 210

boll weevil, 68–69
Brookhaven, Mississippi, 85
Brooks, Daphne, viii, 197, 222
Broonzy, Bill, 201
*Brother Robert: Growing Up with Robert
  Johnson* (Anderson and Lauterbach), xxix,
  xxix–xxx
Brown, Alpheus, 72–74, 77–78
Brown, Benjamin, 209
Brown, Sterling, ix
Brown, Willie, 123–25, 130, 143, 150
Brunswick Record Company, 103
Bryant, Carolyn, 219
Bryant, Roy, 219
Bunch, William, 205
"By Blue Ontario's Shore" (Whitman), 19

Cain, Minerva, 74–77, 79, 86, 89, 209–10
Cain, Virgie Jane Smith. *See* Cain, Virgie
  Mae
Cain, Virgie Mae, 59–64, 67, 78, 84, 189,
  207–8, 220–21
Calt, Stephen, viii, 216–17
Cane, Virgie Jane. *See* Cain, Virgie Mae
Carr, Leroy, 151
Caruso, Enrico, 16
"Casey Jones," 132
Center for Restorative History (CRH), 223
Charters, Samuel, 197, 202, 217
"Chevrolet Blues," 99
Chicago, Illinois, 15, 26–27, 29, 44, 155, 204
Chinese communities, 33, 206
Christian Singers, 201

Civil Rights Movement, ix, 197
Civil War, 26, 68, 133, 168
Clapton, Eric, xxiii, 201
Clark, Alex, 119–21, 141, 150–51, 212, 214
Clarksdale, Mississippi, 31, 44, 69, 192
Cohn, David, 213
Cohn, Lawrence, viii
Coleman, Estella, 207
Coleman, Wade, 67
Columbia Archives, xxiii
Columbia Records, xxiii, 4, 16, *17*, 18, 21–22,
    184–88, 202, 204, 220
"Come On in My Kitchen," 46, 98, 157
Commerce, Mississippi, 113, *113*, 128, *135*, 139,
    158, 162
Como, Mississippi, 38
Conforth, Bruce, xxix, 201, 208, 221
"Cool Drink of Water Blues," 65, 81
Copiah County, 48–87, 96–97, 100, 122,
    137, 209
cotton, 1, 68–69, 133, 164–66, 213n133
country blues, ix–x, xx, xxiii, 14
Craft, Callie, 202, 208
"Cross Road Blues," 17, 82, 142–43
Crowder, Effie Mae. *See* McCormick, Effie
    Mae
Crudup, Arthur "Big Boy," 204
Crystal Springs, Mississippi, 82–84, *83*, 85,
    89, 92, *93*, 208
cultural appropriation. *See* blues: exploita-
    tion of

Davis, Beatrice, 221
Davis, R. D. "Ralph," 221
Davis, Walter, 39, 204
Deal, Otis, 117
death, of Johnson, vii, 3, 23–24, 48–50,
    49, 137–38, 156–59, 164–65, 168–79, 207,
    217–18, 221
Delta blues, x, 44, 69, 134
Dentville, Mississippi, 56, 67–68
"Dixie Boy" hitching posts, 138
Dockery Plantation, 127, 134
Down Beat, xiii, xiv, 217
Driggs, Frank, 4, 16, 204
Du Bois, W. E. B., ix
Dylan, Bob, 201

Ebony (magazine), 17
Edwards, Dave, 160
Edwards, Izena, 190, 217–18, 221
Edwards, Jimmy, 171, 217
Edwards, Robert, 190, 218, 221
"Elder Green Come to Town," 131–32
"Elmo James," 204
Eps, Alpha, 67
Eps, Little Alpha, 67
Equen, Earle, 176–77, 218
Equen, Murdock, 176
Equen, Standard, 176
Escaping the Delta (Wald), 202
Estes, Sleepy John, 150
Ethical Returns, 223
Evans, David, 81

"Falling Rain Blues," 203
Faulkner, William, 166
Festival of American Folklife, xxi, *xxiv–xxv*,
    80, 194
Fictional Blues (Mack), 202
Foster, Brian, 191
Friars Point, Mississippi, 1–2, 5–13, *6*, 203–4
frolics, 73–74, 218
From Spirituals to Swing (concert), *xxii*

Gaitor, Lilian, 218
Gentry, Bobbie, 166
Gibbs, Philip L., 209
Gioia, Ted, 199, 216
Goldblatt, Burt, 141, 148–49
Govenar, Alan, 199
Green, James Earl, 209
Green, Lee, 39
Greenville, Mississippi, 32
Greenwood, Mississippi, 118, 160, 164–81,
    167–68, *170–71*, *173*
Grierson, Benjamin H., 53
Gulfport, Mississippi, 29, 100–101
Guralnick, Peter, vii, xvi–xvii, 184, 202, 217,
    222

Hamber, Jimmie Lee "Smokey," 172, 189, 218
Hamilton, Marybeth, viii, x, 197
Hammond, John, *xxii*, xxiii, 16, 184–87, 189,
    200–201, 220

Hankins, James, 176
Harris, Lewis, 187–88, 192, 220
Hazlehurst, Mississippi, x, 50–60, 62, 65,
   68–78, 76, 100, 139, 207
Heisley, Virginia, 212
Helena, Arkansas, 38–42, 41, 50–52, 51, 81,
   139
"Hellhound on My Trail," 15, 98, 143–45,
   152–53, 211
Henson, Jim, 131
Hernando, Mississippi, 103–7, 147
"Hesitating Blues," 92
Hill, Archie, 67
Hill, L. C., 67
Hines, Bessie, vii, xxviii, 183, 186–88, 192,
   194, 207, 212
Hines, Granville, 187
hitching posts, 138
hoaxes, xx, xxi, 141, 200, 221
"Honeymoon Blues," 9–10, 214
Hooks Brothers Studio, 183, 187
Hopkins, Sam "Lightnin'," xvi, 199, 204–5
Horton, Walter, 158, 160
Hot Springs, Arkansas, 28, 28
House, Son, 48, 103, 123–25, 148, 150,
   160–63, 203, 211, 214–17
Howling Wolf, 154, 214
"How Long Blues," 61
Hudson, Jack, 109, 109–12, 111, 112–13, 211
Hudson, Willie, 67–68, 96, 211
Hughes, Arkansas, 33–35, 150
Hughes, Langston, ix
Hurston, Zora Neale, ix
Hurt, Mississippi John, 48

"I Believe I'll Dust My Broom," 18, 26, 44,
   46, 158, 204
"If I Had Possession over Judgment Day,"
   17, 145
Illinois Central Railroad, 29, 53, 59, 64–65,
   100, 103, 147
imagism, 17
Interstate Grocer Company, 40–43, 42, 45,
   206
"It Makes a Long Time Man Feel Bad,"
   205
"It's Tight Like That," 61

Jackson State University, 209
James, Elmore, 15
Jefferson, Blind Lemon, 151, 156, 199
Jim Crow, vii, xix, xx, 20, 108, 198, 204, 213
"Joe Kirby Blues," 110
Johnson, Blind Willie, xx
Johnson, Clarence, 67
Johnson, Claud, 58–59, 61–65, 84, 88–90,
   125, 188–90, 208, 210
Johnson, Early, 54–55, 97–98, 100
Johnson, LeDell, 92–96, 95
Johnson, Leroy, 206–7
Johnson, Lonnie, 67–68, 94–95, 151
Johnson, Mager, 88, 90–94, 93, 94–96
Johnson, Noah, 75. 7S, 207, 209–10, 214
Johnson, R. L., 59
Johnson, Robert, x, xxix, 38. See also death,
   of Johnson; King of the Delta Blues Sing-
   ers; Spencer, Robert
   childhood of, 98, 121–22, 125, 131, 141, 143,
      150, 162, 213
   death of, vii, 3, 23–24, 48–50, 49, 137–38,
      156–59, 164–65, 168–79, 207, 217–18, 221
   early use of musical instruments by, 162, 213
   legends surrounding, xxix, 18, 33, 155–56,
      216
   Lockwood and, 43
   marriage to Callie Craft, 202, 208
   parents of, 86, 188
   recording sessions of, 36, 98, 117, 145, 151,
      202
   relationship with Virgie Mae Cain, 60–64
   son of, 58–59, 61–65, 84, 88–90, 125,
      188–90, 208, 210
   as underground figure, 17
Johnson, Robert L., 207
Johnson, Tommy, 65, 67, 81, 84, 86, 91–92,
   94, 99, 210–11
Jones, LeRoi. See Baraka, Amiri
Jones, Lewis, ix
Jordan, Cornelia J., 175–76
J. R. Reed Music Co., 212

Kaplan, Ben, viii
Kaufman, Pete, viii
Keeling, Kara, 222
KFFA (radio station), 39–42

"Kind Hearted Woman Blues," 82, 151
King, B. B., 210
King Biscuit Entertainers, 44–46
King Biscuit Time (radio program), 39–40, 42–45, *43*, 44–46, 79, 206
King of the Delta Blues Singers, xxiii, 16–17, *17*, 141–45, *144*, 148–53, 208. See also *Robert Johnson: King of the Delta Blues Singers*
King of the Delta Blues Singers, Vol. II, 18, 21–22
Kirby, Joe, 110
Kitty Cat Cafe, *51*
Klatzko, Bernie, viii, 127

"Last Fair Deal Gone Down," 28–29, 144
Lauterbach, Preston, xxix, xxix–xxx
LaVere, Steve, 183–90, 193–94, 208, 219–20
Law, Don, 201, 221
Leatherman Plantation, 114–15, 117–21, 128, 130, 133, 135, *135*, 137–38, 140, 162
Leflore, Greenwood, 166
Lester, Julius, 25
Lewis, Furry, 150
Lieberson, Goddard, 201
Light Crust Doughboys, 155
Lipscomb, Mance, xvi, 48, 199
Lockwood, Robert, Jr., 40–44, *43*, 44, 46–47, 79, 158, 206
Lomax, Alan, ix, xvii, 197, 202, 205, 214
Lomax, John, xvii
Lomax, Willie, 67
Long, Fox, 212
Long, Phax "Butch," 123, 125–26, 140–41, 146, 151, 212
Long, Sally, 140–41
Loring, Kip, 199
"Lost Girl," 131
Love, Willie, 44
"Love in Vain," 18
Lubin, Ron, viii
lynching, x, 108, 205

Mack, Kimberly, 186, 201–2, 205, 216
Major, Alberta, 85
Major, Julia. *See* Majors, Julia
Majors, Julia, 75, 78, 85, 207, 210, 214
Majors, Madison, 75, 77–78, 85, 210

Majors, Mary, 75, 78, 85
"Mama Just Wants to Barrelhouse All Night Long," 2
Marlowe, Christopher, 22
Martin, Dick, xiii
Martinsville, Mississippi, 59, 65–67, *66*, 67, 72–74
McClain, Anise, 59–60
McClennan, Tommy, 204
McCool, Noel L., 174
McCormick, Effie Mae, xi, xiii
McCormick, Greg, xi
McCormick, Robert "Mack," vii–viii, *xvi*, *xxvii*
    background of, xi–xvii, *xii*, 198
    childhood of, xi
    early jobs of, xi, xv, xv–xvi
    as folklorist, xvii–xviii
    legal troubles of, xiii–xiv, 183–89
    mental health of, xiv, xv, xx, xxi, 184–85, 188–89
    parents of, xi, xii–xiv
    research methods of, xix, xix–xx, xx, xxi, 22–23, 38, 199–200
    self-presentation of, 200
McCulloch, Bill, 215–16
McKune, Jim, viii
"Me and the Devil Blues," 14, 203
Memphis, Tennessee, 32–33, 132–33, 150
Merrimac Plantation, 124–25
Milam, J. W., 219
"Milkcow's Calf Blues," 214
"Mister Charlie," 204–5
Mitchell, George, 81
Monroe, Louisiana, 27–28
Monster, The, 192–94
Moore, Jim, 171–72, 218
Moore, Max, 40–44, 46, 206
Morris, Willie, 216

National Museum of American History, xxvi, *17*, 182, 194, 198, 200, 223
National Museum of the American Indian (NMAI) Act, 222
Negro, use of term, *xxviii*
Negro Prison Songs, 205–6
Newbern, Hambone Willie, 150

New Masses (magazine), xxiii
Newport Folk Festival, xvii–xviii
New Roads, Louisiana, 21–23, *22*
New York Times Magazine, xxi, 200
Nighthawk, Robert, 210
Nix, Susannah, xxviii, 192–93, 222
Norfolk, Virginia, 26, 29

"Ode to Billie Joe," 166
Okeh Records, 202
Oliver, Paul, xiv, xviii, 25, 199–200, 217
Oneida, Arkansas, 36
Opelousas, Louisiana, 23
Origins Jazz (record label), x
Oriole Records, 210

Paramount (record company), 123, 161
Parchman Farm, 93, 179, 205
Patton, Charley, 97, 110, 123–27, 150–51, 156, 211
Pearson, Marry Lee, 215–16
Perfect Records, 210
Perls, Nick, viii, 211
Philippines, 26
Phillips, Phax, 212
Pickens, Edward "Buster," 200
Polk Plantation, 112–13, 119–20
polo, 136
Port Chicago, California, 27
poverty, 108, 204
"Preaching Blues," 14, 144
prison recordings, xvii, xvii–xviii, 29, 205–6

race records, 2–3, 123, 202
radio, 39–40, 44. See also *King Biscuit Time* (radio program)
Rainey, Gertrude "Ma," ix
Red, Tampa, 210
redlining, xix, 204
Reivers, The (Faulkner), 166
Renard, Henry, viii
Richards, Keith, xxiii
Richardson, Benny Will "22," 205
Robert Johnson: King of the Delta Blues Singers, 4, 202. See also *King of the Delta Blues Singers*
"Robert Junior." *See* Lockwood, Robert, Jr.

Robinsonville, Mississippi, 102–3, *107*, 121, 124–28, 131, 139, 147, 160–62, 211, 216
Rodgers, Jimmie, 16
Rolling Stones, The, 18
Roman, Lloyd, 66
Romeo Records, 210
Rosedale, Mississippi, 26
Ruffin, Pete, 123, 212

Scott, Patricia, 187
sharecropping, 41, 44, 108, 134, 206
Sherrill, James, 205
Shines, Johnny, 155–57, 159–60, 204, 215
Ship Island, Mississippi, 29
Simmons, Vanessa Broussard, 193
"Sissy Man Blues," 205
"Sitting on Top of the World," 92
Sledge, Mississippi, 33
Slim, Sunnyland, 160
Smith, Bessie, ix, 97
Smith, Cleveland, 113–17, *116*, 140, 212
Smith, George, 67, 88–90, 118
Smith, Lula, 113–15, *116*, 118, 141, 212
Smith, Virgie Jane. *See* Cain, Virgie Mae
Smithsonian Institution, xxi, *xxiv–xxv*, 193–95, 222–23
Souls of Black Folk, The (Du Bois), ix
Southern National Party, 68, 209
Spencer, Bessie, 125
Spencer, Carrie, 125
Spencer, Charles Dodds, x, 121–23, 198
Spencer, Charles Leroy, 212
Spencer, Leroy, 112, 122–23, 126, 212
Spencer, Robert, 111–13, 115–21, 125–26, 134–35, 141, 214
Spiro, Phil, 211
Spottswood, Dick, 159
Stackhouse, Houston, 44, 79–81, *80*, 82–84, 210
Stokes, Frank, 150
Stonecipher, Norris, 187
"Stones in My Passway," 14, 203
storytelling, xxix, 195, 205, 217
Strachwicz, Chris, 184, 211, 219
Sullivan, John Jeremiah, xxi, 200
"Sweet Home Chicago," 27, 82
Sykes, Roosevelt, 39, 158, 160

tall tales, 205
Taylor, Thomas, 67
"Terraplane Blues," xxiii, 82, 98–99, 117, 143, 158, 212
Terry, Sonny, 201
Thomas, L. V., xxi
Thompson, Carrie, vii, xxviii, 183–88, 190–94, 207, 212, 218–21
Thornhill, Claude, xiv
Till, Emmett, 179, 219
tourism, 28, 191–92
Townsend, Henry, 157, 159–60, 215
"Traveling Riverside Blues," 9–10, 14–15, 203
Tunica, Mississippi, 69, 83, 99, 103, 108, 110, 112, 124–29, *130*, 133–34, 139, 150, 160–62, 212–13, 218
"Turn Your Lamp Down Low," 132

Uncle Tom, 47
Up Jumped the Devil: The Real Life of Robert Johnson (Conforth and Wardlow), xxix, 201
urban blues, ix–x, 15

Vanderbilt, Cornelius, 168
Vicksburg, Mississippi, 27, 91, 132, 146, 168
Victor Records, 94
Vocalion (record label), 3, 210

Wade, Luther, 172–73, 217–18
Wald, Elijah, 197–98, 202–3, 205, 216
"Walking Blues," 158, 214, 216

Wallace, George, 68
Walls, Mississippi, 121, *122*
Wardlow, Gayle Dean, xxix, 199, 201, 208, 212, 217–18, 221
Washington, Mabel, 70–71
Waterman, Dick, 211
Waters, Muddy, ix, 15, 154
wealth distribution, 191–92
Weiss, Stanley, 16
Welding, Pete, 18, 162, 204, 215
West Helena, Arkansas, 38–39
Wheatstraw, Peetie, 34, 205
Whelan, Pete, viii
White, Bukka, 48, 148
Whitman, Walt, 19
Wiley, Arnold, 39
Wilkins, Robert, 150
Williams, Enoch, 124–25, 130
Williams, Henry, 67
Williams, Ira, 67
Williams, Joe, 67
Williamson, Sonny Boy, 41–42, *43*, 44, 46–47, 159
Willis, Dusty, 125, 146, 214
Willis, Julia, 125
Wilson, Al, 25
Woods, Clyde, 197
Work, John, III, ix
WROX (radio station), 44

Yazoo Basin, 121, 127, 133–34, 165